publication supported by
*Figure Foundation*

# BLACK

# SNAKE

STANDING ROCK, the DAKOTA ACCESS PIPELINE, and
ENVIRONMENTAL JUSTICE     Katherine Wiltenburg Todrys

University of Nebraska Press | Lincoln

Library of Congress Cataloging-in-Publication Data
Names: Todrys, Katherine Wiltenburg, author.
Title: Black snake: Standing Rock, the Dakota
Access Pipeline, and environmental justice /
Katherine Wiltenburg Todrys.
Other titles: Standing Rock, the Dakota Access
Pipeline, and environmental justice
Description: Lincoln: University of Nebraska Press,
[2021] | Reports on the experiences of Lisa Finley DeVille,
Jasilyn Charger, LaDonna Allard, and Kandi (Mossett)
White. | Includes bibliographical references and index.
Identifiers: LCCN 2020041573
ISBN 9781496222664 (paperback)
ISBN 9781496227614 (epub)
ISBN 9781496227621 (mobi)
ISBN 9781496227638 (pdf)
Subjects: LCSH: Indians of North America—Political
activity—Standing Rock Indian Reservation (N.D. and
S.D.) | Indians of North America—Political activity—
North Dakota—Fort Berthold Indian Reservation. |
Dakota Access Pipeline—History. | Petroleum pipelines—
Environmental aspects. | Petroleum pipelines—Standing
Rock Indian Reservation (N.D. and S.D.)—Public
opinion. | Hydraulic fracturing—North Dakota—Fort
Berthold Indian Reservation—Public opinion. | Indian
activists—Standing Rock Indian Reservation (N.D. and
S.D.) | Indian activists—North Dakota—Fort Berthold
Indian Reservation. | Environmental justice—Standing
Rock Indian Reservation (N.D. and S.D.) | Environmental
justice—North Dakota—Fort Berthold Indian Reservation.
Classification: LCC E78.D2 T63 2021 | DDC 978.4/88—dc23
LC record available at https://lccn.loc.gov/2020041573

Set in Arno Pro by Mikala R. Kolander.
Designed by L. Auten.

# Contents

# Illustrations

MAPS

# BLACK SNAKE

cost the company money while work was halted. It was a tense time: camps near the reservation were swelling with thousands who had come to be "water protectors," blocking construction of a pipeline they believed would desecrate sacred sites and threaten the water supply for Standing Rock residents and millions of others who relied on the Missouri River for water.

As Tim Purdon spoke to the pipeline company, its representatives asked him a question about his clients' attitude to the project: how much money was it going to take—that is, what would the company have to pay the tribe to make all this go away?

On its face the question may have seemed reasonable. Around 40 percent of the Standing Rock population lives in poverty (compared to 11.6 percent of North Dakota's entire population), the result of centuries of mistreatment by the U.S. government, broken treaties, and generations of continuing trauma.[1] Poverty and woeful underfunding of health services by the U.S. government have also led to myriad health problems; Sioux County, North Dakota, which encompasses the northern part of the reservation, ranks in the bottom five in the United States for life expectancy.[2] High suicide rates; alcoholism; drug use; and physical, sexual, and domestic violence all plague Standing Rock residents, symptoms of its poverty. These are "things you would expect to find in a community that has been on the receiving end of over a century of oppression," concludes the local episcopal priest, Rev. John Floberg.

Further, Dakota Access had found considerable success elsewhere in putting a price tag on the land along the pipeline's route. It had managed to secure voluntary easements from most landowners along the pipeline corridor through four states. But Tim Purdon quickly realized that executives at the pipeline company had no idea that this was a different type of dispute. The Standing Rock Sioux would not be bought off.

Purdon told the pipeline company the story of the Black Hills, the Lakota heartland. The story began generations ago, when the 1851 and 1868 Fort Laramie Treaties established the Black Hills of South Dakota and Wyoming as a part of the Great Sioux Reservation, set aside forever for the use of the Sioux. Gold was discovered in the hills a few years later, and white settlers rushed in. The United States unilaterally took the Black Hills and chiseled the faces of its presidents into Mount Rushmore. But the Sioux never accepted the taking of their land. They filed suit in 1922 and ultimately won perhaps the longest-running legal battle in history. In 1980 the U.S. Supreme Court concluded that "a more ripe and rank case of dishonorable dealings will never, in all probability, be found in our history."[3] Because the U.S. government had taken land that had been set aside for the tribe, said the court, it owed the Sioux just compensation, including interest. But the Sioux refused the money.[4] Since 1980 the money has sat in a Bureau of Indian Affairs (BIA) account in Washington DC accruing interest—and the account is now worth nearly $2 billion. The Sioux don't want the money; they want the Black Hills.

"The Black Hills are not for sale," declared LaDonna Brave Bull Allard, a former Standing Rock tribal historian, "and never will be sold. You don't sell your mother. You don't sell sacred. There is no money in the world. There is no just compensation. That is the center of our heart."

"You have to understand that to understand what is happening with the Dakota Access Pipeline," Tim Purdon concluded. The pipeline company had no idea with whom it was dealing.

On June 1, 2017, oil began flowing through the Dakota Access Pipeline (DAPL). Supporters touted the pipeline as key to safely and reliably transporting U.S. oil from the Bakken oil fields to consumers, essential to both national security and prosperity. Native activists had called it the "black snake," referring to an ancient prophecy about a terrible snake that would one day slither onto tribal land and devour the earth.

The historic demonstrations at the camps near Standing Rock in 2016 stalled the pipeline project and won a major victory for the thousands of water protectors who had taken a stand there during the final months of Barack Obama's presidency. But the victory was short-lived. During his first week in office President Donald Trump fast-tracked the pipeline's remaining permit. Within months oil began snaking its way south through the pipeline. A new generation of activists, galvanized at Standing Rock, had also emerged.

This conflict had been centuries in the making. With the fifteenth-century Doctrine of Discovery, discussed in chapter 4, Europeans rationalized the colonization of Indigenous lands. Fueled by a belief in their Manifest Destiny, Americans justified settling the western United States as their God-given right. First Europeans and then the new U.S. government stole or bought Native lands for trifling amounts. They made treaties. The Sioux and other Indigenous nations signed a treaty of peace and friendship with the United States government in 1805, with more treaties to follow in the subsequent decades. Standing Rock was part of the Great Sioux Reservation, established by the 1851 and 1868 Fort Laramie Treaties and whittled away for years after in a shameful history of misdealing by the U.S. government.

The land that the pipeline was set to cross sat within the boundaries of the 1851 Fort Laramie Treaty and was not ceded by the 1868 Fort Laramie Treaty but had been taken years earlier from the Standing Rock Sioux Tribe.[5] It was also just half a mile from the tribe's modern-day boundaries and directly upstream from its water source.

Overall the United States has the largest pipeline network in the world. Some 2.5 million miles of pipelines crisscross the country—enough to circle the earth one hundred times—transporting such products as oil and natural gas.[6] But pipelines are problematic. Spills, both small and large, are common, and they leave behind land and water that are poisoned and slick with oil. Since 2010 the federal Pipeline and Hazardous Materials Safety Administration has reported more than 6,900 incidents including spills at oil and gas pipelines.[7]

In total the proposed DAPL was designed to cross 437 wetlands and 211 waterbodies, including the Missouri River in two places, one of them north of the modern-day Standing Rock Reservation.[8] The Missouri River is the longest river and largest watershed in the United States, and it has been the region's main artery for food, trade, and transportation for thousands of years. It is a place of both supreme cultural significance and practical importance: around a quarter of U.S. agricultural lands are in the Missouri River watershed. A spill under it could be devastating for the Standing Rock Sioux and for millions of others.

Even if they never spilled, oil and gas pipelines would still present an environmental hazard. Climate change has become an existential crisis for humanity, with global carbon emissions rising despite decades of international negotiations.[9] According to environmentalists, pipelines are key elements of the infrastructure that locks the United States into a fossil fuel–based economy, exacerbating climate change. After companies build and finance an expensive pipeline, they need to pay it off, so they are resistant to systemic change. Energy Transfer Partners (ETP), the parent company of Dakota Access, LLC, has been a leader in creating the pipeline infrastructure that entrenches U.S. dependence on fossil fuels. CEO Kelcy Warren has boasted that "nobody has built more pipelines in the last fifteen years than Energy Transfer. Many of these pipelines are game changers for the nation."[10]

Halting the pipelines at their inception, environmentalists hope, can curb the expansion and entrenchment of fossil fuel dependence. Native Americans, forced decades ago onto ever-smaller patches of land that were considered nearly worthless, now find themselves sitting atop patches of oil and along corridors where some of these pipelines would run.

For more than a decade a fracking boom has harnessed new technology to tap into vast, lucrative, previously inaccessible stores of oil in the Bakken shale oil formation. Affected communities—including the Fort Berthold Reservation in northwestern North Dakota—have paid a heavy price in environmental devastation. This is the head of the "black snake," as activists call the DAPL. ETP sought to build the

February 23, 2017, local law enforcement shut down the main camp, slashing tipis and arresting some lingering water protectors.

These days the site of the camps near Standing Rock stands empty, grasses rustling along the river as the occasional car speeds past on the nearby highway. By the time oil began running through the pipeline in June 2017, the prairie had grown high, and there was no sign of the thousands who had gathered here. A large, ochre-colored statue still sits on one hill: a person, arms clasped, gazing out at the water. The paint on the face is streaked with what look like tears. Called "Not Afraid to Look," the statue was built by Lakota sculptor Charles Rencountre to watch over the camp.

Clearly something significant happened at Standing Rock. On the one hand, it was yet another skirmish in the ongoing war against the treaty rights abuses, racism, and environmental injustice that have long plagued Native Americans. The movement at Standing Rock fits into the long history of Indigenous resistance against settlers, dams, and pipelines.[18] It has echoes of the Indigenous activism, often youth-led, of the preceding decades: the eighteen-month occupation, beginning in 1969, of Alcatraz Island by Indians of All Tribes; the fish-ins of the 1960s and 1970s by Native Americans asserting their treaty rights to fish around the Puget Sound; the 1973 occupation by the American Indian Movement (AIM) of Wounded Knee on the Pine Ridge Indian Reservation; and the Idle No More movement, founded in 2012 in reaction to infringements of Indigenous treaty rights in Canada. The Standing Rock camps also grew directly out of the fight over the Keystone XL Pipeline, which brought Indigenous leaders and environmental activists together.

On the other hand, though, the Standing Rock camp kicked off a movement on an entirely new scale. It inspired thousands around the world to take action. Even Congresswoman Alexandria Ocasio-Cortez credits a stint at Standing Rock with her decision to run for office. Native activists and allies joined together in historic numbers, achieving a stunning (if short-lived) success.[19] Opposition to a single pipeline developed into an Indigenous-led movement that expanded the narrative over environmental issues to include justice to Native nations and highlighted the ways in which mistreatment of Native nations in the United States continues to occur.

Today nearly three million people belong to the more than five hundred federally recognized Native communities and nations in the United States; they descend from the land's fifteen million original inhabitants.[20] Rethinking the national narrative involves recognizing U.S. history as that of settler colonialism—an ideology of white supremacy and a policy of genocide and land theft that has included massacres, military occupation, torture, removal from ancestral lands, and the removal of children from their families.[21] Indigenous peoples have survived genocide, oppression, and misdealing by European and American settlers, the historical backdrop for myriad problems on reservations: multigenerational poverty, unemployment, suicide, alcoholism.

Despite these vast injustices and environmental threats around oil production and transport, Native voices—including those of Lisa DeVille, Jasilyn Charger, LaDonna Allard, and Kandi (Mossett) White—were raised by the movement around the DAPL and today are stronger than ever on the world stage. Meanwhile, the U.S. government led by Donald Trump isolated itself, stepping away from its environmental protections and commitments.

The following chapters tell the story of the movement against the DAPL, beginning on Fort Berthold in 2015 and then gaining force as the camps at Standing Rock in 2016 and 2017 grew. From the perspective of four Native women who were essential to this movement, these chapters aim to answer the following questions: What happened at Standing Rock? How did this movement emerge from the history, lived experience, and determination of these four women? And when they rose up, why was this time different?

This is a story of activists—some only teenagers—who have taken a stand to become the protectors of America's fragile natural resources.

It is a story of Native nations launching an important environmental justice and sovereignty movement that has challenged longtime discrimination and environmental inequity. It is a story of leaders who, despite their own upbringing in some of the most impoverished places in the country, burdened by a history of dispossession and misdealing, are working to decolonize and rebuild their communities. It is the story of the government that finally heard them.

In one sense the victory at Standing Rock itself was short-lived, as oil came to flow through the DAPL. In 2019 ETP even sought to increase the capacity of the pipeline to a million gallons a day, the entire production for the state of North Dakota.[22] By October 2020 the company had received approval from state regulators in all four necessary states and was expecting additional capacity to be in service during the third quarter of 2021.[23] It hoped that increased capacity would "allow for further development in the Bakken, economic growth in North Dakota, and stabilization of costs for the industry and consumers," and it had found "significant interest from shippers" in the plan.[24] The Standing Rock Sioux Tribe adamantly opposed the expansion.[25]

The continued operation of the pipeline, though, is not a foregone conclusion. In March 2020 the Standing Rock Sioux Tribe saw a major legal victory in its challenge to the pipeline: a federal court struck down the pipeline's permits, ordering the Army Corps to conduct a full environmental review. The new EIS process was under way in January 2021, when Joseph Biden assumed the presidency. The change of presidential administration had the potential to prove game changing for the pipeline.

In a larger sense, also, the story of the movement is still being written. The activists who came of age during the DAPL movement have spread to new issues around the globe—championing murdered and missing Indigenous women, challenging pipelines, addressing climate change, and rebuilding communities.

Jan Hasselman likes to think sometimes about the big anti-nuclear protests in the 1970s that came to a head around the Seabrook Nuclear

Power Plant in New Hampshire.[26] In the short term the protests were unsuccessful, he concedes, despite their global attention. That particular nuclear power plant was built. But at the same time, he says, that was one of the last nuclear power plants ever to be built in America. Whether Standing Rock will be a similar paradigm shift is yet to be seen.

Nineteenth-century Lakota leader Crazy Horse prophesied: "Upon suffering beyond suffering, the Red Nation shall rise again and it shall be a blessing for a sick world. A world filled with broken promises, selfishness and separations. A world longing for light again. I see a time of seven generations."[27]

LaDonna Allard remembers as a child when she heard grandmothers talk about the black snake that would come to destroy the earth, when the seventh generation would rise up. At the camps at Standing Rock, she thought that time had finally arrived: "We must stand together and fight the black snake," she charged.[28]

Note on terminology: in this book I use the following terms to refer to Indigenous peoples in the United States: Native, Native American, Indigenous, and American Indian. Wherever applicable, I have tried to use Native peoples' correct names in their own languages, such as Lakota and Dakota, as well as some familiar terms, such as Sioux.

# LISA

# Oil Production in the Bakken

**1**

Our sovereignty, our independence, can be maximized by the number of barrels of oil taken from our Mother Earth. We call it sovereignty by the barrel.

—Chairman Tex Hall of the Mandan, Hidatsa, and Arikara Nation

Just as Lisa DeVille was settling in for a quiet moment in the kitchen of her Mandaree, North Dakota, home, the phone rang. It was December 2010, a cold and snowy time in her tiny town on the Fort Berthold Reservation, but Lisa, thirty-six, had hardly noticed. She had spent her whole life in this desolate northwestern corner of the state and had come to expect frosty temperatures and a white blanket of snow, starting in October. On this day she also had other things to mull over. For over a decade she had worked as a housing administrator for her own Mandan, Hidatsa, and Arikara (MHA) Nation, the three affiliated tribes living on the reservation, but she had recently been laid off—a casualty, she suspected, of internal political maneuvering that had roiled the tribe since the recent chairman's election.

In the past few years the tribe had accepted oil companies' efforts to bring fracking to the reservation, and the new chairman embraced the boom wholeheartedly. The land was beginning to be pockmarked with sinister-looking oil rigs. But the money came in handy in this impoverished place, where around 70 percent of adults were unemployed. Lisa and her husband, Walter, had five children to feed, and the only thing getting them through each month was the money they were starting to receive from oil leases on his family's property.

It was Lisa's neighbor calling, and she was mad. Something funny was happening in her yard, she said; could Lisa come over right way? Lisa hopped in her truck and sped over to the house, about a mile north of her own. Immediately Lisa felt a growing sense of unease: the snow around her neighbor's house had turned an eerie shade of yellow. "What is it?" asked her neighbor, taking a few pictures. Lisa had an idea: "The only thing I can think of is . . . that." They stared at the nearby flare, taller than a person and sending up methane gas in a giant flame. The gas was a byproduct of the oil drilling that was creeping across the reservation, and burning plumes like this one had popped up everywhere alongside the oil rigs.

Lisa knew little about these flares, but troubled by the yellow snow, she went home and started asking questions. She was naturally feisty and inquisitive and called everyone she could think of: the EPA, the MHA Nation's Natural Resources and Homeland Security Departments, and law enforcement. No one had any answers. Not only did she know little about the oil boom that was consuming the MHA Nation, but it seemed that no one else knew anything either. "What the heck is going on?" Lisa wondered. "Were we ready for this?"

Lisa was born in Mandaree—a one-store town on the Fort Berthold Reservation—in 1974. It is a place of stark beauty. To the south and west of Lisa's home are the windswept hills and striped clay buttes of the badlands, which jut out of the earth like the peaks on a meringue pie. To the east are softer rolling hills covered in low-growing grasses; farming equipment, grain elevators, and grazing cattle dot the golden fields. Rows of drying sunflowers sway in the wind.

The middle child of five, Lisa and her siblings were raised by their grandmother, Julia Charging White Eagle, since her mother struggled with alcoholism. She didn't know her father. Lisa grew up knowing hard work. She helped her grandmother dry meat and grind it for pemmican, she ground corn for corn balls, and she washed clothes by hand. Lisa's grandmother did the best she could, but Lisa didn't have much parental guidance and ran with a fast crowd at school.

All around Lisa were reminders of her past, including those who were gone. She had lost both of her brothers, one to diabetes and one to alcoholism. Her ancestors, both Mandan and Hidatsa, are buried along the grassy green banks and red cliffs that overlook glittering Lake Sakakawea, which is also the reservation's water source. She grew up swimming in the cool lake and drinking its water, and today her grandchildren still swim in it on summer days.

Lisa's grandmother, full-blooded Mandan and Hidatsa, predicted that this bucolic landscape would change. In summer when Lisa was a child, she and her grandmother picked plums and juneberries, and her grandmother would look out over the hills. "There's oil under here," she said. "They just got to figure out how they're going to break up all the rock."

Then in the early 2000s, they did figure it out, and life on Fort Berthold changed dramatically. Now the reservation, almost a million acres of land in the heart of the Bakken shale formation, is home to more than two thousand oil wells. In the still night air, when Lisa lets her dogs out to run under the wide sky, she sometimes feels the earth shake beneath her feet. From some spots on the reservation, Lisa can see flames shooting out of the earth in every direction. When she stands on the bluffs overlooking the lake, she hears a roar, like a jet engine taking off, throbbing in the distance. She breathes in the noxious smell of sulfur in her kitchen when the wind turns. The light on the horizon wavers a pulsing red when she drives at night as hundreds of flames burn, torch-like, around her. The result is an apocalyptic landscape where there were once only farms and cattle.

Underlying this change was a controversial—and environmentally devastating—new technology. When oil prices increased in 2002, oil companies began investing in novel ways of tapping into oil reserves, such as horizontal drilling and hydraulic fracturing (fracking). Fracking is invasive and labor-intensive but highly profitable when oil prices are high. First, it involves drilling into black shale, a fine-grained sedimentary rock, often two thousand to ten thousand feet below the earth's surface, that can generate oil and natural gas. Then an army of oil workers injects the rock with sand and millions of gallons of chemical-laced water to break it apart. From 2009 to 2015 U.S. oil production surged to extraordinary new levels as fracking technology improved.[1]

The Bakken region, including Fort Berthold, was on the frontlines of the boom. Its rich shale formation cuts a broad swath through much of western North Dakota, eastern Montana, and portions of two Canadian provinces—around twenty-five thousand square miles in all—under rich agricultural soil. From 2005 to 2017 the number of oil-producing wells in the Bakken region jumped from fewer than two hundred to more than eleven thousand.[2] Production in this region soared to nearly 1.25 million barrels a day in 2018.[3]

While fracking is aimed at extracting oil, natural gas (methane), which sells for far less, is often treated as a byproduct and burned off when oil companies have not invested in the pipeline infrastructure needed to capture, store, and use the gas produced. Methane traps heat and can warm the atmosphere at many times the rate of carbon dioxide. As oil production began in the Bakken, flares began appearing everywhere. Suddenly, an activist says, it became "Kuwait on fire." Indeed in this rural state, the glowing lights from North Dakota that could be seen from space came not from cities but from flares.[4]

Companies investing in the boom have profited royally: Continental Resources, which has leased 1.2 million acres in the Bakken, reported $2.8 billion in net income from 2006 to 2013.[5] Continental's chief, Harold Hamm, estimates that all told, the Bakken fields will ultimately yield twenty-four billion barrels of oil.[6]

North Dakota has also ridden the wave of this prosperity. Since 2012 the state has been the second largest crude oil producer in the United States.[7] Between 2009 and 2015 the state's budget more than doubled as a result of the oil boom.[8] With its newfound wealth, North Dakota found itself boasting a budget *surplus* of $1.6 billion. "The next Saudi Arabia," one oil tycoon concluded.[9] With this free-flowing oil has come change to once sleepy corners of this agricultural state, known for producing wheat and sunflowers. Thousands of oil workers have rushed in from around the country.

The town of Williston, North Dakota, northwest of Fort Berthold, has become emblematic of this new reality. It has dubbed itself "Boomtown USA" as the population has doubled and perhaps quadrupled since 2010. (The transient nature of the workforce makes it hard to track.) The town is practically unrecognizable to long-term residents. Huge oil company complexes have sprung up, surrounded by mud-spattered white pickups and eighteen-wheelers. But one of the most significant changes is demographic: the tens of thousands of new residents are largely men. Indeed North Dakota has a higher concentration of men than anywhere else in the United States outside of Alaska. In Williston a strip club has taken its place among the businesses, fitness centers, fast food restaurants, and apartment complexes that are moving in. One popular restaurant in town has gun-shaped door handles. "Trucks" is stenciled on the men's bathroom; "Garages" is on the women's. An upswing in violence has left observers calling the town and its surrounding area a new "Wild West."[10]

Sweeping changes have taken place throughout the Bakken, nowhere more vividly than on the Fort Berthold Reservation. In 2008, with most of its population living in poverty, the MHA Nation opened Fort Berthold to oil development. Since then the tribe has reaped billions in revenues and taxes, but much of that money has disappeared due to corruption and poor planning.

The MHA Nation has seen many changes throughout its history. The Mandan were a strong and prosperous tribe, with a population of at least fifteen thousand, when they met Meriwether Lewis and William Clark in 1804. Along with the neighboring Hidatsa and Arikara, they lived in earth lodge villages, farming the river valleys and hunting wild game. They also maintained an extensive trading system on the Missouri River, functioning as middlemen for neighboring tribes. After contact with Europeans and several bouts of smallpox, their population was decimated: in 1837 only 125 Mandan remained.

Following the devastation of successive smallpox epidemics, the three tribes joined together for their survival.[11]

After gold was discovered in California in 1848, thousands of settlers began crossing the "permanent Indian frontier" in search of their fortunes, claiming Manifest Destiny. Pressure began to mount on western tribes to cede land and settle on reservations. In 1851 the Fort Laramie Treaty defined the boundaries of the Mandan, Hidatsa, and Arikara territory; the Fort Berthold Reservation was established under the Executive Order of 1870. Traditional territorial lands of the Mandan, Hidatsa, and Arikara people covered more than twelve million acres, but the Fort Laramie Treaty and subsequent executive orders and congressional acts forced the three tribes into just around one million acres.[12]

In 1887 the Dawes Act granted the U.S. president the authority to divide any tribal reservation lands held in trust by the federal government, allotting some plots to tribal members and selling others to non-Natives, in what amounted to an enormous land grab to benefit white settlers. Ostensibly aimed at making Native Americans conform to social and economic norms of rural America by vesting them with private property, the legislation enormously reduced Native land by opening it to white homesteaders. The U.S. government carved up reservations, including Fort Berthold; federal law opened 270 million acres of Native land to white settlement. By 1934 Native Americans countrywide had lost nearly 90 million acres, often their best farmland.[13]

Already confined and reduced, the MHA Nation experienced a second displacement in the twentieth century. In 1944 downstream flooding of the Missouri River led Congress to pass the Flood Control Act, which enacted the Pick-Sloan Plan, a series of dams to reduce flooding, generate hydroelectricity, and irrigate the prairies.[14] It authorized the Army Corps to create and operate five large dams along the Missouri River, with devastating effects for Native communities. Flooding fertile bottomlands served the U.S. aims in this period to terminate federal responsibilities to Native nations and relocate Native peoples off of their reservations. The plan's result was the decimation of 90 percent of commercial timber, 75 percent of wildlife and plants native to the river bottomlands, and thousands of acres of subsistence farms.[15]

On Fort Berthold the Army Corps had already spent $60 million toward the project's completion by the time the tribal chairman, George Gillette, was forced by the federal government to sign the contracts. At the contract signing, weeping and head in hands, Chairman Gillette declared: "With a few scratches of the pen, we will sell the best part of our reservation. Right now, the future does not look too good for us."[16]

The Army Corps constructed the Garrison Dam on the Missouri River, flooding the reservation's richest agricultural lands and forcing 80 percent of Fort Berthold residents from their homes. Bridges, schools, and roads were all inundated. When the dam went up, it created behind it a more than three-hundred-thousand-acre lake—Lake Sakakawea—out of the Missouri River.[17] Tribal elders, who felt that their land had been stolen, looked on with tears as the water began to rise.

As a child, Lisa heard stories from her grandmother about the devastating effects of the dam. Her grandmother, along with much of the rest of the tribe, had had to abandon the reservation's central community, called Elbowoods, in 1953, when the dam was built. The Army Corps relocated residents into six far-flung communities. It could take hours to drive among the reservation's new "segments" to visit former neighbors. Worse still, tribal members effectively lost their way of life. They had left behind the rich soil of the wooded bottomlands, where they had family gardens, for the poor soil of the windswept plains, where they had to try to ranch and farm. The vegetables they had grown were replaced by commodity foods, high in fat and starch. Suddenly they had to navigate a cash economy. Unemployment soared from 5–6 percent to 70–80 percent in the decades that followed, and it stayed there.[18] When families had no way to support themselves, alcoholism, suicide, and violence increased. Life expectancy hovered in the fifties.[19]

ensure that leases are "in the best interest of the Indian owners of the Indian Land"—approved them.[23] Still a 2013 lawsuit that challenged the government for failing in its trust obligations related to approval of oil and gas leases on Fort Berthold allotment lands was concluded in 2016 in the government's favor.[24] No one was held accountable for lowball leases, and tribal member landowners had no recourse. But the oil boom took off.

The deals between oil companies or middlemen and tribal members were leases, agreements that gave an oil company access to the property and rights to the minerals (the oil or gas) under its surface. In exchange for their mineral rights, landowners (or groups of landowners) received an up-front bonus payment, and then a percentage of royalties on the value of any eventual oil production. Typical royalty rates on Fort Berthold in 2008 ran from 16 to 18 percent, depending on the size of the bonus the landowner received. (By contrast, when the tribe began producing its own oil, the tribally owned company, Missouri River Resources, typically gave a 26 percent royalty rate.)

In 2010 Tex Hall, a larger-than-life former tribal chairman, was elected to lead the MHA Nation. Hall had already started a company to collaborate with the oil industry while he was out of public office. Not surprisingly, he took a hard-charging approach to encouraging oil development, arguing that the more oil the tribe pulled from the ground beneath it, the more autonomy it would achieve in its relations with the federal government: "We are a sovereign nation, recognized by treaty with the government of the United States," he said. "Our sovereignty, our independence, can be maximized by the number of barrels of oil taken from our Mother Earth. We call it sovereignty by the barrel."[25]

Drilling began on the reservation without any meaningful environmental impact studies to evaluate the consequences to water, land, and air. Oil production quickly soared—up to 2.5 million barrels per month in November 2011 and then 5.2 million barrels per month in January 2014. Nearly half of it came from the Mandaree community.[26] In April

2017 Fort Berthold had 1,582 active wells producing 187,519 barrels of oil per day, with 114 wells awaiting completion and 507 approved drilling permits.[27] If Fort Berthold were a state, it would be the seventh-largest oil producing state in the country.[28]

Since 2008 the financial rewards for the tribe—twice displaced and more than $100 million in debt, with underfunded and inadequate infrastructure, policing, and regulation—have been breathtaking. From 2008 to 2018 its royalties alone totaled around $1 billion, with tax revenues of around $1 billion more. The MHA Nation has some sixteen thousand members living on Fort Berthold and elsewhere.[29] Many also benefited from individual leases on their own land.

Starting in 2008 an army of oil workers began building drilling pads all around the reservation, and Lisa heard a sound she had never heard before: the little prairie dogs, whose burrows dotted the landscape, were squealing. The oil companies had bulldozed their homes. Kandi White, an activist who grew up on the reservation, started seeing signs that read "For lease, industrial zone" on land that had previously been used for farming. With its sunflower, canola, and wheat fields, the area had long been known as the breadbasket of the country. Cattle and horses grazed on its verdant fields and hills. Now, next to fields that were still in agricultural production, with produce intended for human consumption, oil rigs began to pop up everywhere.

With the boom under way the fabric of the village-like community began to fray. Big trucks driven by sometimes exhausted oil workers began to rattle the reservation's narrow roads, shaking cars they passed. Oil development on Fort Berthold led to a nearly 600 percent rise in truck traffic on the reservation, though many of the sleepy roads were unpaved, having been built to rural agricultural standards.[30] Traffic deaths in North Dakota spiked with the oil boom. The state suffered forty-eight deaths in 2012 involving a large truck or bus (compared to an average of only thirteen in pre-oil boom years), a large truck and bus fatality rate far surpassing that of any other state.[31] Tribal members became afraid to drive. In 2015 sixteen people were killed in motor vehicle crashes on Fort Berthold. More than a quarter of the reservation's reported crashes involved semitrucks.[32] Oil traffic was particularly heavy on the road between Mandaree and New Town, the largest city on the reservation and its administrative center. Roadside ditches were scattered with dead deer and memorials for tribal members lost in accidents. Kandi White's friend Cassi Dee Rensch—only twenty-three, a budding historian with a love of life and gift for working with children—was killed in 2008 when a semi hauling fracking fluids sideswiped her car and drove her off the road near New Town.

When Tim Purdon was appointed U.S. attorney for North Dakota in 2010, he never dreamed of including criminal activity related to oil in the Bakken as one of his priorities. The idea that organized crime would target small towns such as Williston, New Town, Watford City, Dickinson, or Stanley was, in his mind, "a concept that did not exist." In the 1980s and 1990s, when Kandi was growing up on Fort Berthold, merely egging teachers' houses on Halloween had counted as a significant incident.

But soon Tim Purdon's office began to see huge changes; combating crime related to the oil boom became one of its top priorities. Local law enforcement in the "oil patch," including Fort Berthold, was being overwhelmed. A 2013 North Dakota State University study found that the population explosion related to the oil boom had left police departments short-staffed while calls for help doubled or even tripled. Soon officers were becoming concerned for their own safety. Traffic accidents burgeoned, and more drugs came into the area; also on the rise were alcohol-related crimes, oil-field-related domestic violence complaints, and prostitution.[33] Purdon felt that local law enforcement was reactive and overwhelmed, bouncing from bar fights to domestic disturbances to DUIs. Walter and Lisa looked outside and saw unfamiliar vehicles driving around Mandaree in the middle of the night. In 2014 only twenty-three law enforcement officers patrolled the whole million-acre reservation.[34]

At the same time, organized crime did move in along with the oil boom, and people at the tribe's casino in New Town began sporting MS-13 tattoos, indicating their membership in the international criminal gang. Lisa and Kandi began to hear about police chases and shootouts. One of Kandi's cousins went missing in November 2013, last seen with organized crime members. His body was found the following spring under the bridge across Lake Sakakawea.[35] Another cousin, she says, was murdered after giving an oil worker a ride home from a bar one night. The federal government made an effort to respond, with the Federal Bureau of Investigation (FBI) opening an office in Williston as the organized crime, drug, and trafficking cases in Tim Purdon's office began to skyrocket.

The reservation was no stranger to alcohol and some methamphetamine abuse, but suddenly opioids and heroin started to appear. Tribal courts became flooded with drug cases. While forty-seven tribal members were arrested on drug-related charges in 2008, more than eight hundred were arrested in 2015. In summer 2013 Tim Purdon, in conjunction with the FBI and tribal officers, indicted twenty-two people for dealing heroin and meth in the vicinity of Fort Berthold, and later forty more were indicted.[36] Social service officials began to see babies born addicted to opiates and to remove them from their families.

While sexual violence against Native women had long been a scourge in many communities, it increasingly was also linked to the demographic changes that came with the oil boom. Violent crimes in North Dakota increased, particularly abductions and sexual violence in and around the "man camps" that sprang up to house thousands of oil workers in rows of RVs or trailers.[37] Almost overnight the Bakken became a hotspot for human trafficking. A law enforcement officer on Fort Berthold estimated that sexual assaults increased by 75 percent with the oil boom.[38] Lisa began to hear about abductions of Native women—including attempted abductions of reservation kids walking home from elementary school. There was a man camp just a few miles away from Mandaree, on private land. Law enforcement and social services were understaffed and inundated with new cases, a problem compounded by the fact that tribal law enforcement has no jurisdiction over cases in which the perpetrator is non-Native.[39] When a fifteen-year-old boy went missing, police found him being sexually abused in a man camp; the oil workers were passing him around from trailer to trailer. On another occasion in 2014 they discovered a sobbing four-year-old girl running naked down the road outside a man camp after being sexually assaulted.[40]

Lisa and Walter still live in Mandaree, not far from where she was raised. They met at the Mandaree school, when she was in seventh grade; he was two years older. As a junior in high school, she became pregnant with their first son, Michael, and the next year, she was pregnant again, with their son Thomas. Walter went to work for the tribe's buffalo project, caring for the tribal buffalo herd at least ten hours a day. Even with two babies at home, Lisa managed to graduate as valedictorian of her high school class in 1993. As noted, she worked in housing administration for the tribe from 1997 to 2010 while juggling household responsibilities; by 2003 she had five kids. Neither she nor Walter made much money, and financially every day was a struggle. After paying the bills, they often had to decide whether to put gas in the car or eat.

Today Lisa and Walter's modest, ranch-style house is a well-loved family home. They bought it in 2009 and sent all five of their children to school in Mandaree. Lawn ornaments with decorative butterflies and birds adorn their home's windswept front yard, and the DeVilles' children and grandchildren come in and out through the swinging back door. Julia passed away several years ago, but one son lives in a trailer home a few blocks away, and their grandchildren play on the swing set in his yard.

Mandaree, population 596, isn't a big place. A single convenience store selling junk food and a few sandwiches constitutes its entire business district; skinny rez dogs patrol the parking area. When Lisa was growing up, Mandaree had a police station and a court, but by now both had moved to New Town, a forty-five-minute drive away.

Most of the homes are trailers. This seems an unlikely epicenter of an oil boom, but the rigs silhouetted on the horizon, the torch-like flares flaming in every direction, and the giant trucks that barrel through the rolling hills tell a different story. So do the residents. A woman at the convenience store speaks in hushed tones about the dangers of the man camps. One of Lisa's daughter's friends, a freshman in high school, somehow managed to escape when a drunk man threw her into a truck outside that same convenience store.

Tribal members who lived away from the reservation and came back in 2013 found they were stepping into a horror movie. The landscape was marred, housing was in short supply, and strangers from the oil fields were everywhere.[41] No one, especially women, went out alone after dark. People began locking their doors and drawing their curtains. Many acquired guard dogs. Previously a friendly community in which doors stayed open, everyone was suddenly on alert.

Oil leases on land belonging to Walter and his family gave Lisa and Walter some much-needed income. Still Lisa couldn't help feeling that the tribe had been better off when it was poor. Neighbors had looked out for one another. When some were down, the community had come together to get them back on their feet. But suddenly, she says, the attitude around her was, "Well, what are you going to do for me? How much are you going to pay me?"

Indeed there was money to be had from oil. Lisa and Kandi heard from relatives working in the oil industry and signs posted in New Town that oil jobs could start out at $25 an hour and move up to as much as $65 an hour. In twenty-five years working as a laborer for the tribe, Walter had worked his way up from $5 to only $11.71 an hour. Advertisements for everything from truck drivers to engineers to oil field workers began to pop up. The promise of relative wealth lured everyone in. By 2013 North Dakota had the lowest unemployment in the nation.[42] In 2018, after the price of oil had dropped from its peak, the tribal chairman said that unemployment on Fort Berthold stood around 20 percent, down from 70 percent before the boom.

As part of a public relations campaign, the oil industry began visiting the reservation schools. In the Mandaree school Lisa's children heard oil industry representatives paint a rosy picture of the safety of fracking. One oil company even ran an "adopt-a-well" program for eighth graders in 2013, teaching them about the ingredients used in fracking and following the development of a well from start to finish.[43] Kandi's thirteen-year-old niece came home with papers about a school drawing contest in which the winner's name would go on an oil rig, along with the drawing. But when her niece asked to talk in school about her aunt's work as an environmental activist, Kandi says, she wasn't allowed.

The social impacts of the oil boom became obvious fairly quickly. The effect of the boom on the environment, though, was on a slow boil. Lisa's first encounter with it came in December 2010, when she began looking into her friend's yellow snow. When she went to Dr. Kerry Hartman, a science professor at the reservation college, soon after, she finally got an answer of sorts. If she wanted to do advocacy, he told her, he strongly suggested that she go back to school. Lisa hadn't realized that she was doing advocacy, but she agreed. Public speaking made her nervous, but Lisa was no stranger to hard work, and she was a strong writer. Her Hidatsa name, Maheahzah Ahgawgish, means "Accomplishes Everything." In the fall of 2011 Lisa enrolled in Fort Berthold Community College to study environmental science, studying alongside her oldest son, Michael.

Lisa's interest in the water stemmed from her ancestors' creation stories, which involved water's sacredness. In environmental advocacy she had found her passion. For thirteen years working in housing she had worried about families, working to create home ownership programs, but this was different.[44]

Meanwhile, fracking continued to expand across the reservation. When Lisa and Walter drove over to Lisa's grandmother's land in Independence, they saw that all the land around it was pockmarked with oil wells. Her land hadn't been drilled yet, but it was only a matter of time.

In February 2012 Lisa wrote a letter to Tex Hall, the tribe's oil-promoting chairman, asking him how the tribe was preparing its children for the aftermath of the oil boom. She pointed out that since Mandaree was bringing in most of the oil revenue for the tribe, it should receive funding for such civic needs as housing, the community center, roads, and water and sewer lines—all of them in urgent need of attention. She wanted Mandaree to prosper. Also, she noted, "it is time to educate the Mandaree People on the oil and gas development and its environmental issues." At the same time, she wrote to the governor of North Dakota, outlining the Mandaree community's needs and asking how the community could access money set aside by the North Dakota state legislature to help counties cope with impacts from the oil boom. The governor promised to call her, she remembers, but never did.

Lisa already knew Tex Hall, and she didn't expect an answer from him either. "You know, he's got that power. He's not gonna listen to us," she thought. The two of them had history; at one time she had considered him as a mentor. Both from Mandaree, they had met when she was in fifth grade and Hall was a school administrator and basketball coach. Lisa was determined and athletic, and Hall encouraged her in basketball and running. She became a cross-country star in high school. Over time they became close.

When Lisa was a senior in high school, Hall called her and a friend into his office. They were going to fire him, he told her. She was incensed and drove around Mandaree and the Four Bears area of Fort Berthold, collecting some 1,100 signatures on a petition to save Hall's job. But later their relationship soured. Lisa heard that Hall was going to be fired only because he had bought a Corvette with the school's money. Still later, in November 2010, she was one of the hundreds of tribal employees laid off under Hall's administration in what she thought was a politically motivated shake-up. She spoke out about the termination, contending that her rights had been violated.[45]

Indeed Hall did not reply to Lisa's letter, but in a nod to her activism he appointed her in the summer of 2012 to a group developing a strategic plan for the community through a state program called Vision West, aimed at managing economic growth in western North Dakota. In spring and summer 2012 Walter and Lisa also decided to conduct an informal assessment of community concerns. They went house to house, knocking on doors and talking to 149 residents.

The results confirmed what Lisa had suspected: Fort Berthold residents were uninformed about the oil boom and were concerned about its effects. The vast majority of people with whom they talked complained about visible air pollution and incessant flaring. More than eighty said they weren't receiving adequate information about the environmental impacts from oil and gas development; still more were concerned about their families' safety because of the man camps. More than two-thirds of the Mandaree neighbors with whom they spoke were living in overcrowded conditions, in homes badly in need of repair; they asked for a new health clinic, better roads, and updated sewer and water systems.

It became clear to Lisa that the riches of the oil boom were not reaching those who desperately needed help. Amid the ubiquitous rigs and flares, the reservation roads—already in poor repair—were crumbling, undermined further by the constant stream of oil trucks across them every day. Garbage from oil workers littered the reservation. Basics such as improved housing and sewage facilities had been slow to appear, as had improvements in the schools. When Lisa and Walter's first son, Michael, graduated from high school in 2010, he had an English teacher, business teacher, and math teacher. But when their second son's, Thomas's, turn came, there wasn't a single math teacher in Mandaree's high school; Thomas didn't receive any math instruction during his last two years except courses he could do by himself online. In 2012 he was the only student to graduate in his class from Mandaree High School. "So what happened," Lisa wondered, "to the other forty-nine kids who enrolled in Head Start with him?"

Although Tex Hall still lived in the Mandaree area, he didn't seem to Lisa to be prioritizing its development. Infrastructure projects on the reservation were often directly tied to damage done by the oil industry. The tribe itself had been responsible for repairing roads destroyed by oil and gas traffic. In 2014 Chairman Tex Hall said the tribe was planning to spend $100 million to improve reservation roads ruined by heavy trucks, as well as $100 million for a proposed bridge project that would open up the Twin Buttes area of the reservation to additional oil exploration. Another $65 million would be spent to build medical staff housing for an expanded clinic, necessary in part because of an increase in accidents.[46]

Over time other expenditures also came to light. Over in New Town housing prices were soaring as the town doubled in size and added businesses like motels and enormous gas stations to service the oil trucks. But nearby, visitors could also see, sitting on blocks, the ninety-six-foot yacht named *Island Girl*, which had been purchased by the tribe in 2013 in a misplaced attempt at encouraging tourism. The tribal government had spent around $2.5 million on it, but even once it began operating, it spent most of the year in drydock as the cold North Dakota wind whistled around it.[47] Tex Hall was quickly becoming associated with the oil boom's worst excesses.

Hall had served two terms as chairman starting in 1998, leaving office in 2006 before the oil boom began. Then he founded Maheshu Energy LLC in 2007, described in business applications as doing everything from "oil and gas leasing permits" to "cultural surveys and pipelines," supplying fresh water and drilling fluids.[48] When Hall was reelected to the tribal chairmanship in 2010, he retained control of his company. Soon his company was securing more and more contracts from oil companies that ostensibly operated under his tribe's regulation. The MHA Nation's supervising attorney, Damon Williams, concluded to the *New York Times* that "Obviously if you want to do business on a reservation, it's best to deal with the chief."[49] But tribal members had no meaningful way to complain. While the tribe passed an ethics code in 2008, there was no ethics committee to hear complaints until 2015.[50]

Hall's dealings went uninvestigated and unchecked by the tribal government until his personal connection to and financial dealings with an Oregon man with five past felony convictions, James Henrikson, forced their hand. Henrikson built a company to profit off of the oil boom on Fort Berthold that he operated from Hall's garage, exploiting Hall's position and also sharing profits with him. When James Henrikson was later convicted of murder for hire, his connection to Hall, and to the murders, was laid bare.

Affable and with sleek good looks, James Henrikson and his wife, Sarah Creveling, arrived on Fort Berthold in 2011 and insinuated themselves into Hall's life. They signed an agreement with Hall in 2012 and operated a trucking company from his garage, paying him $5,000 a month in rent and also sharing profits. The trucking company worked for both Hall's private oil field company and the tribal government, and it contracted with big oil companies, grossing about $2 million in profits in 2012.[51] James Henrikson and Sarah Creveling also had a personal relationship with Tex Hall and his family. They all vacationed together in Hawaii in 2012, and Henrikson's extramarital affair with the young adult daughter of Hall's longtime girlfriend resulted in a baby whom Hall considered his grandson.[52]

James Henrikson's nefarious dealings turned violent when he felt that his scheme was being threatened. In 2014 he was charged with murder for hire in two deaths: a disgruntled employee of Henrikson and Creveling's company, Kristopher Clarke, who vanished in 2012 after being last seen on Tex Hall's property in Mandaree, and Douglas Carlile, who was murdered in 2013 after he had tried to buy out Henrikson with another investor.[53] Henrikson was later convicted by a federal jury and sentenced to two consecutive life terms in prison.[54] Creveling, who cooperated with prosecutors, received probation and was ordered to pay at least $342,500 in restitution for embezzling money from the oil field truck business.[55] Tex Hall testified and was granted immunity.

This case came to symbolize the dark side of the energy boom. In September 2014 tribal members staged a protest the day before the

MHA Nation's primary elections, demanding release of a months-long investigation into Tex Hall's business activities by an outside law firm (which had been hired by the Tribal Business Council). The report had been presented to the Tribal Business Council on August 14 of that year, but it hadn't been released to the public. Finally, spurred by the clamor, the Tribal Business Council unlocked the administration building and handed out the report, which spread like wildfire on social media.

The report's findings about Tex were damning. It determined that shortly after his 2010 election to the tribal chairmanship, he had used his position to demand $1.25 million from an oil and gas company before signing off on its development plan. Furthermore, it suggested that Hall had used his office to secure more than $570,000 for James Henrikson as payment for water hauling associated with road dust control. The job had not been put out to bid, and Hall had not disclosed his interest in James Henrikson's company. Hall also played a direct role in getting Henrikson and his company hired for trucking work on the reservation. Hall and Henrikson's company had essentially participated in a joint venture, the investigation found, sharing proceeds.[56] "It pretty much shows corruption," Lisa concluded to herself.

Corruption had flourished in an environment with few external checks. In the MHA Nation, as on many reservations, the tribe owned the majority of the newspaper and appointed communications board members. Media scrutiny, therefore, was limited.[57] Under the MHA Nation's 1936 constitution, the tribal government budget wasn't subject to the disclosure and auditing requirements common among many federal, state, and county governments. Large amounts of money (including millions in a "special projects budget" in fiscal year 2014) were disposed of without any public scrutiny.[58] Significant numbers of tribal members have been nominally employed by the tribe in regulatory jobs they are loathe to lose but that have few actual duties as far as Lisa could tell. Tribal staff members are not incentivized to call out abuses. As one resident noted, people who are employed by the tribe have families to support and may look the other way in order to keep their jobs: Once they're on the bandwagon, most people want to stay there.

Frustration with all these things—corruption, the ugly side of the oil boom, and Tex Hall himself—reached a crescendo in fall 2014 with the release of the report. Mark Fox, a former Marine who had a law degree and was working as the tribe's tax director, seemed a safe choice to serve as the next chairman. While Hall called the corruption charges in the report a "smear campaign," he lost the September 2014 primary election to Fox, who went on to win the general election in November 2014.[59] Mark Fox ran on a reformist platform: more government transparency and responsiveness, stricter environmental regulations, improved efforts to address the negative effects of the oil boom, and more oil money to tribal members.

At his 2014 inauguration, Mark Fox announced a Christmas distribution of $1,000 to all enrolled tribal members. "Until now, the boom has brought more negative than positive," he said. "But if we change our mentality, we can turn things around."[60] Quickly he arranged for all members to receive a $1,000 payment quarterly. Fewer than a third of tribal members are landowners who receive royalties from oil leases on their land, and for those who don't personally own land and the associated mineral rights, their ability to benefit from the oil boom depends entirely on how the tribal government spends the money it receives.

Lisa and Walter knew that giving $4,000 annually to each of the more than fifteen thousand (and growing since the oil boom) enrolled tribal members would be popular, but they also felt that such a $60 million payout each year could be used instead to make infrastructure improvements in the community. Further, more than half the enrolled tribal members didn't even live on Fort Berthold. Why, Lisa wondered, did those who had stayed in Mandaree still have to sacrifice everything—living, for example, with water and sewer mains that backed up in the school—while everyone got a payout?

Mark Fox was sworn in as the chairman of the MHA Nation on November 5, 2014, wearing a feathered war bonnet. He had beaten his rival, tribal attorney Damon Williams, by 146 votes out of the 2,334 cast in the previous day's election. Immediately he had to face a new proposal that needed his attention and approval. As oil output had surged, the question of how to ship many thousands of barrels of oil to market had become more pressing. Oil companies had been relying on trains, but train transport for oil is expensive, and train transports have been known to derail and even explode.[61] Behind closed doors in Bismarck hotel rooms, Tex Hall had been meeting with oil executives about a new Bakken pipeline that would help to transport oil from Fort Berthold and the surrounding area.[62] Soon it would become known as the Dakota Access Pipeline.

# Pipelines and POWER on Fort Berthold　　2

I can feel the earth rumble at nighttime
when everything is quiet.
—Lisa DeVille

Chairman Mark Fox inherited a reservation that was literally crumbling under the weight of the oil trucks that, day and night, were speeding across it. The reservation was also swimming in pollutants. In July 2014 a pipeline owned by Crestwood Midstream/Arrow had burst, hemorrhaging fracking wastewater (also known as brine) for days and scorching the surrounding earth. The company estimated that at least one million gallons of fracking waste fluid had pooled, spilling into Lake Sakakawea. Lisa reflected, chillingly, that this spill was just upstream from the Mandaree community drinking water intake.

The spills were mounting. The *New York Times* found 850 company-reported oil-related environmental incidents on Fort Berthold from 2007 to October 2014.[1] More may have gone unreported. As Edmund Baker, the tribe's environmental director, told the paper in early 2014, under Tex Hall's administration, "Our tribal council is so focused on money, money, money. . . . And our tribal chairman is: 'Edmund, don't tell me about spills. I'm busy trying to do things for my people.'"[2] Baker likened living in the Bakken to being the last one left standing at the end of a wild party, surrounded by broken bottles and people passed out on the floor.[3]

Adding insult to injury, Lisa and her neighbors found signs scrawled over the reservation dumpsters for the kids to see: "You're welcome for all of the things us white men paid for you, dirty fucks." Another read simply, "FUCK INDIANS."

Lisa and Walter drove to the site of the 2014 Crestwood pipeline spill site, about five miles from their house, soon after it happened to survey the damage. They found scorched trees, grass, and bushes where lush summer vegetation had recently been growing. With her environmental science training, Lisa knew that fracking wastewater could be devastating. "Our people aren't educated in any of this," she fumed to Walter. "They don't know what brine is, don't know what the pipeline is doing, don't know what radioactive waste is. They're trusting their leaders." Walter agreed: "But those leaders are not looking out for the health or the betterment of the people. They are looking out for their own pocket."

Whenever an oil or wastewater spill occurred, the reservation's health center received dozens of worried phone calls; some patients were particularly anxious because they were immuno-compromised. "What should we do?" they would ask. But the doctors had no idea what to recommend following a spill; they weren't trained to deal with this problem, and there was no protocol in place. Meanwhile, Walter and Lisa were shocked at Crestwood's simple remediation efforts; to them it appeared that Crestwood had decided that dilution was the solution. A video from the MHA *Times* showed the company simply washing the wastewater down the hill into Lake Sakakawea as then chairman Tex Hall looked on.[4]

Mark Fox, sitting in Hall's old office in the low-slung brick tribal headquarters building west of New Town, agreed that the reservation's pipelines were problematic. To the media he admitted that shoddy construction—under the previous administration—had been commonplace: "Some of these pipes were put into place too soon, too fast—prior to my administration. . . . The integrity is questionable in many areas."[5] When the price of oil dropped in December 2014 and January 2015, soon after his inauguration, Fox spun the slowdown in oil development as a relief, allowing the tribe to take a breath and reassess its quick development.

But even as Mark Fox acknowledged the problems besetting some of the reservation's existing four thousand miles of pipelines, he was quickly swept into meetings about a new one—one that might completely change the way Bakken oil reached consumers around the country.[6] In January 2015 Mark Fox sat down with a representative from the company seeking to build a pipeline. "So, what's going on?" he asked.

As Fox discovered, the Dakota Access Pipeline, also called the Bakken pipeline, was a mammoth $3.8 billion project designed to carry up to 570,000 barrels of crude oil a day from the Bakken oil fields to Illinois. At existing production volumes, the pipeline would transport half the total oil produced in the Bakken. A pipeline was the "safest, most efficient and reliable mode of transporting crude oil," the company claimed.[7] Its goal was to lower transportation costs and decrease the use of rail and truck transport. Moving oil out of the Bakken by rail was costly and accident-prone; a new pipeline promised an efficient solution to the problem of how to transport the millions of barrels of oil coming out of the Bakken's productive ground. It would even free up rail capacity for transportation of grain and other crops out of the Dakotas, the company argued. Pipeline supporters hoped that it would generate millions of dollars in taxes and thousands of temporary construction jobs.[8] In December 2014, even before the meeting with Mark Fox, Dakota Access had filed an application with the North Dakota Public Service Commission to build the new line.[9]

The DAPL would primarily be owned by Dakota Access, LLC, which, in turn, was majority-owned by ETP. Co-founded in 1995 by billionaire businessman Kelcy Warren, ETP was a Texas-based Fortune 500 company worth $24 billion. Its main business was the transport and storage of crude oil, natural gas liquids, and refined products. And business was booming: in 2002 it operated two hundred miles of pipelines; by

2018, more than seventy-one thousand miles.[10] Kelcy Warren, the CEO, was an affable, soft-spoken Texan with a taste for expensive real estate and rock music. The son of a pipeline worker, he had accumulated vast wealth as he capitalized on the shale oil boom.[11] He owned an island off the coast of Honduras and a Texas ranch where he kept giraffes.[12]

ETP was seeking to route the pipeline under some four miles of land that the tribe owned adjacent to the reservation. But the plan hadn't gotten much attention, and in fact only a handful of people were talking about DAPL at all. Nicole Donaghy, an organizer working on the oil and gas task force of the nonprofit Dakota Resource Council, a membership-based organization that works with communities to push for responsible development, had only recently become aware of it. She drafted a resolution to oppose the pipeline because it would run so close to water. Acutely aware of his campaign promises to protect the tribe's water, Mark Fox was determined to sit down and negotiate hard to make sure that if the land was ceded, the tribe would be compensated. But immediately he was struck by the implicit threats of condemnation in the negotiations. The land was owned by the tribe, but it was not on the reservation—and thus was subject to state laws and state courts.

At the same time, some MHA Nation members were beginning to worry about what fracking was doing to their land and animals. Ranchers were losing cattle and horses to truck accidents on the roads. And people were starting to notice strange things: Kandi heard stories of cattle born deformed, something no one had ever seen before.

Then came another chilling realization: quietly but surely, the birds were disappearing. Migratory birds mistook uncovered waste disposal pits for ponds and died after becoming covered in oil waste. Rather than installing netting that would prevent the birds' deaths, companies often chose instead to pay a $350 fine for a citation issued by the Fish and Wildlife Service. In 2011 U.S. attorney Tim Purdon had tried to hold oil companies accountable for the dead birds, charging seven companies with misdemeanor violations of the Migratory Bird

Treaty Act.[13] Both from the state government and the oil industry, the reaction was overwhelmingly negative. Within twenty-four hours of filing the cases, Purdon received a call from a friend with a message from a top state official: "If Tim thought he would be a federal judge someday, that's done."[14] ("You'd have thought I put on Birkenstocks, went out to a well site, and bike locked myself to the derrick," Purdon mused.) Staunchly he pressed forward with his prosecution. Three of the companies signed plea agreements; Continental Resources decided to fight it as unreasonable government overreach and filed a motion to dismiss. Federal Judge Daniel Hovland agreed. He even refused to accept the guilty pleas of the companies that had already signed plea agreements and dismissed their cases.[15]

Continental Resources' CEO Harold Hamm went on to become Governor Mitt Romney's energy adviser during Romney's 2012 presidential campaign; in the second presidential debate Tim Purdon was watching with his wife when Governor Romney accused President Barack Obama of having so much of an animus against domestic oil that his U.S. attorney had indicted oil companies over some duck deaths.[16] Clearly, Purdon thought, the prosecutions had hit a nerve. Four years later presidential candidate Donald Trump—whose energy adviser was also Harold Hamm—came to Bismarck and called out the prosecution as an example of overreach by the Obama administration.[17] Upon taking office, the Trump administration set out to explicitly change the way it interpreted the Migratory Bird Treaty Act to prohibit these types of cases.[18] However, Purdon took pride that his prosecutions had increased the pressure to eliminate open pit waste disposal in the state.

In winter 2015 Lisa received a text message from a friend asking her to come over right away. When Lisa arrived at her friend's home in the reservation's Little Shell community, she could see the full horror of what had happened. Six of the woman's horses had died, and they lay stiffly on the frozen grass, covered by a thin blanket of snow. The animals looked to Lisa like they had been starved, but her friend was dismayed at the suggestion: "I was feeding them every day," she assured Lisa. The horses just weren't eating. Glancing around, Lisa noticed a number of fracked oil wells and a pipeline near the home, and she encouraged her friend to get the horses tested. The results, she said, showed evidence of toluene, a volatile organic compound found in petroleum. Even at low levels, it can lead to a galaxy of symptoms including confusion, weakness, nausea, and loss of appetite.[19]

No one was examining the long-term consequences of fracking for the health of people living on Fort Berthold, but research pointing to fracking's serious health effects was growing and undeniable. Multiple peer-reviewed studies from scientists at such institutions as Yale University, the University of Pennsylvania, and the University of Colorado show that the wide array of chemicals used in the fracking process can contaminate air and water and have severe long-term health implications for oil workers and surrounding communities—including such problems as cancer and disorders related to the respiratory, cardiovascular, brain, and nervous systems—the extent of which may not become clear for years.[20] Exposure to benzene, a carcinogen, is particularly worrisome. One study near fracked shale gas fields in Canada found that levels of benzene, which has been linked to low birth weights and some birth defects, were far higher for pregnant women in an area of intense fracking activity than in the general Canadian population.[21]

Water pollution is especially dangerous to human health, and the fracking process presents myriad opportunities for contamination to occur.[22] Fluids used in fracking or the resulting wastewater can spill, chemicals can migrate from fracked wells to aquifers, wastewater pits can leak, and workers can release inadequately treated wastewater.[23] Wastewater can be particularly difficult to clean up—even harder than oil—and it contains a toxic brew of chemicals, oil, and radioactive materials that can destroy farmland and pollute surface waters for years, as contaminants such as radium remain.[24] After spills of fracking wastewater, radium can persist in the water, killing fish, long after remediation efforts have begun.[25] Studies have pointed to the sudden death of animals after exposure to fracking fluids and cattle giving birth to stillborn calves after exposure to fracking wastewater.[26]

In North Dakota, however, the effects of the fracking boom on water quality were not being carefully monitored or documented. A 2016 North Dakota State Department of Health report on water quality monitoring referenced fracking only to note briefly that wastewater from man camps was a concern and to laud the increased use of such wastewater in the fracking process.[27] In the same reports from 2008, 2010, 2012, and 2014, fracking was not mentioned at all.[28]

Access to clean water on Fort Berthold was further complicated by the fact that individuals with water on their lands were selling it as a commodity. Fracking an oil well takes millions of gallons of water, so fresh water for fracking began to fetch a premium. The sheer quantity of water consumed by fracking is a concern. North Dakota receives only about fifteen inches of rain each year, while the EPA has estimated that for horizontal wells in shale formations, each well needs two to four million gallons per well.[29]

Amid the frequent spills on Fort Berthold, federal and tribal regulatory enforcement were proving wholly inadequate. Further, the problem was growing. North Dakota's oil and wastewater spills per well almost tripled from 2004 to 2013 as oil production ramped up.[30] In 2015 Edmund Baker reported seeing at least one spill a day—and sometimes more—of fracking fluids, crude oil, or human waste. But he had only six officers responsible for the nearly 1,500 wells and million acres of reservation land, far from the number needed to provide adequate oversight.[31] When the boom started, the closest EPA detectives charged with investigating environmental crimes were stationed in Helena, Montana, a twelve-hour drive from the oil patch; Tim Purdon pushed to bring those kinds of agents to North Dakota. In 2015 Edmund Baker admitted to journalists from Al Jazeera that he had issued only two fines, despite dealing with spills and dumping incidents on a daily basis. He estimated that with a larger staff educated in environmental regulations, the office would issue at least one fine a week.[32] Tribal member Dave Williams, head of the tribe's own oil company, said the problem was simple: low or nonexistent fines didn't present enough of a deterrent to big companies. On Fort Berthold a legal question of jurisdiction over non-Natives on reservation land also complicated enforcement, and the MHA Nation faced an uphill legal battle in holding oil and gas developers and their employees accountable for many wrongs.[33]

The Tribal Business Council is the governing body of the MHA Nation, establishing such regulations as minimum rates for oil and gas leases, royalties, and road and pipeline easements. But the tribe had lacked the capacity—and at times the desire—to adequately regulate the oil boom on its land. At first the Tribal Business Council was slow to adopt basic regulations. Now that it has enacted some, it doesn't always have jurisdiction to enforce them. Furthermore, Mark Fox was increasingly frustrated that tribal regulations weren't considered primary on the reservation by the federal government; he felt that he was constantly lobbying to be the regulator on the tribe's land, arguing that the tribe's interest in protecting its home should supersede all others.

The federal rules on gas capture, which permitted the incessant flaring on the reservation, were infuriating to both Mark and Lisa, who found them weak and permissive. State and federal authorities also allowed disposal pits for deep, underground injection wells for wastewater disposal on non-tribally-owned lands within the boundaries of the reservation. All together federal control of fracking was incomplete at best. A 2005 act of Congress exempted fracking from the Safe Drinking Water Act's provisions on underground injection, a measure that environmentalists called dismissively the "Halliburton loophole" after then vice president Dick Cheney's oilfield services company.[34] This loophole removed the EPA from regulating fracking, leaving regulation to the states.[35] Furthermore, oil companies were exempted by the Energy Policy Act from environmental statute provisions that would require them to reveal the stew of chemicals they shot into the ground as part of the fracking process.[36]

In the absence of adequate regulation, the reservation's water supply was clearly under threat. Kandi White, who, as noted, grew up on the reservation, spent her summers swimming in Lake Sakakawea and picking chokecherries, filling big white five-gallon buckets to make syrup or jam. During lazy afternoons fishing, her dad would dip a cup into the lake and drink the water. "This is the best water out there," he would say.

With pipelines crisscrossing the lake bed under Lake Sakakawea and horizontal drilling underneath, the previously crystal-clear lake water now looked silty and murky to Walter and Lisa. Sometimes it even glowed. Kandi's sister was swimming in the lake when she realized the water was bright turquoise. Kandi got a sample tested by the North Dakota Department of Health and learned that the color was the result of a blue-green algae bloom that can produce dangerous toxins. As fracking proceeded, the reservation's health center received still more calls from patients asking about the safety of drinking water as well. Dr. Kathy Eagle, the CEO of the health center, thought that other tribes posted water testing results in their newspapers, but if the MHA Nation was doing water safety testing, the health center wasn't seeing the results, and the doctors didn't have any information to share with patients. Uneasy herself, Dr. Eagle drank bottled water at home.

Lisa and Kandi saw trucks spill the chemical-laced toxic wastewater right on the roads. But even if a tribal police officer managed to get to the scene, the officer didn't have legal authority over a non-Native driver, and a sheriff with that authority might not show up for hours.

Walter DeVille was a volunteer firefighter, and when a truck that contained fracking fluids or wastewater was involved in an accident, he was one of the first people standing in the mess. His volunteer team formed in 2014 because fire departments in neighboring communities were becoming overwhelmed by calls and increased road traffic and sometimes took hours to arrive at the scene of an accident. His group decided, he said, "If we can get there first and do what we can, maybe we can save a life." They had seen mangled bodies, slick with oil spewed by tankers in a crash. Whenever Walter drove down the road, he tried to stay as far away as he could from the trucks.

Walter had heard that the fracking wastewater was radioactive, and he feared contamination while he was working. Along with his fellow volunteers, he tried to take precautionary measures, but none of them really knew what they were exposing themselves to. Walter had found himself at the scene of accidents involving huge trucks engulfed in flames, with unknown substances leaking out—probably fracking wastewater or diesel fuel. He had been to spills where there was fracking fluid all over the road, puddling or quickly seeping into the ground. A Hazmat team would come out three or four days later, but at that point the liquid could have made its way anywhere, he thought. At the scene of one accident to which Walter responded, a truck full of crude oil had come around a corner too fast and lost control. The young driver and his fiancée, both oil workers, were in the truck. The truck rolled, covering the driver and the truck in oil. His fiancée was thrown through the front windshield and lay in a ditch, covered in oil, for hours before the coroner arrived.

On May 7, 2015, another Crestwood pipeline burst and spilled 220,000 gallons of wastewater into a pasture in Mandaree. By that point Lisa was becoming even more nervous, and in July 2015 Lisa, Walter, and Nicole Donaghy took Dr. Avner Vengosh of Duke University and a team of researchers to spill sites in the Bakken so that they could collect water and soil samples. The team mapped more than 3,900 wastewater spill sites in North Dakota, most of them caused by the deterioration of pipes intended to transport flowback water from fracked pipes to injection wells for disposal underground. What these scientists found confirmed Lisa's worst fears. They said that contamination from fracking was widespread and persistent, and they had clear evidence that fracking had directly contaminated the water. Unlike spilled oil, which eventually breaks down in the soil, the chemicals, metals, and salts in the spilled wastewater don't break down, creating a legacy of radioactivity. Indeed contamination associated with wastewater spills was remarkably persistent, with high levels of contaminants even four years after a spill.[37]

Something else had started popping up all around Fort Berthold. Oil drillers use mesh tubes to strain solid waste from wastewater so as not to clog injection wells; those mesh tubes—called "frack socks"—become contaminated with radium from the shale.[38] Radioactive frack socks were required by state regulations to be shipped or transported to special processing plants equipped to handle them. But some oil operators simply dumped them in fields or community landfills to save money. In 2010 state health officials began receiving complaints from landfills about oily waste materials, including frack socks, that had been bagged and discarded illegally at conventional landfills. In the McKenzie County landfill, located just thirty-five miles from the Fort Berthold Reservation, almost one thousand radioactive frack socks were found in 2013.[39] In 2014 thousands of pounds of frack socks turned up at an illegal dump site in Watford City, twenty-five miles from Fort Berthold.[40] North Dakota regulators estimated in 2014 that as many as seventy tons of frack socks were discarded in the state every day.[41] In Mandaree toddlers were found playing with radioactive frack socks that had simply been dumped in a field.[42]

As the New York Times reported, when Tex Hall's property was about to be searched in July 2013 as part of the investigation into murders committed by Tex Hall's friend James Henrikson, Hall texted Edmund Baker and asked him to remove "a few frack socks" from his yard. Baker surmised the reason for this request: with the removal, searchers wouldn't come across an illegal radioactive dumpsite on Hall's property. Baker and his crew found some two hundred frack socks in Hall's field; they were "sun-baked" and looked as if they had been there a while.[43]

At the same time, Lisa and her neighbors were worrying about the air they were breathing. Air contamination from sand in fracking fluid and airborne chemicals from wastewater often occurs around fracking sites.[44] It causes many of the same problems as water pollution: respiratory and nervous system disorders, birth defects, blood disorders, and cancer.[45] Indeed asthma attacks have been shown to be more common when asthma patients are living in an area with fracking.[46] Flaring also poses significant health concerns, increasing the risk of premature births among pregnant women.[47]

There is no active surveillance of asthma on the reservation. Dr. Kathy Eagle at the reservation's health center had heard speculation about an increase in asthma and other respiratory problems, but she found it impossible to tease out whether emissions from oil development or smoking might be the culprit. She hadn't heard of any air quality testing, and she worried that conditions like Respiratory Syncytial Virus (RSV, a common respiratory ailment that can be serious for infants or older adults) might be exacerbated by air quality issues, particularly given the reservation's omnipresent flaring.

Lisa had also heard about people from her community—in their thirties, forties, and fifties—getting cancer. When she pushed, they brushed it off: "Mom or Dad or Grandma or Grandpa had cancer. So, you know, that's probably the reason I got it," she would hear. The tribe was not doing active surveillance on cancer rates; still Dr. Eagle observed that the reservation's health center was seeing more cancers, though it was hard to tell whether the incidence was up or more people were seeking care. Cancers and reproductive problems could take years to develop, and it could be difficult to definitively link them to an environmental risk factor.[48] While the social impact on the reservation from road accidents, man camps, and drugs was easy to see, Kandi lay awake at night worrying about the day—even twenty years hence—when the long-term health effects from fracking, especially cancers, would finally show up.

Sadly Fort Berthold residents were used to getting sick. When the reservation flooded in 1953, it lost its hospital, which the U.S. government—despite promises—never rebuilt. Instead it gained a legacy of inadequate medical care, particularly for emergencies and serious conditions like cancer. Only a tiny clinic, built fifteen years after the flooding and only open during business hours from Monday through Friday, was available to reservation residents for decades. During this time health on the reservation underwent a steep decline. Anyone injured or sick after 5 p.m. or on a weekend had to travel at least eighty-five miles from New Town to an off-reservation hospital. Then if the federal Indian Health Service (IHS) later deemed that visit a non-emergency, the resident would be faced with a staggering and potentially ruinous bill. After 1953 health problems on Fort Berthold, including cancer, heart disease, and diabetes, reached epidemic proportions in the absence of preventive care. Chairman Tex Hall declared in 2003 that cancer rates were up to seven times the national average. Many patients might have benefited from screening to detect the cancer early, but the reservation's clinic lacked screening capacity.[49] Finally, a larger health center, funded by the tribe and the federal government and later headed by Dr. Eagle, was built in 2011, with some screening capacity.[50]

The tribe contracted with the IHS to provide its own health-care services. The U.S. government has committed by treaty and law to provide health care for Native Americans. However, the IHS is chronically underfunded to near-catastrophe on an annual basis—federal funding covers only about half of the MHA Nation's expenditures on health—leading to grossly inadequate coverage that the MHA Nation has felt compelled to supplement. An old adage about IHS is, "Get seen before June, before the money runs out." Journalists studying South Dakota IHS hospitals have found mistaken amputation of limbs; an incident including doctors restraining and pepper spraying a man overdosing on meth, causing a fatal heart attack; a suicide attempt by a twelve-year-old in the emergency room; and mold on hospital walls that make health-care workers and patients sick.[51] The standard of care may mean that unless loss of life or a limb is immediately threatened, treatment is deferred. With a high poverty rate and low insurance rates, many Native people rely exclusively on the IHS for health services, leading to major disparities compared to the general population, including high incidences of alcoholism mortality, diabetes, and tuberculosis.

Even before fracking came to the reservation, other kinds of pollution were undermining the residents' health. Environmental groups have long complained that coal plants upstream were contaminating waterways in the area with mercury, which is particularly harmful to children and developing fetuses (causing irreversible deficits in verbal skills, damage to attention and motor control, and lower IQs).[52]

While Kandi White was growing up, she saw cancer diagnoses all around her. She thought that was normal until she left for college on the other side of the state, in Grand Forks. There her new friends were surprised to hear her casually talk about acquaintances back home with cancer. When one friend finally asked, "Why do you know so many people with cancer?" Kandi was surprised. "Don't you?" "No, that's not normal," the friend said. Then she began to wonder: was there something wrong on the reservation? In Fort Berthold it seemed that everybody had cancer when she was growing up—prostate cancer, liver cancer, lung cancer, uterine cancer, brain cancer. Were environmental pollutants even then causing these cancers?

Whatever the cause, poor health care certainly exacerbated the cancer problems, as Kandi herself discovered. A decade before the oil boom, Kandi was home from college on Thanksgiving break when she discovered a pea-sized lump in her stomach and saw a red and purple bruise on the skin. She instantly realized, "This is bad; this is cancer." She went to the reservation's health clinic because it was the only health insurance she had, but the clinic wouldn't refer her off the reservation to have the tumor diagnosed. The doctor told her to come back in thirty days; she came back in just six, but the tumor had already grown from pea to walnut size. She had a stage 4 sarcoma tumor, often a death sentence. Six surgeries later at hospitals off the reservation, Kandi was a survivor, though she had lost friends to other cancers.

Fracking compounds the already fragile health situation on the reservation, posing a major new threat to community members. But it also endangers the oil workers themselves, who work in close proximity to hazardous chemicals—hydrogen sulfide and silica, which can cause silicosis, an incurable lung disease—and face such daily risks as explosions, fires, and vehicle collisions.[53] Medical facilities in North Dakota have been overwhelmed by casualties of the oil boom in the Bakken: bodies torn apart by accidents on roads full of trucks, accidents on the oil rigs, an increase in sexually transmitted disease. Many of the workers are uninsured.[54] The health center on Fort Berthold serves only the Native population. Hospitals off the reservation were struggling because they could not deny care to anyone in an emergency situation, but the transient oil worker population was not paying its bills. Meanwhile, those hospitals relied more than ever on the MHA Nation to reimburse them for after-hours and emergency care for tribal members.

A flaring well stands half a mile from Lisa and Walter's home, and the smell of rotten eggs permeates their house when the wind blows in their direction. Since oil extraction started, they have experienced frequent respiratory illnesses, sometimes suffering for weeks from uncontrollable coughing and congestion. In summer 2017 Walter fell ill with a cough, runny nose, and congestion. Lisa came down with the same thing, and they went to the health center on the reservation, where they got some medicine. But they didn't get any better, so they finally drove forty-five minutes to an off-reservation clinic in Watford City. "It's a virus," the doctor told them. She gave Walter a steroid shot and Sudafed to Lisa. Then she added something that resonated: "You know," she said, "we see a lot of what you guys have got. You have the same symptoms as the oil field workers." She called it the "Bakken cough." It took eight weeks for them to heal.

By 2015 Lisa had finally earned her B.S. in environmental science, graduating alongside her son. As environmental incidents on the reservation mounted, Lisa and two local residents, sisters Theodora and Joletta Birdbear, began asking more and more questions about the environmental impact of fracking. Lisa had begun to write essays to raise awareness, becoming a regular fixture in the local newspaper.

With the help of the Dakota Resource Council, Lisa and the Birdbear sisters, along with a handful of other tribal members, founded Fort Berthold Protectors of Water and Earth Rights (POWER). Fort Berthold POWER was the latest incarnation of two earlier organizations. Years before a small group of residents had formed an environmental awareness group to fight a proposed oil refinery that was never built. Next a group called Save Our Aboriginal Rights (SOAR) spun off, working with local landowners concerned about the environment. Now they had a new name and a new mission: POWER aimed to push back against local officials and corporations, bringing Native and non-Native people in the surrounding communities together to advance environmental and political goals. The group's first meeting was at the tribal museum in New Town. Some prospective members were hesitant to join for fear of retaliation. "Yes, it's rough and hard out here," declared Theodora Birdbear to journalists. "But this is our land, darn it, this is what we've got left and we've got to fight."[55]

One of POWER's first acts was to speak out against the DAPL. ETP had applied to the North Dakota Public Service Commission (PSC) in December 2014 for a route permit.[56] The company was working through the process of seeking easements from affected private landowners. In May 2015 Dakota Access's parent company said it had already obtained some 55 percent of the land easements needed in North Dakota. The company held three public hearings that May and June, soliciting public comment that would become part of the PSC's official record as it considered Dakota Access's permit application. The North Dakota Department of Health wrote to the PSC, concluding that "environmental impacts from the proposed construction will be minor and can be controlled by proper construction methods." It did caution that care was to be taken with construction near water.[57] But some North Dakota landowners were wary.

Elsewhere the pipeline company was reportedly using aggressive tactics to get the land it needed. On its proposed route from North Dakota to Illinois, the pipeline would include a 343-mile diagonal route across Iowa. In May an Iowa landowner claimed that a land agent working with Dakota Access, LLC had offered him a sex worker in exchange for allowing the pipeline to cross his land, and he had an audio recording to prove it.[58] Company officials told landowners they would use eminent domain laws if landowners refused to sign voluntary agreements. Some North Dakota landowners also called the PSC, reporting that they had been bullied by the company and threatened with the specter of eminent domain. Dakota Access filed civil lawsuits to gain access to several landowners' properties to conduct surveys.

On a lovely warm day in June 2015 Lisa DeVille drove thirty miles past the oil rigs and flares surrounding her home across the reservation boundary to testify at the second of the three public hearings on DAPL in Killdeer, North Dakota. More than eighty people were in the room that day, but Lisa and the Birdbear sisters were the only MHA Nation members who had come. Almost all the faces in the crowd were those of white landowners, mostly men, who would be affected by the pipeline.

The hearing began at 9 a.m. and lasted all day. Dakota Access first presented its case, and then—after almost six hours—private individuals were finally permitted to make their comments. The public commissioners were polite; they encouraged people to ask questions, and landowners did express their concerns. But it became clear that the commissioners were assuming that the pipeline would be built. Its creation seemed non-negotiable; particulars such as the exact route were the only ones on the table. One farmer and rancher, pushed by the commissioners to suggest the best location for the pipeline on his land, protested: why was there a presumption that he had to come up with a solution?[59]

After more than eight hours, Lisa was able to speak. She talked about pipeline malfunction, the Crestwood spills, and spills upstream on the Missouri River. She urged the commission to reject the pipeline. Lisa's written statement was entered into the hearing's formal record: "It is up to you to use your influence to reject [the] Dakota Access

Pipeline and support clean, renewable, and sustainable solutions for our future ahead," her testimony read.[60] Theodora Birdbear also spoke forcefully about the dangers of the pipeline to water, while her sister Joletta Birdbear urged the commissioners to reject the pipeline. "We don't want to be desecrated, so don't hand us documents that lead to that," she said.[61]

Finally the hearing concluded. "This is a tough place to be . . . it's impossible to make everybody happy," one commissioner acknowledged. She pointed out that they had all driven to the hearing using gasoline and noted society's dependence on fossil fuel. Thus, she said, the commission faced the challenge of balancing a "God-given resource" with minimal impact.[62] In North Dakota, says Nicole Donaghy, testifying at a public hearing is not often a fruitful process since the commissioners usually have their minds made up. But Lisa and POWER had succeeded in making their opposition to the pipeline part of the public record.

The pipeline had already faced opposition from Native nations in Iowa. Two tribes, plus Dakota Rural Action and the Indigenous Environmental Network (IEN; an international nonprofit that had been involved in several pipeline battles) had joined forces to oppose the pipeline in South Dakota. But supporters were also galvanizing: at the final North Dakota hearing, just a week or so after the one Lisa attended, a labor union made its case for the pipeline.

While Lisa and the Birdbear sisters were in Killdeer, the MHA Nation was forging ahead with its own effort to produce oil, which it planned on having the DAPL carry to market. In June 2015 Missouri River Resources, a newly incorporated company owned by the tribe and with a 75 percent Native American work force, produced its first barrel of oil, and a year later it was pumping around one thousand barrels of oil a day. Missouri River Resources' head, tribal member Dave Williams, had experience in the oil industry; he wanted to help the tribe to produce its own oil and start a workforce program. He was also ceding more profits to the landowners. When the tribe and individuals on the reservation had leased their lands to private oil companies for drilling, the landowners received royalties of just 16–18 percent of the money generated by the oil on the property.[63] Missouri River Resources generally gave 26 percent, depending on how much the landowners needed up front as a bonus. Still it scrambled to acquire land since almost all of it had been leased already. It cost between $6 and $8 million to drill a well, a cost that had to be recovered through the oil. Dave Williams still keeps a little bottle of the oil that came out of the company's first well; a *Star Trek* fan, he jokingly summarizes his company's mission: "To boldly go where no Indians have gone before."

In July 2015 Mark Fox and his full Tribal Business Council went down to the Dakota Access headquarters in Houston to negotiate. He got into a heated argument with executives there about what he saw as the company's transparent efforts to take advantage of the tribe. "You want to negotiate?" he asked. "Or do you want to fight? Because if we negotiate, it's going to be on behalf of our people." Fox was frustrated that Dakota Access wanted tribal members to take what he saw as pennies in compensation for their land. But he also knew that the company held a trump card. The tribe's land, under which the pipeline would pass, was not federal trust land on the reservation; since it lay across the reservation boundary, it was subject to state jurisdiction. If the state supported condemnation of the land, he thought the tribe stood to lose a lot. And in their negotiations there was an undertone of the threat of condemnation.

At the end of July 2015, after its three public hearings had concluded, North Dakota's PSC met to discuss the pipeline. From the first meeting, the question of whether the pipeline should go forward in North Dakota was not even under consideration. One of the commissioners deemed the project "pretty good." They sat down to the business of working out reroutes, where trees needed to be cleared, and what reclamation would be necessary.[64] At another work session in late August, the commission noted that Dakota Access had secured voluntary easements on close to 70 percent of the land on its path through the state.[65] The company was moving quickly: at the end of August at least one North Dakota landowner heard that he had a week to accept the company's compensation offer for the easement on his land, or the offer would be withdrawn and the company would go to court.[66]

In November 2015 the South Dakota Public Utilities Commission approved the pipeline in a 2–1 vote—the first state to do so. The dissenting commissioner, Gary Hanson, blamed the company for "trampling on citizens' property rights" and using "abusive" practices to sue landowners to survey their properties.[67] Two days later the Illinois Commerce Commission unanimously approved that state's portion of the pipeline. The pipeline route was still under review in the other affected states, including North Dakota, but momentum was building.

Lisa knew that the tribe was making a deal. Chairman Fox told the Tribal Business Council on November 12 that the tribe had come to an agreement with the company for the right of way through the tribe's land.[68] Then on December 2, 2015, the Tribal Business Council officially approved construction of the DAPL under the tribally owned land.[69] There was no opportunity for public comment, and Lisa didn't think people on the reservation knew much about the pipeline. The exact terms of the twenty-five-year lease were protected by a non-disclosure agreement (Mark Fox simply described the amount as "significant" and "a good deal" for the tribe), but the figure reportedly ran into the tens of millions. Fox was pleased that the tribe had avoided legal costs as well as condemnation.

Lisa was upset when she heard the decision. She suspected that some Tribal Business Council members had accepted bribes to close the deal, but she couldn't prove it. Kandi was also frustrated. Mark Fox was her relative—her stepmother's brother—but she didn't agree with his decision. "Why did you do this to us?" she asked Fox. His reply rang all too true, given the tribe's history: "'Look, they were threatening condemnation. They were threatening eminent domain. They were going to do it anyway. We might as well get the money for it.'" In 1953 the MHA Nation had fought back against the Garrison Dam and lost, seeing its best land flooded and way of life stolen; a century earlier it had fought against being forced onto a reservation and had lost then too.

Dakota Access began building the pipeline just a few miles over the reservation line from Fort Berthold. These striped, clay buttes jutting to the sky, mixed with patches of green grass, were the badlands; the tribe had intended to turn this stretch into a buffalo ranch, but the necessary fence had never been finished. When Walter and Lisa drove by the site just a few miles from their Mandaree home, they saw bull-dozers clear-cutting the trees and starkly beautiful clay buttes. Over the course of months Lisa and Walter saw an entire habitat vanish before their eyes.

After it finished the agreement with the MHA Nation, the pipeline company filed twenty-three condemnation lawsuits against 140 land-owners in North Dakota.[70] Mark Fox felt vindicated. But the tribe didn't know when it voted that the company was also planning to cross under land near the Standing Rock Reservation, just 150 miles to the south of Fort Berthold. A few months later, in early 2016, Mark Fox found a notice on his desk from the tribal government down at Standing Rock: it was planning to take a stand.

# JASILYN

I knew I had to help them. These people weren't from my tribe, and I didn't know them personally, but I felt I needed to be there. It was like gravity. It just pulled me there.

—Jasilyn Charger

In summer 2015, as the MHA Nation's Tribal Business Council was working to strike a deal on DAPL, nineteen-year-old Jasilyn Charger returned to the town of Eagle Butte, South Dakota, on the Cheyenne River Reservation, south of Standing Rock, which is home to four bands of the Lakota people. She flew home after several friends on the reservation had attempted or committed suicide. But Jasilyn, who is Lakota, had her own demons: she was addicted to cocaine and alcohol. She had always been tall and striking and considered herself chubby, but lately she had dwindled to a skeletal eighty pounds.

Her cousin Joseph White Eyes, nineteen, took her for a drive and attempted to intervene. He pulled the car over and shouted: "Look what you're doing to yourself!" Jasilyn and Joseph had grown up together, living with family members when their mothers were too troubled to take care of them, and they were close. Joseph was soft-spoken, with a ready smile, and seeing him so upset hurt Jasilyn. "See, you're crying," he said. "The pain you're going through, this is the pain you're putting us through. We have to watch you do this." His intervention came at a crucial time: the night before Jasilyn had been so strung out on cocaine that she had ended up in a bathtub and couldn't remember how she had gotten there. In the past she had sometimes

a couple, and he assured her she had the strength and courage to do anything she wanted.

Buoyed by this encouragement, Jasilyn moved to Rapid City, where she got a job as a video editor at a local Fox news station and lived in her own apartment. But the news station was all middle-aged white men, and she grew tired of what she saw as their undisguised racism. Jasilyn returned home to Eagle Butte in the summer of 2015, when her cousin Joseph helped her turn her life around.

Possessed of a quiet strength that seemed nothing short of miraculous given her turbulent childhood, Jasilyn was a talented singer. She considered herself a "two-spirit," a term used to describe the embodiment of two genders residing within a person. She loved animé and the television show *Game of Thrones*. She was also wise beyond her years, a compelling and gifted speaker, and with an understanding borne of hard experience.

At last by early fall 2015, Jasilyn felt reborn. She began to see with greater clarity the lives of her friends in Eagle Butte. They were coming of age in an environment marked by poverty, meth addiction, and alcoholism. The pain from which they ached was hereditary pain, passed down through generations after decades of misdealing by the U.S. government. She still struggled with depression, but she wanted to help the youth of Cheyenne River. She decided to start small.

Jasilyn, now off drugs and working with reservation youth, channeled her troubled childhood into community activism. She helped Joseph to form a youth group called the One Mind Youth Movement. At least eight regulars met every Sunday at the local college library. Jasilyn dragged Kalen to meetings, and Jasilea brought her boyfriend. At first Kalen sat quietly and listened, but the discussion captivated him too. They talked about things they wanted for the community: more recreational facilities, greater use of the Lakota language, a safe house for youth, legal marijuana. Life on Cheyenne River could be hard; even the tribal chairman readily acknowledged that high poverty, unemployment, and poor infrastructure were challenges. But the issue at the top of everyone's mind was suicide.

Many recent attempted and completed suicides at the Pine Ridge Reservation in South Dakota had been getting a lot of attention, but Joseph knew there were other cases in Cheyenne River that the media hadn't covered.[2] Eagle Butte had twenty-eight recent attempts and two completions, and Joseph wanted to draw attention to the issue. He and Jasilyn saw their friends leaving them at such an alarming rate that they needed to do something. Jasilyn reached out on Facebook to people who might be afraid to speak up about their depression. The group's first act was to hold a prayer vigil following a wake for a girl who had committed suicide. A local car dealer loaned them a microphone system, churches donated candles, and they lined Eagle Butte's Main Street with marchers. More than a hundred people showed up. Jasilyn saw that they were starting to create a support system.

Eagle Butte has a population of 1,300, and though it is the biggest town on the Cheyenne River Reservation, it is a small place and opportunities there are limited. Yapping rez dogs bark and circle the housing developments and trailers in town; cigarette butts discarded on the ground are quickly picked up by passersby in case there is a smoke left in them. Since jobs on local farms go mostly to family members, the main options left for employment are fast food work, day labor, and some tribal jobs.

Many of the kids Jasilyn knew in Eagle Butte used drugs, especially Triple C (the cold medicine Coricidin HBP Cold and Cough, which contains the hallucinogen dextromethorphan). At $3 a pack, it would curb their appetites for eight hours while giving them hallucinations. A sandwich cost nearly $5, so doing drugs had become cheaper than eating. Others would use Robitussin to get high—it numbed them, Jasilyn thought, and sometimes it was easier not to feel.

Jasilyn saw her friends losing hope. While their families wanted them to get good jobs, the youth couldn't find any—and certainly not meaningful ones. Even those who did find employment saw the years stretching before them with low wages that would never be enough. Jasilyn heard her friends saying, "Well, if I get a job, I'm going to be stuck working there for the rest of my life, and it ain't ever going to mean nothing. I'm never going to keep moving forward; my family's never going to flourish." And so some decided not to even try. They didn't see a road that would work for them. "If this is what I'm here for, then I don't want to be here," she heard them saying.

The Eagle Butte youth were not alone. From 2000 to 2016 suicide rates rose across the United States.[3] Among American youth aged 15–24, suicide was the second-leading cause of death in 2013.[4] Native youth suicide has been at crisis levels for years and an epidemic on reservations.[5] Indeed even though likely undercounted, Native American youth aged 18–24 have the highest suicide rate of any racial or ethnic group, with Native young men more than twice as likely to commit suicide as their peers in other racial and ethnic groups.[6] The high rate of suicide among Native youth, says Dr. Donald Warne of the University of North Dakota School of Medicine, is strongly related to trauma, both the historical trauma from when populations lived under stressful, toxic conditions that could cause changes even to their DNA and the personal trauma related to adverse childhood experiences.

On Cheyenne River, as on many reservations, along with violence, inadequate housing, unemployment, and addiction, poverty is the legacy of historic wrongs. Native youth are disproportionately represented in foster care and have high school graduation rates lower than those of non-Native youth. Trauma, discrimination, lack of access to mental health services, and family breakdown all contribute to the risk of suicide. Generations of Native exploitation and genocide—the appropriation of Native lands by European and American settlers, destruction of their traditional lifestyle, treaty violations, and the introduction of abusive boarding schools—have taken a heavy toll on Native youth, stripping them of their culture and contributing to suicides today.[7]

With the creation of the One Mind Youth Movement in 2015, Jasilyn and Joseph were eager to give the youth on Cheyenne River a sense of belonging and hope. The youth group raised funds by shoveling snow, at first for community elders and the disabled. From summer to fall 2015, Jasilyn went from looking for marijuana to buy on Facebook to posting inspirational messages, photos of marches, and her number to those who needed help.

As experts agreed, the key to halting the suicide epidemic was countering feelings of hopelessness. A program on the Pine Ridge Reservation used tribal traditions and culture to prevent suicide, while another on the Rosebud Reservation in South Dakota used traditional Lakota cultural education to rehabilitate juveniles caught in the criminal justice system.[8] On Cheyenne River there wasn't any treatment facility for youth who tried to commit suicide; they were sent to jail, then on to the Yankton Reservation, a four-hour drive away, where the mental health facility was located. As Jasilyn and Joseph's One Mind Youth Movement grew, it gave youth in Eagle Butte a sense of belonging.

Jasilyn and Joseph began organizing marches and raising community awareness about the Keystone XL Pipeline. The more immersed she became in this work, the more Jasilyn began to feel as though she could take back power over her life. She was excited to be a part of something that felt real and could lead to substantive change on an issue in which she believed. The group began receiving invitations from around the country. Jasilyn, Joseph, and Jasilea took part in the Indigenous Climate March in California in September 2015. With the help of IEN, Jasilyn traveled to Washington DC for her first protest in November. She spoke in front of a crowd for the first time, talking about environmental justice, immigration reform, and racial justice. She had found her voice.

One chilly day in November 2015, as the MHA Tribal Business Council was on the verge of approving DAPL's route upstream, Josephine Thundershield—a Lakota youth worker and mother of eleven living in the town of McLaughlin, South Dakota, on the Standing Rock Reservation—learned a disturbing fact. A friend who worked at the PSC in Bismarck showed her plans for a pipeline, and she saw that it would pass perilously close to the Standing Rock water supply. That evening Thundershield gathered a few friends to talk over the news. She was alarmed. She had heard stories coming out of Fort Berthold about what oil had done to that community that had made her sick—man camps, women disappearing, children sexually abused. Like Thundershield, her friends were concerned.

One of their first calls was to Joye Braun from the Cheyenne River Reservation. Beset with health problems, including rheumatoid arthritis, stroke, and fibromyalgia, Braun sometimes used a wheelchair, but it didn't hold her back. She was a former journalist and veteran community organizer who had gotten her first taste of activism when she helped save her tribe's buffalo herd from liquidation in order to pay tribal debts. She went on to protest the "megaloads"—giant truckloads, hauled by a rig and trailer, that filled both lanes of a two-lane highway—crisscrossing the reservation. The megaload traffic was a result of the oil boom in the Bakken and the tar sands of Alberta, Canada; the tribe had banned fracking and had passed a resolution against the megaloads but didn't have the resources to enforce it.[9]

Braun was involved in the fight against the Keystone XL Pipeline, which TransCanada (later TC Energy) sought to build from the tar sands of Alberta to Nebraska, where it would connect to existing pipelines. Braun had already been following the progress of DAPL closely, and that very month she had traveled from her home in Eagle Butte to a hearing on the pipeline in Boone, Iowa. "We will stop the second snake from coming for our land," Braun said.[10] She worried that this pipeline would bring other social problems—man camps, rapes, murders, and drugs—like fracking had brought to the Bakken. When Thundershield contacted her, Braun was ready to take the fight to Standing Rock, but she needed more support. She called on young friends and former allies in the Keystone fight: Jasilyn and Joseph.

Working with the youth, thought Braun—who was a grandmother—kept her young.

When President Barack Obama denied the proposed Keystone XL Pipeline permission to cross the border with Canada in November 2015, effectively halting the project, Jasilyn, Joseph, and their fellow activists felt jubilant. But within weeks their celebrations ceased. Joseph received a message from Joye Braun asking him to get the youth council together to go to Standing Rock. "You guys want to get involved in another fight?" she asked. He called up Jasilyn, and they agreed that they did. Braun had begun attending meetings all over the Standing Rock Reservation to talk about the DAPL—in McLaughlin, Cannon Ball (a town near the Cannonball River), and Fort Yates—to spread awareness about the plans. Jasilyn thought they could share their Keystone XL experiences with the youth on Standing Rock to help them to become more involved.

Meanwhile, DAPL was steadily securing all the necessary approvals. The North Dakota PSC approved the permit for the pipeline in January 2016, following on the heels of Illinois's approval. Construction on parts of the project was already beginning.[11]

The Standing Rock Sioux Tribe itself had been working behind the scenes since 2014 to combat the pipeline. LaDonna Brave Bull Allard—whose Native name is Tamakawastewin, Her Good Earth Woman—a Standing Rock Sioux tribal historian and a fiercely elegant woman with flowing black and silver hair, remembers she had first heard about it in 2014, when the tribe's historic preservation officer, Wasté Win Young, had come to her one day, plans in hand. "LaDonna, did you see this project?" she asked. "Look at the map. I think you're the closest landowner." Studying the plans, LaDonna realized that her family land was close to the proposed pipeline, and her mind went blank except for one thought: "My son is buried there. How *dare* they?" Her first obligation in life, she believed, was as a mother. Even though her son had left for the spirit world, it was still her duty to protect his grave. "They're having a meeting," Wasté Win Young said. "You'd better come."

The chairman of the Standing Rock Sioux Tribe, Dave Archambault, was a serious and thoughtful business owner and educator who chose his words carefully. Archambault had grown up on the Pine Ridge Reservation in the 1970s and entered politics to help the Standing Rock Sioux Tribe move out of a state of dependency on the U.S. federal government.

Starting in September 2014, Archambault had been clearly stating in meetings with the company building the pipeline that the tribe opposed it. DAPL was slated to cross under land to which the tribe had never ceded its rights, he insisted, adding that members felt incensed by the threat to their water supply and sacred sites.[12] But LaDonna felt that the tribe's comments fell on deaf ears, and she resolved to oppose the pipeline. "I'll be standing here," she thought to herself. "Even if I'm alone, I'll be standing here." Pretty soon, she noticed, the company stopped inviting tribal members to meetings.

The tribe knew that another entity would also have to play a role in the pipeline approval process: the Army Corps. Building a pipeline in North Dakota requires a state permit, but no federal agency has jurisdiction over oil pipelines, and there had been no broad environmental analysis conducted for the project. (By contrast, the Keystone XL Pipeline had had a full EIS because the proposed pipeline crossed an international border and required a federal permit.) But the Army Corps has regulatory responsibilities relevant to pipelines under Section 404 of the Clean Water Act and Section 10 of the Rivers and Harbors Act. Under these statutes a permit from the Army Corps is required for any point at which a pipeline touches water, such as a wetland, stream, or river. The Army Corps analyzes each of these contact points separately, ignoring the hundreds of miles of pipeline that connects them because its jurisdiction does not extend to them, and it streamlines the permit in a system called Nationwide Permit 12, which avoids extended environmental review.

The majority of oil pipelines subject to the Army Corps' regulation are authorized under Nationwide Permit 12. As the Congressional Research Service describes it, "A nationwide permit essentially pre-authorizes a group of activities similar in nature that are likely to have a minor effect on waters and wetlands both individually and cumulatively."[13] The system has been heavily criticized, and environmental lawyer Jan Hasselman thought of it as little more than a joke. However, legal challenges have been largely unsuccessful.[14] Dakota Access had applied to the Army Corps for a permit for the 202 proposed water crossings in North Dakota, South Dakota, Iowa, and Illinois.[15]

Buoying the tribe's hopes for careful consideration in the permit process was the obligation of the Army Corps to conduct a meaningful consultation with the tribe.[16] The National Historic Preservation Act (NHPA) was passed with the objective of fostering conditions for modern society and historic property to coexist. Section 106 of the act explicitly recognizes the right of Native nations to be consulted when a federal agency approves or commences a construction project that impacts property to which Native tribes attach religious and cultural significance, even if they live far away from it. In effect it is a "stop, look, and listen" statute. In order for the pipeline project to move forward, the Army Corps would have to issue a permit. So the tribe began demanding a meeting with the Corps. Noting the presence of historic sites, the tribe asked for a full EIS and archaeological survey.[17]

Dakota Access had also applied to the Army Corps for easements allowing the pipeline to cross Corps-managed federal land.[18] An easement and permission for the pipeline was necessary for it to cross beneath the Missouri River at Lake Oahe, which is managed by the Corps, half a mile upstream from the Standing Rock Reservation and seventy-three miles north of the Cheyenne River Reservation.[19] By its own analysis, the Corps had acquired the lands through condemnation as part of the Oahe Dam project. Previously it had been in private hands, after "the State of North Dakota claimed ownership of these lands through its statehood on February 22, 1889." The 1868

Fort Laramie Treaty, which established the Great Sioux Reservation, did not cede the area of land required for the easement. However, the Corps noted, "it is unclear from our Corps records how the Sioux tribes became divested of this property after 1868," though the treaty did include a clause on allowing utility works.[20]

The proposed path under Lake Oahe ran only a few miles from the tribe's existing water intake. An oil spill under the river would be devastating for the Standing Rock Sioux and for the rest of the eighteen million people who rely on the Missouri River for water. The right of everyone, without discrimination, to sufficient, safe, acceptable, accessible, and affordable water is a fundamental human right.[21] The Standing Rock Sioux rely on the Missouri River for their water supply, and the tribe was desperate to avoid problems with its water. Several years earlier, over the Thanksgiving holiday, the reservation's water plant intakes malfunctioned, and for a week the entire community was without water. People had to travel to buy drinking water; health facilities had to move their patients. An oil spill in the river promised even more devastation.[22]

Because of their own experience with pollution of the Cheyenne River, Jasilyn, Joseph, and Joye Braun had deep sympathy for the risks to the Standing Rock Sioux. When Braun was growing up, she would turn on the tap in the spring, and the water would come out brown, full of silt. That silt was poisonous; the Cheyenne River had been polluted by the Homestake Mine, the largest gold mine in America, which was near the headwaters of the Cheyenne. It closed in 2002 after a century of gold mining in the Black Hills of South Dakota. During that period millions of tons of tailings had washed downstream and left high levels of arsenic and mercury in some of the river sediment.[23] Studies have shown that arsenic in drinking water can cause cancer; further, in places where naturally occurring arsenic contaminates the groundwater, research has suggested that chronic exposure to high levels of this substance can also contribute to diabetes, cognitive deficits, and cardiovascular disease.[24] Mercury exposure can lead to nervous system damage, along with learning disabilities and developmental problems in children.[25] As Jasilyn and Kalen knew, the presence of mercury in their water meant there was a strict limit on how many fish they were supposed to eat—as on Fort Berthold—but they also knew that no one on Cheyenne River listened. Because of the reservation's poverty and the importance of fishing to Lakota culture, tribal members frequently ate mercury-contaminated fish. Kalen recalled finding a fish with three eyes in the river. Suspecting that the dirty water she drank had contributed to her myriad health problems, Braun was determined that her children and grandchildren wouldn't face the same future.

In December 2015 the Army Corps of Engineers published a draft Environmental Assessment (EA) of the pipeline, prepared by Dakota Access, LLC. It emphasized that the pipeline would, as much as was practical, follow the route of existing pipelines. It opened up the plan to public comments, including those on environmental and cultural impacts, but the draft EA did not assess the potential impact of the pipeline on the Standing Rock water supply.[26] Its related map didn't even note the existence of the reservation, a mere half mile away.[27]

In the early months of 2016, when Jasilyn, Braun, and Joseph were planning their trip to Standing Rock to meet with Dave Archambault and the tribal administration, Archambault himself was working feverishly, for the most part behind the scenes, to respond to the draft EA. He traveled to Washington DC to meet with government officials, including the Army Corps and Department of Defense, and he met with district-level Corps officials on the reservation. On February 5, 2016, he released a statement outlining the tribe's opposition to the proposed pipeline and criticizing the Corps for failing to consult with the tribe. He also described the cultural resources that could be impacted by the project and warned that an oil spill was a serious risk.[28]

At the same time, the One Mind Youth Movement was trying hard to get a youth safe house up and running on Cheyenne River. The group celebrated its first anniversary with pizza, sodas, and a birthday cake in early 2016. Joye Braun, who had been traveling to Standing Rock for meetings related to the pipeline—raising funds for gas money by selling home-baked loaves of banana bread or cinnamon rolls—was gearing up for a battle. After a meeting in McLaughlin, she urged relatives to get ready to fight the pipeline. "It only takes a few [people] to start a revolution," she remarked on Facebook.[29] On February 25 she issued a call: "Pipeline fighters . . . Dakota Access pipeline is threatening our homelands. . . . Are you ready??"[30] LaDonna Allard exhorted people to stop by the tribal offices the next day to tell the Army Corps not to issue the permit for DAPL, the "black snake."

On February 26, 2016, Braun brought Jasilyn, Kalen, and Joseph to Standing Rock for a meeting with the tribal administration. Braun sat outside the administration building next to the others, wearing a black beret and waving a Cheyenne River Sioux Tribe banner. "No Pipeline, No Problem," declared Joseph's sign. Braun thought that people on Standing Rock were starting to wake up to the dangers of the pipeline to their water supply. "You can't eat money and you can't drink oil," she said to a reporter from the *Bismarck Tribune*.[31] When it came time for the meeting, the room was packed.[32]

After meeting with the tribal administration, Jasilyn, Joseph, Joye Braun, and Kalen went to another meeting with Standing Rock community members. Even though the Standing Rock Reservation was only a few hours' drive from Cheyenne River, Jasilyn had not visited it often—only to watch her high school-age sisters play basketball or for powwows. But her father's mother was from Cannon Ball, so in some ways the meeting was like coming home. When she walked in, she was expecting a crowd of kids to be there to talk with them, but there weren't any young people at all. Instead she felt a ripple of surprise at her age from the tribal elders who were present. "You guys are all children," one of the Standing Rock members said. Jasilyn agreed. But when they spoke, the Standing Rock community members seemed impressed that such young activists were involved in community organizing and tackling a problem on another reservation. "Where's our young people?" she heard them ask.

Joye Braun, Joseph, and Jasilyn all spoke, sharing their experiences of community organizing. "How far are you willing to go to stop this when it comes?" Joseph asked the room directly. He talked about nonviolent actions, about interactions with the police, and about organizing. Then someone in the room asked, "Well, what should we do?" "Start a camp," replied Braun immediately. They asked if anyone would be willing to start one. The room was silent.

LaDonna Allard came up to them after the meeting. "I have land right at the mouth of Cannonball River," she told them. "and you can use it for this camp." Her land was carpeted in summer with fragrant sage, wild buffalo berries, plums, juneberries, wild grapes, and chokecherries. It also contained the burial site of her father, her aunts and cousins, and her son, who had died in 2007 of a heart attack at age thirty-four. LaDonna hadn't planned to start a camp—in fact she had recently resolved to focus the rest of her life on becoming the best grandmother in the world. She had spent her career as a historian, not an activist, but this cause was personal to her. In addition to her family connection, the land was where a Mandan village had bustled centuries earlier, where unmarked graves lay along the tops of the hills, where a spirit had put medicine in the ground to make the land sacred. Jasilyn felt that LaDonna was pleading with the youth to stand with her, and she knew they needed to help.

After the meeting they left for a house in Fort Yates, the largest city on Standing Rock, to attend a *yuwipi*, a traditional Lakota healing ceremony. The doors were locked, the windows blacked out, everything reflective was covered, and the lights were shut off so that it was pitch black. Everyone sat in the dark, singing together. Some of the elder men asked permission to create the camp. Joseph felt the spirits coming in.

It had been a long day but a good one. That night Joye Braun's voice was so tired and raspy that she thought she could have passed as a blues singer. But she was pleased with the way things were going.[33]

Soon after the meeting, LaDonna Allard took the others to her land in Cannon Ball so they could see the prospective campsite. "This is my home. This is where we have our picnics," she told her visitors as they surveyed the grassy landscape. "Nice," Joye Braun answered, looking it over. "When do you want to open the camp?" LaDonna wasn't sure. "Let's start it April 1," Braun suggested. When LaDonna was a child, she remembered seeing the river littered with huge round sand stones created by the whirlpool when the Cannonball River hit the Missouri.[34] Lewis and Clark had thought they looked like cannonballs, and the name stuck.[35] The campers decided to call it "Camp of the Sacred Stones," after the area's precolonial name, the Place That Makes Sacred Stones, and it came to be known as Sacred Stone Camp.

In the early months of 2016 Dave Archambault made another important connection. The tribe had heard about Jan Hasselman and Kristen Boyles, attorneys at Earthjustice, the largest nonprofit environmental law organization in the United States, who had represented Washington State tribes in a case involving the TransMountain pipeline in Canada. The tribe's lawyer emailed Jan Hasselman. Hasselman had never heard of the Standing Rock Sioux or the DAPL. But he started to investigate and became puzzled: here was a pipeline almost as big as the Keystone XL, and nobody seemed to be doing anything about it. Now it seemed late and the case big; the legal tools might be too weak. He knew from experience that pipelines were difficult to block. Other efforts to attack pipeline approvals granted by the Army Corps had largely been unsuccessful. But he felt that it was important to stand with the tribe and highlight the injustice it was facing. The tribe was also taking a leap of faith in trusting its case to Earthjustice.[36] Hasselman agreed to pay the tribe a visit.

Jan Hasselman, who was well aware of the legacy of environmental discrimination faced by Native nations, also felt concerned about the environmental justice implications of placing a pipeline so close to the Standing Rock Reservation. Initially ETP had proposed an alternative route that would have run some ten miles north of Bismarck, the North Dakota state capital, which is 92 percent white and a relatively affluent community.[37] Yet when the Army Corps evaluated the Bismarck route, it determined as part of its EA that the route was not a viable option; one of the reasons cited was the potential threat to Bismarck's water supply. The Bismarck route would also have been slightly longer and costlier; it would have crossed over environmentally sensitive areas.[38] The Corps rerouted it to a crossing downstream, saying that the route would be shorter, involve fewer water crossings, and be farther from residential areas. By the time Dakota Access had submitted its application to North Dakota state regulators in December 2014, the company had selected the route that crossed just a half mile up the Missouri River from the Standing Rock Reservation, 84 percent Native and one of the lowest-income communities in the country.[39]

Back home in March, Jasilyn, Joseph, and Joye Braun, plus a growing group of other activists, continued mulling over plans for fighting the pipeline. One small group started strategizing in a Facebook messenger group. Braun, Nicole Donaghy from the Dakota Resource Council, and Kandi White from Fort Berthold joined LaDonna and others—about twelve people in all—in finding ways to connect with other tribes to oppose the pipeline, brainstorming about ways to get the word out.

Following Jasilyn and Joseph's visit, the youth of Standing Rock began to get involved too. More than half of Standing Rock's population of fifteen thousand is under the age of eighteen. In late March Standing Rock members Bobbi Jean Three Legs and Waniya Locke organized a "Run for Water" event, and several dozen runners, walkers, and horseback riders traversed an eleven-mile stretch to draw attention to the pipeline threat. In March the youth also mounted a "Rezpect Our Water" campaign. Tribal members began visiting the reservation schools and asking kids from kindergarten through high school to write or film short videos about what water meant to them. They put these videos on social media, with the kids leading the way on Twitter, Instagram, Facebook, and live streams. Youth began to approach Tribal Council members, asking for direction, and their elders were impressed.

Part of the pipeline's route was especially significant to tribal members because while it didn't touch the official modern-day boundaries of the reservation, as the Army Corps recognized, it crossed lands within the boundaries of the 1851 Fort Laramie Treaty and was unceded by the 1868 Fort Laramie Treaty. Back in September 2015 the Tribal Council had passed a resolution declaring that the pipeline violated Article 2 of the 1868 Fort Laramie Treaty, which guaranteed the tribe "undisturbed use and occupation" of its permanent homeland, the Standing Rock Reservation.[40]

While Dave Archambault was aware that the treaty boundaries were not binding under modern American law, he and other tribal members also knew they had never ceded their land, so they felt they should have a say over which infrastructure projects were going to damage it. Over and over again, Archambault thought, infrastructure projects had had a negative impact on the lives of his people: in the nineteenth century, when the railroad came through and nearly wiped out the buffalo; in the mid-twentieth century, when the Pick-Sloan Plan flooded the fertile bottomlands of Fort Berthold and also inundated Standing Rock. Every time an infrastructure project came through treaty lands, it negatively affected the tribe, he thought, without providing any benefit. The Standing Rock Sioux had lived with so many broken promises. This time would be different. "It is not right," he concluded. The project was going to have a lasting impact on his people, so he wanted to have a seat at the table.

Throughout that bleak March LaDonna and Joye Braun both had pipelines on their minds, especially as the first day of camp approached. LaDonna recalled her peoples' history on the rivers; she reflected on the many ways in which water is the center of their lives and how it needed to be protected. Did her people have the strength to fight another battle, she wondered? But her preparations also focused on the practical: she planned to set up a tent for supplies, as well as a lodge for prayer. Braun was calling on pipeline fighters and landowners who had been coerced into taking money for the pipeline to join forces. To raise money for her planning trips to Standing Rock, she sold cinnamon rolls and Indian tacos over Facebook. Joye Braun also focused on the daily necessities of a camp—a prepaid cell phone, batteries, tarps, propane, an air mattress, and much-needed coffee—along with getting tipi poles to Cannon Ball. For prospective campers the rules were clear: bring your own necessities, but leave weapons, alcohol, and drugs behind.

April 1 arrived, an overcast and frosty early spring day, the ground damp and soft. Dana Yellow Fat, a Tribal Council member, had helped to coordinate a ceremonial horseback ride to the campsite to raise publicity for the pipeline fight. Both of his sons and one of his daughters participated in the ride, with his teenaged son leading the pack for the first half. In prayer, they burned sage before starting off. The ride began in front of the tribal administration building in Fort Yates, then continued twenty miles north to the site of the camp at the confluence of the Cannonball and Missouri Rivers. Everyone was in good spirits. Around fifty riders from the Standing Rock Sioux and Cheyenne River Sioux, including the chairmen of both tribes, galloped through the snowy air, many of them carrying flags. Chairman Harold Frazier of the Cheyenne River Sioux Tribe came to lend support to Standing Rock and also because Cheyenne River itself had such strong ties to the Missouri River. Neither ETP nor the Army Corps had consulted with Cheyenne River about the pipeline, despite the fact that the tribe's only fresh water source was now the Missouri River.

The riders formed a circle when they arrived at the camp. Elders blessed the ground with a pipe and water. Everyone prayed. LaDonna followed the horses to the site. By the time she arrived, people were already putting up tipis while Joye Braun, wearing a lavender jacket and her customary black beret, called out directions. Prairie McLaughlin, LaDonna's adult daughter, approached Joye Braun. "I need help setting up the tipi," she admitted. "I've never set one up." The ground at the camp was snowy and slushy. "We'll do it together," said Braun. They set up seven tipis as the evening sky turned to pink. Braun stayed alone that night, keeping warm with a sacred fire.

"I am not expendable. My grandchildren are not expendable. We have to fight to live," LaDonna declared to a journalist at the top of the hill.[41] Most went back to the Cannon Ball community center to eat, but Joye Braun knew that once they opened the camp, someone had to stay behind to watch it.

The next morning LaDonna went out to the camp to take coffee and breakfast to a half-frozen Braun. She returned home to Fort Yates and told her husband, Miles, she was going to dedicate half of her paycheck to the camp. "Okay," he said. "We tighten our belts."

Joseph was sick on April 1 and couldn't make it to camp. But he called to check in and discovered that Joye Braun was the only person staying there. He and Jasilyn agreed that she shouldn't be alone. Jasilyn believed they had the power to change the system. So Jasilyn (still just nineteen), Kalen (sixteen), Joseph, and a few friends got some gas money from their tribe, borrowed Joseph's grandmother's van, bought a week's worth of groceries, and drove to the camp to join Braun on April 3. They were planning to be there for only a week, but after a week they went home, washed their clothes, and went straight back.

A fire had recently swept through Cannon Ball, incinerating some homes and damaging the schools. But even though the town, already poor, was in the process of rebuilding, the residents were generous. The camp's first donations came from the people of Cannon Ball, who cooked for the campers, brought them water or wood, or appeared bearing pots of soup and blankets. Jasilyn felt deeply touched to see them giving what they could to people who were taking a stand for them. The power of community members rallying around them felt like a gravitational force, tugging at Jasilyn to stay. At night drumming echoed in the camp, and a bonfire crackled. There were no drugs or alcohol, no leaders. Campers prayed every day. For the first time in her turbulent life, Jasilyn felt healed.

# Seventh Generation Rising

**4**

We nourished the youth, and we gave them a place to call
their own. We said, "Whatever you think, whatever you feel
passionate about, you have the power to change it." We were
trying to encourage them and build them up when so many
things in their community tear them down. They were able
to get out of that environment and go to a different place and
become who they wanted to be—not just who their family is,
or what side of the town they live on, or what kind of job their
parent has.

—Jasilyn Charger

"Everyone welcome Sacred Stone Camp" declared a cheerful sign on
the prairie. As the spring chill began to soften in April 2016, campers
sat around the smoking elder and cottonwood fire, eating fish, discussing their problems, or listening to a friend sing. Jasilyn Charger,
nineteen, felt that in a few weeks they had quickly become a family,
living and standing together. They had learned to see each other as
people without any judgment or comparisons, now focused instead
on what they could do to help each other. The work was physical, and
it could be hard—gathering wood, herding the cows that wandered
into camp—but it felt more meaningful than office work or flipping
burgers. Awed by the majestic rivers nearby, the campers called themselves "water protectors."

Although coyotes, wild turkeys, and buffalo roamed close by, the
camp was peaceful and quiet. As the slush on the ground melted and
flowers began to dot the prairie, Jasilyn and the campers settled into a

routine. They pitched more tents and tipis as fifteen to twenty people trickled into camp—more as the days warmed. They did laundry at people's houses in the community. Many of them were new to this sort of activism, so at first they needed a lot of training: in nonviolent resistance, media, and security. Honor the Earth, an organization founded by former vice-presidential candidate Winona LaDuke, offered help with the training. Camp life was lived in ceremony, with the intention of maintaining purity; there were daily water ceremonies, a sacred fire, prayers, and absolutely no drugs or alcohol. Time in the camp had given Jasilyn a chance to think. Her life had taken an unexpected turn, but she felt comfortable that she was the person she was meant to be. Camp was the safe haven that she and the Eagle Butte youth had been yearning for.[1] She felt happy.

The complete absence of drugs and alcohol at the camp was critical to Jasilyn's well-being. Her body was still craving them, and she found it easier to abstain when they simply weren't available. Even when she and Kalen made the occasional trip home, they didn't stay long. It was too easy to become addicted again to soda and sugar when they were away from their healthy camp diet—to say nothing of other temptations.

While the campers maintained their vigil, the pipeline they hoped to stop was moving relentlessly forward. In early April Iowa regulators issued a permit to Dakota Access. The company now had approval from all four states through which the pipeline would pass, but it was still waiting for approval from the Army Corps. Construction had begun on tank farms in North Dakota (which would provide oil storage at the head of the pipeline), and the company was already preparing for construction in all four affected states. Dakota Access said it had secured 93 percent of the land it needed.[2]

Dave Archambault also reached out to his old friend Nick Tilsen, who had founded the nonprofit Thunder Valley Community Development Corporation (CDC) on the Pine Ridge Reservation in South Dakota. The tribe had only 40 percent of one person's salary focused on PR, media, and communications. Tilsen helped the tribe to craft messages and immediately put together a team to keep up with demand as interest in the camp developed. Even down on Pine Ridge, the pipeline's impact in the case of rupture would be immediate: the reservation's drinking water, including that of the community Tilsen was building, came entirely from the Missouri River.

Jan Hasselman from Earthjustice came to visit Standing Rock in April. LaDonna Allard took him around the small group of tipis and tents on her land. "These people," she said, "aren't leaving until this pipeline is blocked." To himself Hasselman worried: "They are in for a long wait." The spring was still cold, and the tipis were holding up fine, but the tents were beaten by the incessant wind.

Hasselman also met with Dave Archambault and the Standing Rock Sioux Tribal Council when he visited. Cautioning them that it could be a tough fight, he tried to keep expectations low. Lawsuits could be an effective tool to generate some public interest and draw attention to the issue, but a lawsuit was unlikely to actually stop the pipeline. He was struck by the fact that every single person with whom he met—Tribal Council members, staff, tribal members—brought up the flooding of the reservation by the Army Corps when the Oahe Dam was created. "This had been so traumatic in the life of the tribe and cast such a shadow on their current situation even though it was so long ago," he realized. Memories of the tribe's mistreatment at the hands of the government were sharp.

Behind the scenes Earthjustice went to work to convince the Corps not to issue the permit for the Missouri River crossing above the reservation. Chairman Archambault was also active, meeting with the EPA, the U.S. Department of the Interior, and the Army Corps. A spill, he argued, would threaten the very existence of the eighteen million people who rely on the Missouri for their drinking water, farm irrigation, and cultural and spiritual life.

Dave Archambault was right to be concerned about the possibility of a spill. Dakota Access had been quick to stress the standards that the steel pipeline had to meet, the safety of pipelines compared to rail and truck transport for crude oil, and the fact that the DAPL would not be the first to run under Lake Oahe, which was already crisscrossed by eight pipelines.[3] Oil pipeline spills are common.[4] Tioga, North Dakota, just off the Fort Berthold Reservation, experienced one of the largest on-land oil pipeline spills in recent U.S. history in September 2013: about 865,200 gallons.[5] In the year ending May 1, 2017, North Dakota's oil and gas industry reported 745 oil spills—one every eleven hours and forty-five minutes.[6] Pipeline spill cleanup can take years and in some cases can never be fully completed.

Indeed the company seeking to build the pipeline had an especially problematic record. A Reuters analysis of government data concluded in 2016 that Sunoco Logistics Partners, the future operator of the DAPL, had spilled crude more often than any of its competitors, racking up more than two hundred leaks since 2010. Spills in 2009 and 2011 on Sunoco's lines drew censure from the EPA in a settlement announced in 2016.[7] In its own 2016 annual report, ETP (the company building the pipeline) acknowledged that "Contamination resulting from releases of crude oil . . . is not unusual within the petroleum pipeline industry and had resulted in impacts to the environment, including soil and groundwater."[8]

With their behind-the-scenes arguments, Earthjustice and the tribe succeeded in slowing things down. Dakota Access had wanted the Corps' permits by April or May to meet its construction schedule, and the government faced a lot of pressure.[9] But the tribe and its lawyers were also pushing the conversation in the administration.

As April wore on, the few dozen campers at Sacred Stone Camp also maintained their quiet presence. Some days it was a struggle to provide everyone with enough necessities, but the people of Cannon Ball donated supplies. Every day LaDonna stopped by the camp, bringing supplies and picking up a list of requests for her next shopping run to Bismarck. Kandi White, the activist from Fort Berthold, would also drive down to drop off blankets or food and water and then stay to chat by the fire. Standing Rock Tribal Council member Dana Yellow

Fat and his wife, Glenna Eagle, collected money for firewood. Friends of Standing Rock Tribal Council member Phyllis Young, who had participated in the American Indian Movement, donated bags of rice and beans to the camp; others brought folding chairs and sleeping bags. One day someone donated a live cow, which the campers had to shoot and butcher. They used surplus five-gallon plastic containers from the casino for waste. Chief Arvol Looking Horse, the spiritual leader of the Lakota, Dakota, and Nakota people, even came to perform a water ceremony.[10] The Cherry Creek singers, a band from South Dakota, stayed for two nights to sing for the campers.

Such community support bolstered the resolve of the campers, but Kalen still had moments of reluctance. He was just sixteen and had dropped out of high school to live in the camp. Occasionally in those early weeks he would think of his old life and say, "Man, I don't want to be here. I want to go home." One day he said it more seriously. On his grandfather's birthday he wanted to be with his family to celebrate. Jasilyn called Kalen's grandfather and said they were going to leave camp. "No, no," he replied. "Stay there. You're not missing nothing. I'm going to have one next year." Strengthened by his support, Kalen jumped back on board. "All right, then," he resolved. "We'll stay."

Jasilyn rarely wavered in her commitment to the camp. Its emphasis on the sanctity of water appealed to her because, she reasoned, water was healing and rejuvenating, a key element in the human body. To convince other youth to care about pipelines and water, though, was harder. "Why should I care about that? No one even cares if I have somewhere to sleep right now," she heard. But Bobbi Jean Three Legs from Standing Rock had an idea. Her two-year-old daughter woke up every morning asking for a cup of water, she told a journalist. One morning, she thought to herself, "What am I going to do when we wake up and I can't give her a cup of water because our water will be damaged?" She decided to take action.[11]

In the middle of April Joseph White Eyes received a message from Standing Rock member Waniya Locke about a run she was organizing with Bobbi Jean Three Legs in the style of a "crow hop," a traditional Native relay-running method to spread a message. The relay would end in Omaha, where the runners would deliver a petition to the Army Corps of Engineers' district office. The petition called on Col. John Henderson, commander of the Omaha district of the Corps, and the Army Corps to conduct a full EIS on the effects of the pipeline, address environmental concerns, assess the potential impact to cultural and historic sites, and consult and coordinate with affected tribes before issuing a permit to Dakota Access.[12]

The runners would trade off running and resting in an accompanying vehicle, stopping at reservations along the way and bringing together representatives of the Oceti Sakowin, the Seven Council Fires of the Great Sioux Nation.[13] The Oceti Sakowin included seven divisions, which are Dakota-, Lakota-, or Nakota-speaking, each one made up of bands related to kinship, dialect, and proximity.

On April 24 a group of runners left Cannon Ball for the five-hundred-mile relay, starting with an eighty-mile route through the Standing Rock Reservation.[14] Jasilyn and Joseph planned to meet them at the border between Standing Rock and Cheyenne River and run the fifty miles through Cheyenne River. When, late at night, they finally joined the throng, the Standing Rock runners were dead in the legs, so Jasilyn and Joseph took the lead. When they reached Cheyenne River's southern border, they looked at each other. "You wanna keep running?" was the question in their eyes. They kept running.

Along the route Joseph had to leave for a pre-planned trip to Australia with IEN, and Jasilyn began mulling over the idea of staying with the group for the full relay. She was the only one from her tribe who could keep running, and she felt an obligation to represent it. On the other hand, she wasn't a runner, and many of the other kids on the run were strangers. She spoke to Kalen's grandfather, seeking his advice: "You do what you feel like you need to do," he counseled her. "Don't let anything hold you back." "I can't *not* represent my community," she decided. She kept going with only the clothes on her back.

The days seemed endless. They ran from 9 a.m. to sundown, and often later, and endured nearly nonstop rain. They carried a heavy staff that represented their ancestors. But Jasilyn heard that her community and friends were proud to have her representing them, and she felt deeply alive.

After a grueling two weeks, a group of ten determined runners finally reached Omaha. At the office of the Army Corps, they delivered their petition, which asked the Corps to conduct a complete EIS before issuing a pipeline easement for the Missouri River crossing.[15] They met with another colonel who they thought had tears in his eyes as he accepted their petition.

On April 29, while the runners were on their way to Omaha, Colonel Henderson met with concerned tribal members at the Grand River Casino in Mobridge, South Dakota, for a public forum to discuss their pipeline objections. Native people came from all over: Joye Braun from the camp, happy to get a real bed and a shower the night before the meeting; Lisa DeVille and Joletta Birdbear from Fort Berthold; Kandi White from Montana; LaDonna Allard from Standing Rock. Dave Archambault presided over the head table with an impassive Colonel Henderson, who was dressed in military fatigues.

Sitting in the conference room, the women encircled by the men, the visitors shifted in their chairs, awaiting their turns to speak. Joye Braun made a powerful speech on behalf of Cheyenne River. "This black snake is not going through," she declared. A short time later came Kandi, who had arrived at the meeting wondering, "Are they actually listening to us? Is this just to appease people?" She had always gone strictly by the book in challenging environmental issues but often had ended up losing anyway. Now she wanted to speak her mind as part of the public record. But she was also looking closely at Colonel Henderson: "Oh God, I hope this guy has some sort of power and clout." Holding her two-year-old daughter, Aiyana, she gave an impassioned talk. The Army Corps had flooded traditional tribal lands, creating reservoirs like the one under which the pipeline would run, and now it was coming back to force people to do something *else* they didn't want to do? "Be prepared for a fight," Kandi warned.

Lisa had come to the meeting armed with the study—authored by Dr. Vengosh at Duke University—of the lingering effects of fracking wastewater spills in the Bakken. She was certain that the pipeline company and the Corps would assure everyone that pipelines never spilled, but she had documented proof of the damage that such spills had already caused. In her mind she thought: "They are lying to us." All of the speakers strongly urged the Corps to prepare an EIS.

Meanwhile, Dakota Access was progressing in obtaining necessary approvals. By late May it reported another milestone: it now had 100 percent of the easements it needed in North and South Dakota. Though it was still waiting to receive Corps approval for water crossings, bulldozers began clearing land along the pipeline route in North Dakota.

Back in camp in May after the run to Omaha, Jasilyn began to think of herself as a part of the seventh generation, a concept from a Lakota prophecy from the time of nineteenth-century leaders Sitting Bull and Crazy Horse. After seven generations, the prophecy said, the youth would awaken and rise up. Another prophecy foretelling that a terrible black snake would enter the Lakota homeland and spread death and ruin across the earth, beginning with the water, also suggested historic resistance.[16] Jasilyn believed they were living in that time, when the seventh generation had risen to stand against pipelines running under the earth and water.

Kalen had grown up hearing about the seventh generation; his elders had always told him, "In your time, you guys are going to go through something, you know, very 'moving.'" He didn't know what they meant; he thought they were crazy. But at camp it all came together: the youth would rise up to fight this battle for their water.

One evening in May, Jasilyn, Joseph, Bobbi Jean Three Legs, and a few other friends were sitting around the fire after fishing. As Joseph filleted the fish, they all laughed about how much fun the first run had been. "Let's run to Washington," said Three Legs. "We *should*," Joseph realized. Just like that, Bobbi Jean Three Legs and Joseph began to organize another run. Their goal was to support thirty-six runners on a $21,000 budget. At Standing Rock the youth faced some backlash from elders for their decision to undertake the run.[17] "We don't send our children and our women to war, to go meet with officials," one elder told Jasilyn.[18] But they went forward with the run.

On July 15 twenty youth set off on a nearly two-thousand-mile run from Cannon Ball to Washington DC. "The seventh generation is here, and it is time to uphold the prophecy and restore balance to our mother, the earth," Joseph declared as they left.[19] As they passed through Cheyenne River, Jasilyn woke up her twin sister, Jasilea, quickly packing her a bag and encouraging her to join the runners.[20]

On July 25, ten days into the run, the U.S. Army Corps of Engineers approved most of the permits necessary for pipeline construction, including more than two hundred water crossings. The 1,261-page report on the approval asserted, "No significant comments remain unresolved." Colonel Henderson wrote that he had evaluated the effects of the river crossing and determined they were "not injurious to the public interest." The Corps' EA found that the project had no significant impact.[21] But the Corps didn't issue one crucial piece of permission: the easement for the pipeline to cross under Lake Oahe.

Just as they reached the Mississippi River, Jasilyn and the other runners found out about the permits. They felt discouraged but resolved to go on.

LaDonna was at a meeting in Albuquerque when she heard the news. "Oh my God," she thought to herself. "I'm not even there. What do I do? What do I *do*?" At the end of a long day, she went to her hotel room alone, picked up her phone, and pushed "record." Choked with emotion, she pleaded: "I'm asking *everyone* to stand up. . . . This is not a time for egos and petty differences; it is a time for people to stand together. It's a time to fight something greater than ourselves. It is time to protect the future of our grandchildren." She called on people watching over Facebook to join her at Sacred Stone Camp to stop the black snake. She hoped for fifty people.[22]

On July 27, in the aftermath of the Army Corps' decision, the Standing Rock Sioux Tribe filed a lawsuit against the Corps. Among other things, the suit claimed that the Corps had violated the NHPA, the Clean Water Act, and the National Environmental Policy Act (NEPA) in issuing permits for the pipeline. The suit noted that the tribe's traditional territory extended well beyond the current reservation's boundaries and included the lands at issue. Cultural resources were located on these lands, the suit argued, and construction of the pipeline would destroy crucial "burial grounds, sacred sites, and historically significant areas in its path." It also expressed concern that the proposed pipeline's route ran half a mile upstream from the reservation under Lake Oahe, and any leak or spill would flow directly onto the reservation, with dire impacts to its water. Consultation on the pipeline, the suit argued, had been "profoundly inadequate."[23]

A broad coalition of tribes, landowners, and environmental groups—including Jasilyn's own tribe, the Cheyenne River Sioux, which drew its water downstream on the Missouri River—joined in the legal challenge. Fort Berthold POWER was one of the organizations involved in the lawsuit: "This pipeline could have been rerouted, but, as usual, communities of people of color are always first for sacrifice," declared Lisa DeVille.[24]

The strategy for Dakota Access, attorney Jan Hasselman thought, was to get the pipeline permitted as quickly and quietly as possible so that potential opponents would not know what had hit them. But there were a couple of problems with these permits as Hasselman saw it. One key issue was the lack of an EIS. Under NEPA, a project with significant impact on the environment requires an EIS, a study that evaluates risks, consequences, and alternatives; with impacts uncertain, an EA is prepared to determine either the necessity of an EIS or whether the impacts are not significant.[25] Hasselman had seen environmental impact statements done for dog parks, restoration projects, and drinking water plants. Surely, he thought, a thirty-inch pipeline carrying almost six hundred thousand barrels of crude oil a day under a waterway serving millions would merit an EIS. He assumed the company was trying to avoid one because when the Keystone XL Pipeline had had an EIS done because it crossed an international border, the increased scrutiny hadn't worked out well for the company. A second issue Hasselman saw with the permits was related to treaties. The U.S. government is obligated by law to protect the integrity of the reservation, including the water on which Standing Rock residents rely.

Jan Hasselman still worried that the case would be hard to win on its legal merits but hoped that the tribe could also use it to help raise awareness and leverage political opposition.[26]

Even as the tribes and their supporters filed suit, construction was kicking into full gear. By the end of July the North Dakota portion of the pipeline was 44 percent complete.[27] Jan Hasselman went to court seeking an emergency injunction against continued pipeline construction, hoping to stave off confrontations.[28]

Amid the backdrop of ongoing pipeline construction in North Dakota and the tribe's legal battle, Jasilyn and the runners continued to Washington DC to deliver their petition. Some of the runners had never been off the reservation before, and as they passed through cities, they were shocked to see the skyscrapers and traffic. They also encountered opposition. At a gas station where the runners were getting something to eat, a man stepped out of his diesel truck and strolled over to them. He told them their run was a waste of time and that they should go back to where they had come from. The runners were angry and taken aback until a two-year-old named Wiconi, who was accompanying her mother on the run, toddled up to the man, saying simply, "Mni wiconi." Water is life.

Eastward they ran, making slow progress through small towns: Long Creek, Illinois; Crawfordsville, Indiana. They aimed for thirty to seventy miles per day. Actor Shailene Woodley, wearing black Converse high tops, joined them for a stretch of the run in Ohio and helped to supply the group with necessities. "We run . . . for our brothers, our sisters!" "We run . . . for water, for life!" "We run . . . for our people, for our nation!" they cried as they ran. Wrapped in the Standing Rock and Cheyenne River Sioux tribal flags, runners picked up trash along the side of the road. For Jasilyn and the others each day began and ended with a prayer circle, and they carried a sacred staff as they ran.

On August 4 the group finally arrived in Washington DC with more than eighty runners and eight chase cars. The following day they ran to Army Corps headquarters. Jogging through the streets of Washington, Bobbi Jean Three Legs called to anyone who would listen: "We ran for our people; we ran for water!" During their meeting with the Army Corps, the conversation ranged from treaties to the impetus for the run to the importance of water. The runners delivered their petition, which by that point had garnered 160,000 signatures.[29] On the same day the tribe asked the court for a preliminary injunction barring pipeline construction.[30]

After their meeting in Washington, Jasilyn and the other runners stopped by New York for a pipeline protest in Union Square, and then they headed west, back to North Dakota. On their way home, they could already see that things were changing at the camp. Live videos on their phones showed police gathering as the pipeline construction came nearer. They were astonished and dismayed.

On August 8 Dakota Access issued a notice to the Standing Rock Sioux Tribe that construction would begin two days later near the reservation. As construction began, the crowd sang and prayed. The first arrests came on August 11, when eleven people, carrying a hand-painted "NO DAPL" sign and several flags, were arrested for sitting on the gravel access road to be used for construction vehicles. "Mni wiconi," one called as he was led away. "Keep it in the soil!" Most were charged with misdemeanor disorderly conduct. Morton County Sheriff Kyle Kirchmeier contended they were not staying within boundaries set by law enforcement and were getting in the way of pipeline surveyors. Police arrested four more before the end of the day.

On the same day, the runners—sweaty but triumphant—finally returned home. For Jasilyn the run had been an empowering experience, allowing her to take control of her life and her future.[31] She also came back to a changed camp: hundreds of new water protectors had started flooding in, and the cluster of tents, tipis, and vehicles in the grass was quickly growing. LaDonna—near tears as she saw so many people pouring in—credited the runners.[32] Jasilyn was stunned by the size of the camp. She had never seen so many people coming together—from different nations, ethnicities, and regions.

The runners finished their run with a lap from the Cannonball River to nearby Highway 1806 as a few hundred tribal members and supporters prayed and sang. Happily many of those who had joined the run also came back to stay. One of them was a young Lakota man, Danny Grassrope, who gave up his job at the courthouse in Lower Brule, South Dakota. His mother, who had coped with domestic violence and alcohol abuse in her own life, had taught him to be a fighter and to use his voice. Now it felt good to get in touch with being Lakota—to acknowledge it, accept it, and embrace it.

Still despite the arrests and new arrivals, construction continued on a roadway into the Cannonball Ranch worksite. More arrests followed. But it seemed to Dana Yellow Fat as though the arrests weren't accomplishing much. The water protectors were caught in a sort of stalemate. "Why are people getting arrested and nothing is being done?" he wondered. The arrests weren't even attracting significant press coverage or attention on social media. Yellow Fat told Glenna Eagle that for people to take more notice, he would have to be arrested.

On August 12 Yellow Fat gave Dave Archambault a serious message: "There's a lot of people here, but we have almost zero news coverage," he said. "I'm going to cross their lines, and I'm going to go to jail. But when I do," he warned, "make sure people know. Get it out there that now they're arresting leadership. That'll get people here." When they met later that day, he says, Archambault told him, "I'll go with you."

As people gathered along Highway 1806, singing and praying, a rumor started circulating that the construction vehicles had uncovered human remains. Dana Yellow Fat decided that his moment had come. He and Dave Archambault ran toward opposite sides of the police line and were quickly arrested. Glenna Eagle hung back, watching. As soon as Yellow Fat was arrested, she posted on Facebook: "Free Councilman Yellow Fat and Chairman Archambault." That single post spread like wildfire, shared more than ten thousand times. Suddenly friends and family began calling, asking what needed to be done. People who had not taken part in the camp now messaged Glenna Eagle, "We're getting in a car right now; we're on our way."

Police loaded Dana Yellow Fat and Dave Archambault into a van, their hands secured with zip ties. As the police van drove on to Morton County, the policewoman transporting them turned around: "Excuse me, guys; I have a question for you. Who are you?" Yellow Fat gave her their names and titles. "Oh, my God, okay," she replied, getting on the radio to call ahead. They were booked into the Morton County jail, charged with disorderly conduct, and quickly released on bond. The whole process took only an hour and a half, but they had made their point.

The episode had a longer-lasting effect. After the arrest Dakota Access went to federal court to obtain a restraining order against Yellow Fat and Archambault that prevented them from interfering with construction of the pipeline.[33] Yellow Fat remembered feeling scared and thinking, "Wow, these guys must be pretty powerful. How can they do this?" But he soon concluded, "You know what? I don't care. They can try whatever they want, but I still have to do what I have to do." A week later he was back on the front lines—though he felt as if he had a big target on his back.

For representation Dave Archambault contacted Tim Purdon, the former U.S. attorney who had taken on oil companies in North Dakota for violations of the Migratory Bird Treaty Act and who had also worked to combat crime associated with the oil boom. Purdon and Archambault knew each other from Purdon's time as U.S. attorney, and Purdon thought Archambault one of the greatest leaders in Indian Country in his generation. "Of course," Purdon replied when asked to represent Archambault and Yellow Fat. He thought their case boiled down to the First Amendment right to free speech.

A couple of days later, Purdon drove down to the Standing Rock tribal headquarters to meet with Archambault. As he walked in, he ran into Moe John, president of the Seneca Nation. "President John, what are you doing here?" Purdon asked. "Ah, you know, the DAPL protest. I came to support it," John answered. As Purdon left the meeting, he noticed a flatbed truck with a twenty-two-foot northwest tribal totem pole in the back, a gift for the camp from eight Washington tribes; then he saw the top-ranking leaders of the Yakama Nation exit the truck. Purdon realized that this protest would be different from any other he had seen. "If they arrest two hundred people," Purdon thought to himself, "There are going to be two thousand here the next day. And if you arrest them, there will likely be twelve thousand."

In the days that followed Archambault and Yellow Fat's arrests, hundreds of water protectors prayed and burned sage at the entrance to the pipeline route as they tried to maintain a stance of prayer and peaceful protest. Dana Yellow Fat and Glenna Eagle, meeting people from as far away as Missouri who had come to stand with the camp after seeing Yellow Fat arrested, felt their message was reaching faraway places. But on the construction site nothing changed; as several days passed, the arrests continued. Then on August 15 a group of women—including Ta'Sina Sapa Win, a young Lakota woman who had come to the camp from Cheyenne River after being inspired by the runners—holding sage and tobacco, scaled the barbed wire fences and advanced toward the construction equipment, effectively halting construction.[34]

Relations between the camp and the local sheriff's office soured. The Morton County sheriff started routing traffic away from the protest area. Sheriff Kyle Kirchmeier spoke to the media and declared brusquely that the protests had turned "unlawful."[35] He claimed his officers had been threatened; they had heard gunshots, he said, and received reports of pipe bombs, fireworks, vandalism, and assaults on private security personnel. Officers around the state had been called in, and there was no longer any chance that his department would be the one to provide water protectors with dumpsters or water. "I don't know if we need to provide them supplies when it has turned into an unlawful protest," said Sheriff Kirchmeier. "We are just going to make sure that it remains safe."[36]

Frustrated by these accusations, Dave Archambault repudiated the weapons reports and objected to road closures.[37] On August 18 Sacred Stone Camp, Honor the Earth, and IEN issued a joint statement strongly refuting the claims of violence: Weapons were not allowed in the camp, they said, and "we reject this fear-mongering tactic being used by the local police and media that paints our actions as violent and misguided." The only pipes in the camp, they said, were peace pipes.[38]

But tensions continued to rise. On August 19 Governor Jack Dalrymple issued an emergency declaration for southwest and south-central North Dakota, prompting additional funding for state agencies to deal with the protests. Morton County also declared its own state of emergency. North Dakota Highway Patrol troopers were instructed not to wear name tags near the pipeline demonstrations because of concerns that they might be individually threatened.

Meanwhile, Sacred Stone Camp had swelled to capacity by late August. The colorful collection of tents, tipis, cars, and trucks on the grassy hillside had grown. The campers, still known as water protectors, spilled over into the surrounding area, about three thousand of them in all by the end of the month. Dana Yellow Fat alone was fielding fifty to a hundred calls a day from people across the country who said they were on their way or wondered how they could help. Worried, the Tribal Council held an emergency meeting. The members looked at a map, trying to find a place to accommodate these crowds. While the land along the river technically belonged to the Army Corps, they believed it really belonged to the tribe under the Fort Laramie Treaties. The council decided to set up the new camps there.

In this main overflow camp—called Oceti Sakowin—trailers, tipis, and tents soon dotted the landscape. Located within the boundaries of the 1851 Fort Laramie Treaty and unceded by the 1868 Fort Laramie Treaty on land claimed by the Army Corps when it built the Oahe Dam, Oceti Sakowin was organized with seven tipis of the horn and a council lodge.[39] Camp leaders lit a sacred fire. Water protectors erected banners reading "No pipelines," "Treaty land, take a stand," and "Water is our first medicine."[40] Nearby reservations organized school buses to transport people to the camps, and others had driven themselves there or hitchhiked across the country. The community was growing larger than most North Dakota small towns but maintained its joyful and cooperative atmosphere. Residents pitched in to cook pots of soup, fry bread, and boil corn for the thousands who were gathering. The camp even had a Medic and Healers Council. One camp medic—an EMT who had served in Desert Storm—described the camp's medical philosophy as follows: to see patients, protect their privacy, and treat them as humans.

Phyllis Young helped to coordinate the new overflow camp; additional camps included Rosebud and Red Warrior Camps. Winona LaDuke set up her tipi—painted with animals threatened by climate change—at the Red Warrior Camp. She was a veteran of the successful Sandpiper pipeline fight against the Enbridge company in Minnesota. The nonviolent, peaceful, and prayerful character was essential to camp organizers.

Word spread by social media, and donations flowed in. Standing Rock leaders created an emergency management task force, coordinating a supply of water tanks, dumpsters, port-a-potties, a medical trailer, a wash station, and a helicopter pad for emergencies. Afterward what visitors most recalled from their experience was the collaborative, prayerful atmosphere.

Behind the scenes the tribe had to quickly make decisions. Usually the Tribal Council met weekly, trying to decide on the next steps and strategize about how to keep things peaceful. Council opinion on the camp was mixed. The last thing the members wanted was for anyone—water protector or pipeline worker—to be injured or killed.

Religious leaders also began to get involved. The Episcopal Church was the first to go on record that summer saying that it stood with Standing Rock; church leaders brought their flag to the Oceti Sakowin sacred fire as they read a statement of solidarity. Episcopal Church presiding bishop Michael Curry (who later officiated the wedding of Meghan Markle to Prince Harry) also visited. The support was not surprising. The Episcopal Church had also been an early leader in repudiating the Doctrine of Discovery, a concept that still justifiably infuriated Native people. Originating in a fifteenth-century papal bull that allowed the Portuguese monarchy to seize land in West Africa, the doctrine legitimized Christian European countries' claims to lands they "discovered" belonging to people outside of Europe and provided legal cover for settler colonialism that devastated Indigenous nations from the mid-fifteenth to mid-twentieth centuries as much of the non-European world was colonized.[41] Thomas Jefferson had claimed the doctrine to be international law also applicable to the fledgling U.S. government in 1792. In the 1823 U.S. Supreme Court decision *Johnson v. McIntosh* Chief Justice John Marshall agreed that "discovery" and "conquest" gave the federal government ownership of land within its boundaries. Indigenous inhabitants had lost their natural rights to it.[42]

The Right Reverend Dr. Carol Gallagher arrived in August. Dr. Gallagher was the first Native American woman to become an Episcopal bishop and had a Cherokee ancestor who walked the Trail of Tears. Her parents had been involved in the civil rights movement, and she had even met Dr. Martin Luther King Jr. as a child; she was struck by the similarity of the nonviolent protest at the camps to the spirit of the civil rights movement. There was a generosity, a grace and gentleness, to it as camp organizers cared for everyone who showed up—helping to set up tents, feed people, make sure there were lessons for the kids. In fact, she thought, it almost seemed like holy ground.

During the second week in August, Kandi White arrived with her young daughter, alternately staying in a tent, a yurt, and the nearby casino hotel. She had been working on the Fort Berthold Reservation, trying to draw attention to the toxic impact of fracking, but everyone there was talking about Standing Rock. Lisa and Walter DeVille drove down from Fort Berthold to visit, bringing cases of water and canned food. They donated $200 to a Tribal Council member to buy whatever the campers needed.

Up to this point Joye Braun had been crisscrossing the country, building alliances with environmental organizations, returning to camp as home base. In August she realized that she was ready to dig in and stay. The society she saw rising up around her was astonishing. Every day different tribes and groups would come in and find a warm welcome at the camps, all without any exchange of money. She was in awe. Never in her entire lifetime had she expected to see the rising of the Oceti Sakowin.

Support from other tribes was flowing in quickly, even from such longtime rivals as the Crow Nation, who were early supporters, walking hand-in-hand into camp. The American Civil Liberties Union (ACLU) of North Dakota and other organizations also threw their support behind the movement, as did municipalities across the country. Dennis Banks, cofounder of the American Indian Movement, had arrived. All together some sixty tribes were represented at the camps, and leaders began to call it the largest gathering of Native Americans in modern times.

Chairman Mark Fox of the MHA Nation had paid a quiet visit to Sacred Stone Camp back in July. He knew Dave Archambault well, and they had discussed logistical issues: feeding people, keeping them warm, making sure no one got hurt. In late August he issued a formal letter supporting Standing Rock's opposition to the pipeline: "DAPL should find an alternative means and method of transporting oil to market that has less potential for negative impact to Standing Rock," he wrote.[43]

Mark Fox traveled to the camps again in late August with his full Tribal Business Council and a caravan of a hundred vehicles. On a sunny, breezy day drums played as they entered with flags flying. As gifts, they brought food—hundreds of pounds of beef and sweet corn. They also donated thousands of dollars for portable toilets. Mark Fox knew that some people wouldn't understand how the MHA Nation could be so heavily involved in extracting oil and still support Standing Rock in its pipeline opposition, but he saw it as a show of support from one nation to another. He believed Standing Rock had a right to choose whether to be impacted by oil and gas, just as the MHA Nation had made its decision. At Standing Rock the MHA Nation message was: "We're a fellow nation, and we're here to support you, whatever you choose to do."

Kandi White, however, was incensed at Fox, even though he was her relative and she liked him. When the MHA Nation marched into camp, she publicly complained about the tribe's decision to approve the pipeline crossing near its own borders. She felt that she had a responsibility to hold her own leaders accountable.[44]

Jasilyn, immersed in camp life, was traveling to the pipeline construction site every day. One day in August, when she and Joseph were at the front line—the area near pipeline construction where water protectors conducted protest actions—they heard drumming and saw some riders in beaded regalia gallop in, doing a horse dance just in front of the police line. The police backed up again and again, and Jasilyn saw that the riders were "counting coup"—an old plains Indian tradition of touching enemies without harming them, an act that requires great courage and skill. Watching them, she felt a surge of pride and longed to do more.

Back in camp, Jasilyn and Danny Grassrope called for the youth to gather at the sacred fire that evening. About a dozen met and talked about how they saw the camps, what they wanted, where they had come from, and why they were there. As the camps grew, it was getting more difficult for young people to be heard. They were frustrated that the elders wouldn't let them attend council meetings—it could be difficult to start generation-to-generation conversations—and so they decided that night to create their own council.

One source of frustration for all members of the camp was the roadblock on Highway 1806, twenty-five miles north of the camp. Vehicles bound for the reservation were detoured, while those heading to destinations north of Standing Rock were permitted to pass. Amnesty International called on state and local authorities to remove the roadblock, which hindered access to the construction sites and camps. Native officials agreed. "Rerouting the traffic is an attack on our economy, our schools, our nation and our race. It's not fair, and it's not right," said Dave Archambault.[45] Relations between the tribe and state officials had worsened. On August 22 North Dakota's homeland security director, Greg Wilz, pulled state-owned trailers and water tanks from the camp, suggesting they could be damaged. Tribal officials were left scrambling to find a new drinking water supply for the camp in ninety-degree heat.

On August 24 a federal court in Washington DC heard the tribe's request for an injunction to stop pipeline construction. Some five hundred people, including Dave Archambault, Joseph White Eyes, Bobbi Jean Three Legs, and actors Shailene Woodley and Susan Sarandon, gathered outside the courthouse.

The judge, James Boasberg of the U.S. District Court of the District of Columbia, decided to take a few weeks to consider the injunction request; he said he would have a ruling by September 9. Boasberg was an Obama nominee to the court. A former federal prosecutor, he stressed the importance of following the law and facts to the outcome they dictated, rather than focusing on a desired outcome or using an "empathy standard."[46] Boasberg had previously ordered the Obama administration to stop detaining immigrants solely for deterrence purposes; he had also ordered the U.S. State Department to release emails from Hillary Clinton's tenure as secretary of state.

Back at the camp, officials shouted the judge's decision to an eager crowd of campers. "I guess we stay," Johnelle Leingang, the tribe's emergency manager, concluded resolutely to journalists. Joye Braun was also undaunted: "Two weeks more. What is that? Nothing to save the lives of the people." Hundreds settled in for the duration.[47]

With rumors of violence and a state of emergency swirling around them, the campers also tried to reclaim the narrative of the demonstrations, making clear that they and their movement were peaceful. Chafing at the false contention that they were violent, water protectors insisted that the camps were nonviolent and dedicated to peaceful prayer; they also said the roadblock perpetuated the misconception that their activities were violent. Amnesty International sent a delegation of observers to monitor the law enforcement response to the camps.[48]

On August 24 Dave Archambault published an opinion piece in the *New York Times* laying out the tribe's case. The tribe had opposed the pipeline since it had first learned about it in 2014, he said, and there had been no meaningful consultation by the Army Corps. The resistance was growing—over ninety tribes were represented at the camps—and their cause was just. Indeed the story was a familiar one for Indian Country. The U.S. government had taken the Sioux Nation's land and resources following the Fort Laramie Treaties and again with the damming of the river. "Whether it's gold from the Black Hills or hydropower from the Missouri or oil pipelines that threaten our ancestral inheritance, the tribes have always paid the price for America's prosperity," Dave Archambault charged.[49]

On August 25 a slew of environmental groups—among them Kandi's IEN, Honor the Earth, 350.org, Greenpeace, and the Sierra Club—signed a letter to President Obama urging his administration to deny the remaining permits for the DAPL and revoke the existing ones, in the absence of adequate environmental review.[50] The next day former presidential candidate Senator Bernie Sanders declared his support for the tribe. Obama himself hadn't spoken out on the issue yet, though he had a history as a friend to Standing Rock. In June 2014 President Obama had visited Cannon Ball with Archambault, only the eighth sitting U.S. president to visit an Indian reservation. Dave Archam-bault's sister, Jodi Archambault Gillette, had worked in the Obama administration as the special assistant for Native American Affairs, and he admired the president.[51]

Jasilyn and Danny Grassrope's new youth group—now called the International Indigenous Youth Council (IIYC)—was quickly becom-ing a significant presence in the camps. It was helping to give youth the tools to use their voices. Many had come to the camps broken, looking for themselves, and trying to become stronger. The IIYC nourished them, gave them a place to call their own, and tried to encourage them. After their meetings Jasilyn was totally exhausted. Sometimes she wanted to give up, thinking, "I want to be a normal kid, a normal teenager. Go for a walk. Make mistakes." But the group that swelled on the banks of the Missouri River came together partly in a cathartic way to reclaim its cultural heritage and give young people a sense of shared purpose.

As the camps grew, people sometimes bragged about how long they had been there and asked Jasilyn and Kalen when they had come. Jasilyn was humble: "Yeah, we've been here for a while." LaDonna had come to be surrounded by supporters and reporters, but she always made time for Jasilyn and Kalen—stopping to talk to them, helping them out, taking them out to dinner, giving them money for gas. Jasilyn wondered whether LaDonna would forget about the first campers as the encampment grew, but she never did.

In the evenings the camp fires burned bright, and the prairie was still filled with laughter, stories, music, and drumming. Jasilyn marveled at all the tribes that had gathered in one place, for the first time in hundreds of years. Some were even historical enemies, with centu-ries of bitter grudges and stereotypes—the Crows, the Apaches, the Pawnees, all gathered with the Sioux. They had come to fight for their joint future, to dispel the old hatreds and heal.

The IIYC was also working to heal its participants. The members became fast friends, some almost like siblings. One member, Andreanne Catt, seventeen, came to Standing Rock from the Pine Ridge Reservation in August with only the clothes on her back, just a week and a half after attempting suicide. She had seen videos of the police line at Standing Rock and made a last-minute decision to hop on a bus there with only her purse. She ended up staying until December. Many youth council members had attempted suicide. They understood each other, and spent considerable time listening to each other—learning, healing, and growing. They were working to overcome years of trauma while coming together as a family. In a momentous ceremony Chief Arvol Looking Horse and the Seven Council Fires gave the youths a *chanupa*, a sacred ceremonial pipe.[52]

But still pipeline construction continued. By the end of August, Dakota Access reported to the North Dakota PSC that the project was 68 percent complete. The company said it was working hard to meet the projected mechanical completion date of October 31.[53] Behind the scenes the tribe's attorney, Jan Hasselman, was surprised that the pipeline company had adopted such a hard line: it wasn't going to delay construction, no matter what. Hasselman began to worry that if construction continued, there was a risk of violence. He called the attorney for Dakota Access, pleading with him to convince his client to stop construction—at least right near the camps—until the preliminary injunction could be resolved. The lawyer hung up on him.

Frustrated by continuing construction, activists were stepping up their tactics to include lockdowns to construction equipment. Although construction had paused near the Cannonball River crossing, it continued only twenty miles away, with crews clearing topsoil in the early stages of pipeline construction. On August 31 two men—one from Standing Rock and one from the Rosebud Sioux tribe—bound themselves to pipeline construction equipment, immobilizing it and delaying construction for hours. One of them was Dale "Happy" American Horse, who spent more than six hours attached to a digger. He clutched the equipment, his hands fastened to it by a lockbox made from PVC piping, duct tape, poultry netting, and tar. "All this for clean water," American Horse mused as he was arrested. "Why does it have to come down to this?"[54]

Meanwhile, the court fight was moving along. Jan Hasselman gleaned from Judge Boasberg's questions that he was concerned about a lack of evidence of significant cultural and historic sites in the construction area.[55] In response Tim Mentz, the former tribal historic preservation officer, surveyed some two miles of the pipeline corridor and discovered at least twenty-seven burials, sixteen stone rings, and nineteen effigies.[56] He considered the findings significant; some might even be eligible for listing under the NHPA, and one might be among the most significant archaeological finds in the state for years. Hasselman told journalists that this discovery underlined the need for a more complete study of the pipeline route: "The whole area is rich in cultural heritage, but the tribe never had the chance to go out and do this work," he said. While the firms hired by Dakota Access hadn't found any significant sites along the route, Hasselman argued that "the pipeline's hired guns don't get to decide what is sacred to the tribe."[57]

Jan Hasselman was convinced that Tim Mentz had made remarkable discoveries. On Friday, September 2, just before the Labor Day weekend, he filed Tim Mentz's supplementary declaration with the court, detailing the discovery of sacred and culturally significant sites along the pipeline's route. On Saturday bulldozers moved in and destroyed them.

# LADONNA

## Militarization of the Response 5

What happens when the pipeline breaks? What happens to our water? It's the same old story—government, agencies, big oil. We don't matter. So we have to fight to live.

—LaDonna Brave Bull Allard

On the warm late summer morning of Saturday, September 3, 2016, LaDonna Allard settled in to give a history lesson. She was speaking with journalist Amy Goodman of *Democracy Now!* about LaDonna's great-great-grandmother, who—like the ancestors of many Cannon Ball residents—was a survivor of the Whitestone Massacre, the U.S. Army's September 3, 1863, slaying of hundreds of Native Americans in what is now southeastern North Dakota.[1]

As she calmly laid out the scene of the massacre, LaDonna's phone rang. A friend from Cannon Ball was on the line, breathless: "LaDonna, the bulldozers are here; they are taking out the grave sites; what do we do?" She was incredulous: "Stop them!" Politely she turned to Amy Goodman: "I'm sorry; I can't finish the interview. I have to go now." "I'm coming with you," declared Goodman, who had heard the call. LaDonna jumped in her pickup and drove to the front line.

As LaDonna pulled up, she saw women and children lined along a chain link fence. Three bulldozers worked beyond the fence, churning up the earth. A helicopter circled overhead. As she got out of her truck, a friend came running up to her, crying. "They're digging up the graves," she lamented. LaDonna continued walking. A man got out of a white truck and pepper sprayed the whole line.

Young men, water protectors, pushed the fence down and inserted themselves between the pepper spray and the women and children. When the fence came down, water protectors swarmed the construction site where the bulldozers were running.

Private security contractors advanced toward the water protectors, their dogs lunging and biting. People were screaming. LaDonna saw two great German shepherds, their mouths dripping with blood. "Where the hell am I?" she wondered with astonishment. "Is this America? Is this who we are?"

LaDonna ran up to a policeman standing on the road: "Stop them!" she called, indicating the dog handlers. "I'm only here to direct traffic," he replied. She stood in place, closed her eyes, and prayed. In that moment LaDonna felt her whole life change. She decided that there was no justice in America, that there was no law—or at least that the law served only certain people. In that moment she stopped being the historian. She became mad.

LaDonna Brave Bull Allard was born in 1956 in Fort Yates—the biggest town on the Standing Rock Reservation—the oldest of seventeen children. Growing up, she moved from an abusive Indian boarding school to a foster home in Massachusetts to high school in Vermont, but she always returned to her grandmother's home on the reservation, right at the mouth of the Cannonball River.

LaDonna's heritage was Dakota, like many of the people of Cannon Ball, and Lakota. The Standing Rock Reservation is home to members of both the Dakota and Lakota language groups and is one piece of what settlers had called the Great Sioux Nation.

The first international treaty between the Sioux Nation, among other Indigenous nations, and the U.S. government was executed in 1805, in the aftermath of the Louisiana Purchase. Many more followed in the succeeding decades. The Sioux had proven themselves adaptable and resourceful in the face of Euro-American contact. From the 1600s to the 1800s the Lakota transformed from foragers to farmers to hunters to pastoralists, leaving their historic homelands in the eastern woodlands to move westward to the Missouri Valley. They became accomplished horse riders who hunted bison, and they became the most powerful Indigenous nation in the Americas, controlling a vast swath of land.[2] After the 1848 discovery of gold, prospectors traveled west to California across the plains in ever-increasing numbers.[3] The 1851 Fort Laramie Treaty defined the relationship between the Sioux and the government but was followed by a decade of war, as tens of thousands of settlers continued to stream west, protected by the U.S. military. Confrontations were common, with the Sioux proving an effective fighting force and winning decisive victories.[4]

The 1868 Fort Laramie Treaty brought peace and again defined the Great Sioux Reservation land and hunting rights. In the treaty parties agreed that the Great Sioux Reservation, including the Black Hills, would be "set apart for the absolute and undisturbed use and occupation of the Indians."[5] But when gold was discovered in the Black Hills only a few years later, the U.S. government abandoned its treaty obligations to preserve Sioux territory. The Lakota tried to evict gold prospectors in accordance with the treaty, leading to the Battle of Little Bighorn and the defeat of Custer and the Seventh Cavalry in 1876.[6]

Switching tactics, the U.S. government instead focused not on military confrontation but on more insidious actions: encouraging the encroachment of settlers, failing its treaty obligations to provide food and clothing, and engaging in the systematic destruction of the buffalo herds of the plains. Indeed by the late 1870s around five thousand bison were killed per day, with their hides and bones sent east for use in products ranging from blankets to china.[7] The estimated thirty to forty million buffalo who roamed the western plains midcentury had been reduced to fewer than four hundred by 1893, the result of a deliberate campaign of slaughter to defeat the Native nations who depended on them for survival.[8] Weakened by attacks, disease, starvation, and forced movement, the Sioux dependence on buffalo and trade left them vulnerable to the purposeful extermination campaign. They were forced onto reservations in order to survive. The Sioux were starved into dependence on the U.S. government for the rations and commodities agreed upon by the 1868 treaty.[9]

Like the MHA Nation, the Sioux were subjected to still more efforts to take their land. The Dawes Act of 1887 promised to encourage individual ownership and farming, fund an Indian boarding school system with the sale of "surplus" land, and open land for white settlers by allotting individual plots of land. It amounted to an enormous land grab: between 1887 and 1934 Native landholdings dropped from 138 million acres to 48 million.[10]

Even before the Dawes Act was implemented, a government commission descended on Sioux territory in 1888 to split the Sioux Nation into smaller reservations. It was unable to garner the necessary signatures to alter the 1868 treaty. On a second try General George Crook offered the Sioux people $1.50 an acre, managing to secure the necessary signatures by manipulating the leaders of starving people. The Great Sioux Nation was broken apart and reduced, and reservation land itself became a checkerboard of allotments. "Nearly all prime grazing lands," concludes historian Roxane Dunbar-Ortiz, "came to be occupied by non-Indian ranchers by the 1920s."[11] On Lakota and Dakota reservations in 2012, non-Natives controlled almost 60 percent of agricultural lands and received 84.6 percent of all agricultural income.[12]

The Great Sioux Reservation was broken into five smaller reservations. The 2.3-million-acre territory of the Standing Rock Reservation (of which 1.4 million is tribally owned) was defined in 1889, straddling North and South Dakota. It is the fifth-largest reservation in the country. The tribe has an enrollment of 15,568 and the reservation a population of 8,250. With the buffalo nearly eradicated, a plains people were expected to farm and raise livestock in the semi-arid Dakotas. Their former homeland became home to cities with largely white populations—Bismarck, North Dakota; Rapid City and Sioux Falls, South Dakota.

The tribe's legacy of dispossession continued into the twentieth century, when, as it did upstream on Fort Berthold, the Pick-Sloan

Plan authorized the U.S. Army Corps of Engineers to create a dam on the Missouri River that would flood the land on Standing Rock.[13]

Construction began before the negotiations were complete. Standing Rock lost over fifty-five thousand acres of land and 190 housing units. Completed in 1962, the Lake Oahe Dam above the reservation destroyed 90 percent of the timberland on the Standing Rock and Cheyenne River Reservations, in addition to grazing and agricultural lands. More than one thousand Native families were displaced as the tribes lost over three hundred thousand acres of rich bottomlands.[14] Roads, villages, bridges, and infrastructure were all destroyed. Compensation had been grossly inadequate, and Standing Rock residents had even been excluded from any of the power revenues for the dams that were built.[15]

LaDonna remembered the time before the Army Corps built the dam, when her grandmother, Alice—like Lisa's grandmother on Fort Berthold—had lost her land to flooding. The fertile bottom lands had been filled with trees and gardens, and Standing Rock members pastured their animals there and gathered plants to use in medicines. The dam changed all that, as Standing Rock residents were forced to move onto higher ground with bad soil. Many lived in cookie-cutter government-issued homes, with paper-thin walls that couldn't withstand the wind or the cold winters but had exorbitant electricity costs. LaDonna's own father had to live in a tent for a couple of years after the flooding because there was no home ready for him. Tribal Council member Phyllis Young, who grew up on the river during the time before the flooding, experienced homelessness and hunger—ostensibly because the dam was in the national interest—when her grandparents' home was inundated and destroyed.

The pre-flood town of Cannon Ball had boasted a train depot and a proper business district—a feed store, post office, grocery store, and bakery, along with a community softball field and pow wow grounds. Today it doesn't even have a gas station. Cannon Ball residents have to drive twenty miles to get to a dollar store. The landscape is largely flat with lots of sky, stunning and with a cinematic feel; scrubby trees dot low green and yellow hills. Sunflower fields, hay bales, cows, horses, and occasional buffalo are scattered across the landscape. But Cannon Ball is a poor town, with boarded up houses, graffiti, and few working street lights.

LaDonna's father was a tribal police officer with the BIA, and they moved from reservation to reservation as he was transferred, including a year in Los Angeles on the relocation program (a 1956 law intended to encourage Native people in the United States to voluntarily move from reservations to cities). But her grandmother Alice always took her home to the mouth of the Cannonball River.

One place LaDonna's grandmother rescued her from in the 1960s was a mission boarding school—the St. Francis Mission on the Rosebud Reservation in South Dakota. St. Francis has been accused by former students of physical and sexual abuse and has been subject to numerous lawsuits alleging abuse.[16] LaDonna was left-handed; in boarding school she was relentlessly beaten and even locked in a closet when she used her left hand. She remembers spending half of first and second grades in a closet at the school.

Abusive Indian boarding schools had been a particularly insidious force operating for generations, from the late 1800s to the 1970s, when they closed or came under tribal control. In 1879 Richard Henry Pratt opened the Carlisle Indian Industrial School in Carlisle, Pennsylvania; boarding schools for Native students proliferated, with attendance becoming coercive. The schools aimed at a type of cultural erasure, indoctrinating students into Euro-American culture—cutting their hair, forbidding them to speak Native languages, and often subjecting them to brutal physical and sexual abuse.[17]

Small infractions—speaking a Native language, neglecting to flush the toilet, crossing a chalk line on the playground—lead to lashes with a leather strap, and some punishments were even worse: young boys were handcuffed to basement pipes or forced to kneel on sharp stones or stand outdoors in freezing temperatures. The punishments for those who ran away could be even more brutal: solitary confinement for weeks or months, beatings, rape. Indeed the school grounds at these schools included graveyards because—according to the Meriam Report, a 1928 U.S. government investigation of Indian administration, health, and education—Native children were six times more likely than other children in America to die in childhood while at boarding schools. For three generations of Native Americans, significant numbers of children died at boarding schools, and many others were broken by them. Those who survived carried with them a legacy of discipline based on pain and humiliation that bore no relation to traditional Native discipline.[18] As historian Roxanne Dunbar-Ortiz describes, "The experience of generations of Native Americans in on- and off-reservation boarding schools, run by the federal government or Christian missions, contributed significantly to the family and social dysfunction still found in Native communities. Generations of child abuse, including sexual abuse—from the founding of the first schools by missionaries in the 1830s and the federal government in 1875 until most were closed and the remaining ones reformed in the 1970s—traumatized survivors and their progeny."[19]

Over centuries the tribal members had suffered unspeakable abuses, and the tribe had lost much of its land, much of what it considered sacred. When the bulldozers rolled over the area where sacred sites had been discovered that Labor Day weekend, with dogs snapping, it hit a nerve.

In the aftermath of the attack on the water protectors, all parties traded accusations: Morton County sheriff Kyle Kirchmeier called it "more like a riot than a protest." Dave Archambault called the destruction of cultural sites "devastating."[20] He claimed construction workers had moved equipment at least fifteen miles to bulldoze the area where the graves and sacred sites had been found. A tribal spokesman said that the dogs had bitten six people, including a young child; at least twenty were pepper-sprayed.[21]

The video taken by journalist Amy Goodman and her crew, showing dogs with bloody mouths, went viral, was viewed millions of times, and was replayed by all the major networks.[22] Commentators—including leading environmentalist Bill McKibben—compared the images to violent crackdowns during the civil rights movement.[23] It was their Bull Connor moment, Jan Hasselman thought, referring to the Birmingham, Alabama, official who ordered the use of fire hoses and attack dogs against peaceful civil rights activists in 1962–63 to the horror of the people around the world who saw the images. The whole world also saw what had happened to the water protectors. Even 1,200 museum directors and archaeologists took the unusual step of signing a letter to President Obama denouncing the bulldozing.[24]

On the night of the dog attack a line of cars arrived at the camps as people poured in from around the country. Newcomers gathered in a circle and prayed for the graves that had been desecrated. As LaDonna looked at the circle, at the tall feathers of Aztec dancers, she asked herself: "Am I standing in the middle of prophecy? Am I a part of this prophecy?" LaDonna remembered as a child hearing about a black snake that would come to destroy the earth. She had been taught that when eagle and condor—the Indigenous people from North and South America—came together, they could heal the world, that the seventh generation would stand up, and that when the black snake came to devour the earth, they would stop it. She decided that the prophecies were alive. The black snake was the pipeline, and the broader darkness or sickness, a disconnect in American life.[25]

Jan Hasselman at Earthjustice immediately requested a temporary restraining order to halt pipeline construction in the area until a decision was reached on the injunction.[26] Judge Boasberg issued a restraining order for the pipeline corridor closest to the Missouri River but did not ban construction on the part of the pipeline route the tribe had identified as a sacred burial ground.

People also started to ask questions about the dog attack incident. Why was the company doing work on that spot, and had it deliberately damaged the sites the tribe had flagged as sacred? Who were these private security contractors with the dogs? As to the former question, attorneys swore in court documents that the work had been long planned. Jan Hasselman didn't think they would ever know whether that was true, and the issue was never definitively resolved in litigation. As to the latter question, Frost Kennels of Hartville, Ohio, claimed credit on Facebook. It had been working under Silverton, a private security company employed by Dakota Access. Sheriff Kirchmeier, for his part, disclaimed all prior knowledge of the dogs: "It's a private company. Protecting their personnel as they see fit," he said.[27]

The security company's actions quickly drew censure from the ACLU and even from specialists who trained police dogs. The North Dakota Private Investigation and Security Board, a state licensing board, opened an investigation, and the Morton County Sheriff's Department also vowed to investigate, ultimately determining that the dog handlers were not properly licensed.

On the gray, cool Labor Day Monday, a brief calm descended at the camps. The energy seemed to have shifted; campers' resolve and resistance grew stronger. At the open mic, the overwhelming message was about prayer, peace, unity, and nonviolent action. "I think things in Indian Country are changing," Dave Archambault told journalists. "No more are we going to let things happen to us."[28]

Central fires burned night and day as more people arrived at the camps, driving into Oceti Sakowin down the dirt road lined with flags fluttering from Native nations. Phyllis Young went to the flags every morning. "Flag Avenue" was the spot where Russell Means, a Lakota activist and prominent member of the American Indian Movement, had been shot by a policeman decades earlier. She prayed and thanked him because she thought he had brought them back to that sacred place.

Small groups of white tipis and colorful tents were clustered around the fires. The movement had quickly become a sprawling encampment of thousands. The number fluctuated daily, but LaDonna thought five thousand lived at Sacred Stone in the early fall and some estimated ten thousand overall—with more than three hundred tribes represented. Oceti Sakowin, which started as an overflow camp, had become like a small city, with tents holding donated supplies, a school, multiple kitchens, free meals, daily trainings in nonviolent direct action, and tribally provided water and port-a-potties. Environmental groups like 350.org were there too, helping to set up an art tent. Prayers, songs, and dances from Native nations mingled with hip hop and country music.

All summer LaDonna continued to work full time for the tribe while helping to sustain the camps. She didn't sleep much. At 5 a.m. she would get up, load her car with water and food, and drop it at camp before driving into Fort Yates and working all day. At 4:30 p.m. she would get back into her car and drive to the camps, where she would cut up meat—cow or buffalo that had been donated—and cook. She would stay until one or two in the morning before returning home and repeating the cycle.

For LaDonna Sacred Stone Camp had started as a way to support other people's activism and idealism. But then something clicked for her. She went down to Sacred Stone one evening in September, and as her truck pulled in, she saw two women working. Someone had brought a deer, and people were hanging its meat to dry. Men were sitting around the fire, roasting food. Kids were running and playing hide and seek and climbing trees. She thought of life on the river before the Army Corps had flooded the reservation. She thought: "This is how we're supposed to live. This is what we're supposed to be doing." It felt like home. She began to believe that her people could survive by living with the earth again.

The message of water protection was especially important to LaDonna. She believed that as a woman, she understood water—through water, women bring children into the world, bathe their children, care for their children, feed their families. Through water, plants and animals drink.

On September 8 North Dakota governor Jack Dalrymple announced that armed National Guard officers in fatigues were taking over the roadblock on Highway 1806. "Why?" LaDonna asked herself. She also stopped one of them to ask. "For safety," the national guard member replied. But she didn't believe it. She thought they were there to protect the oil company's equipment.

On the same day Morton County authorities issued an arrest warrant for Amy Goodman, the journalist who had documented the dog attack, for a charge of criminal trespassing. She called the charges a violation of freedom of the press and a clear message not to return.[29] But she did return to North Dakota the following month, to fight. The trespassing charge was dropped as Amy was arriving, and the judge refused to sign a complaint against her for an additional charge of engaging in a riot. But law enforcement continued to target other journalists covering the camps.[30] A few days later, two journalists from the nonprofit media collective Unicorn Riot were arrested while covering the movement and charged with criminal trespass.[31]

More people were starting to take notice though. Presidential candidate Jill Stein was charged (and later pleaded guilty) for spray-painting construction equipment. On Twitter Stein quipped that she hoped North Dakota would also pursue charges against the company that had bulldozed sacred sites.[32] Senator Bernie Sanders offered legislation to prevent the Army Corps from granting the easement for the pipeline before conducting an EIS. Meanwhile, President Obama still declined to take a stand on the pipeline and avoided a question on it from youth at a town hall in Laos, an indication of how internationally prominent the movement was becoming.[33]

Everyone was highly anticipating the court decision on September 9; it would decide the tribe's request for a preliminary injunction to halt construction. The day brought a stunning series of developments. First, Judge Boasberg made the ruling that Jan Hasselman had been expecting: he denied the tribe's request for a preliminary injunction. Judge Boasberg concluded that "the Corps has likely complied with the NHPA and . . . the Tribe has not shown it will suffer injury that would be prevented by any injunction."[34]

Hasselman was in his office reading the court's disappointing decision, not even halfway through, when he received a press release without comment. He read it, then reread it twice. The Departments of the Army, Justice, and Interior had issued a joint statement promising that construction under Lake Oahe would not be authorized until the Army Corps conducted additional review. They also urged the company to voluntarily halt construction twenty miles east and west of Lake Oahe.[35]

This stunning move changed the equation. Dave Archambault considered it a crack at the door. In court the tribe was quick to file notice of appeal.[36] It was still asking for a full EIS. Dakota Access wouldn't comment on whether it would stop construction in that area. But Hasselman was optimistic when speaking to journalists: "Considering they need a permit from the Army Corps to cross under Lake Oahe, thumbing their nose at the Army Corps sounds like a bad strategy," he said.[37]

What had happened? Hasselman thought there were a few possible explanations. The camps were in full glory. While tribal leaders and the vast majority of participants were there as an act of prayer and peace, a few of the camp residents seemed primed to explode. The government's decision may have been intended to reduce confrontation, to let passions cool. Another interpretation, though, was that the tribe had been right: there were issues that hadn't been given a suitable amount of attention, and someone thought the government needed more time to consider, even if it was not on the company's schedule.

On September 12 Hasselman filed an appeal of the lower court's decision and requested an injunction pending appeal. The injunction asked the court to make the government's request for a voluntary cessation of construction twenty miles around Lake Oahe a legal requirement while the appeal was under consideration.[38]

LaDonna remained skeptical. "This is not a victory," she cautioned. "Until Dakota Access is stopped, we stand."

The government reversal was big news and made the front page of the *New York Times* the next day (it drew criticism in other outlets).[39] Within a few days ETP's Kelcy Warren had circulated an internal memo vowing to meet with federal officials to reiterate his company's commitment to the pipeline.[40] The company's stock was falling; it had gone from $42.53 a share on August 3 to $36.47 a month later.

Dave Archambault, in a letter to Jo-Ellen Darcy, assistant secretary of the army for civil works, was grateful for the government reversal. But, he wrote, "the fundamental question is this: do Tribal interests matter in federal decision making regarding a crude oil pipeline, in former Treaty lands of great cultural and historical importance that were taken away, but are immediately adjacent to an Indian Reservation?" The September 9 statement suggested to the tribe that they did but that they hadn't been given adequate consideration thus far.[41]

If nothing else, the government's announcement made clear that a speedy resolution was not imminent. The state started to ramp up its response in preparation for an extended duration of the camps while expressing frustration at the lack of federal assistance. The North Dakota Department of Emergency Services requested and was granted up to $6 million in borrowing authority from the Bank of North Dakota as it reeled from what it determined to be the cost of responding to the camps. The governor's office estimated that the state had spent $1.8 million in assisting law enforcement to date.[42] The Morton County Sheriff's Department was claiming around $100,000 in weekly expenses; the state, around $263,000.[43]

Life in the camps continued to thrive and grow richer as pipeline construction moved inexorably forward. Some worried, though, that another problem was emerging: a backlash of racism in the surrounding communities as a result of the camps. Some tribal members had been sensing an increase of racism—an insidious fact with which LaDonna had dealt her whole life—as a result of changes in the broader world. The 2016 presidential election was heating up that summer, with Donald Trump and Secretary of State Hillary Clinton as the presumptive nominees of their parties. Already the Trump candidacy was creating ripples in North Dakota. Dana Yellow Fat had found himself outside a Trump rally in late May, where he noticed men giving Nazi salutes to the protestors who had gathered in the street. He felt that the quiet daily racism Native people experienced in North Dakota—people following them in stores or refusing to rent to them—was coming out into the open.

But backlash against the camps had made the harassment far worse. Because of threats against Native people on social media, the Standing Rock community school board had voted in August to request school resource officers or BIA law enforcement to escort children whenever they traveled off the reservation for extracurricular activities.

Being a spokesperson for the IIYC and on the front line for the youth put a target on her back, Jasilyn thought. Increasingly she was being asked to speak about the camps and attend meetings. She found that when she traveled to the Bismarck airport, she would always get pulled over and searched. She credited her "Water Is Life" bumper sticker; cops were targeting anyone with NoDAPL insignia on their cars, she observed. Often she would leave five hours before her flight time to allow for time to be stopped and searched on the way to the airport; even so she had missed two flights. She had also been stopped and asked to leave stores in Bismarck by security and management. It pained her to see other IIYC members unable to go to Bismarck, to the mall, to Walmart for supplies, or to a movie without fear of being treated differently.

All fall, racism continued to erupt in the surrounding community. Passersby harassed Native women driving on the streets of Bismarck with children in their cars. Water protectors at hotels in Bismarck were threatened and met with profanity. A volunteer firefighter wrote on Facebook that he would stack up water protectors' bodies and burn them in his driveway.

But the water protectors held their ground. Pipeline frontline actions—while nonviolent—were continuing just outside of the twenty-mile zone. On September 14 Nick Tilsen, the NGO leader from Pine Ridge, was one of three water protectors to chain themselves to a piece of construction equipment, aiming to stop construction, cost the company money, and delay the project. Construction was shut down for the entire day as Tilsen remained chained to the equipment for an uncomfortable five hours (he had a broken foot at the time). He felt empowered, like a modern-day warrior, as though his ancestors were with him on top of the machine. But he was also one of the first to be charged with a felony (reckless endangerment, a charge that could lead to five years in prison and/or up to a $10,000 fine). Law enforcement officials were looking for charges that would discourage actions like Tilsen's.[44]

When LaDonna had first started the camp at Sacred Stone, her daughter, Prairie, told her she didn't want to participate. But it didn't take long before Prairie showed up at camp and stayed for a few days. Soon after she moved in with all of her kids. She started her own camp of frontliners, Heyoka Camp. "What do you want me to do, mom?" she asked, looking for guidance. LaDonna answered: "Be Crazy Horse." Prairie didn't know what that meant. "Duck and dive," LaDonna told her. "Never stand still. Don't let them see you, but always be on the front lines." After that Prairie always was, LaDonna noticed. She was everywhere, and she was nowhere.

LaDonna's husband Miles had taken on a quieter role in the camps—hauling supplies, cutting wood. He worried about LaDonna. Miles was born in 1948, in Williston, North Dakota, right in the heart of the Bakken, decades before the oil boom. He had lived in San Francisco with the relocation program and was in the U.S. Navy during the Vietnam era. They met when they each already had four children but quickly became soulmates. They had settled into a comfortable life together in Fort Yates, Miles as a public school teacher and LaDonna working as a tribal historian.

After the camps took off, they hardly saw each other. At night when they got home, Miles would kindly tell her, "Just go to bed." When she rose in the morning, he would have breakfast waiting for her and would see her off with a simple, "Be safe."

When LaDonna looked up from her daily work at Sacred Stone, she was hopeful: "I see a nation standing up because it is time; I see the young saying that they are proud of who they are; I see the grandmas standing for their grandchildren," she wrote. "I see that our nation can heal."[45] She was in awe of what was happening around her and knew the world was watching. The youth looked to her for guidance. Jasilyn considered LaDonna a teacher, showing by example how to be a warrior for her people.

On Friday, September 16, the tribe gained a temporary win: The U.S. Court of Appeals for the DC Circuit ordered Dakota Access to halt construction within twenty miles of Lake Oahe while the tribe's lawsuit against the Army Corps was pending. In court documents Dakota Access stated that all construction beginning twenty miles east of Lake Oahe was complete and that all but two miles to the west had been cleared and graded.

Meanwhile, in a federal court in North Dakota, U.S. district judge Daniel Hovland lifted the temporary restraining order on Dave Archambault and Dana Yellow Fat that had been in effect since their mid-August arrest, concluding that it no longer served a "legitimate purpose." (Ultimately Judge Hovland dismissed the suit.)[46]

As the beautiful mid-September days passed and the leaves changed color, LaDonna and her grandsons dried corn and stored it for winter. They needed tipis with liners, wood stoves, yurts, more wood. She told the campers at Sacred Stone to start preparing.

LaDonna made sure everyone at Sacred Stone Camp worked. "If you don't want to work, go over to Oceti," she said. She called camp meetings regularly. Sacred Stone campers were building semi-permanent hoop-shaped structures as gathering spaces; framed in wood and draped with tarps, they were warm and water proof. Marty Brave Bull, LaDonna's sister, cooked for seventy-five to a hundred people a day using donated food.

Preparation for winter, as Sacred Stone grew, also included financial planning. The camp had a financial committee, a bookkeeper, a CPA, and a separate bank account for camp funds, with receipts for everything. LaDonna had started out supplying tents, sleeping bags, blankets, cooking pots, walkie-talkies, and even hats and gloves herself. Her electricity had been shut off three times that summer because she hadn't been able to pay the bills.

Eventually donations started rolling in. While LaDonna was at the camp, Miles was often at home organizing the packages that arrived. The house was inundated with donations. Rumors about the amounts of donations swirled around camp, and LaDonna thought that the pipeline company was trying to divide the campers with the gossip. GoFundMe sites for the camp proliferated. After they were able to tap into those donations and subtracted GoFundMe's sizeable cut, they were able to buy tipis, yurts, stoves, vehicles, and gas cards. They bought wood from Minnesota because local retailers wouldn't sell to them. Just supplying the camp cost $7,000 a week.

Meanwhile, Dakota Access was consolidating its landholding. In late September the company bought more than seven thousand acres north of the camps, including Cannonball Ranch, from cattle ranchers David and Brenda Meyer. The sale included the portion of the pipeline route where the Standing Rock Sioux claimed sacred sites had been disturbed. In practical terms the sale didn't change much; the Meyers had previously signed easements with Dakota Access for construction of the pipeline. But privately the sale hit hard. LaDonna knew the Meyers, and they had a friendly relationship. She heard that ETP had sued them and threatened to take everything they owned. In the negotiations that ensued, the Meyers ended up selling the ranch. LaDonna felt they had been pushed into a corner.

The legality of the sale was questionable. Attorney Sarah Vogel, a former head of the North Dakota Agriculture Department, claimed that the sale violated anti-corporate farming law, which permitted corporations to own farmland only when "necessary." But the pipeline company already held an easement for the land. The state attorney general, Wayne Stenehjam, got involved, asking Dakota Access to explain how it planned to use the land. (He later determined that the purchase was "temporarily necessary for commercial development.")[47]

ETP also seemed to be using increasingly aggressive tactics. Water protectors were beginning to feel that they were being watched. Back in April, Jasilyn, Kalen, and LaDonna had started to see drones, helicopters, and airplanes circling above them almost daily, and big white trucks parked across the road, with people inside watching through binoculars or even from boats on the river. As time wore on, small planes, drones, and helicopters began to fly over the camps twenty-four hours a day, circling noisily at low altitude even at night. In August LaDonna had started receiving anonymous threatening calls and letters.

Jasilyn stayed vigilant, sleeping in one place, then another, giving information to only a core group she could trust. The IIYC members communicated by walkie-talkie, so their conversations couldn't be picked up, and every few weeks they rotated the frequency. LaDonna changed her phone number.

The campers were not paranoid. In fact, as award-winning online news publication *The Intercept* later detailed using an extensive collection of leaked documents, in the aftermath of the dog attack in September, ETP had hired TigerSwan, a shadowy international security firm with experience in counterterrorism operations in Iraq and Afghanistan, to respond to the growing presence at Standing Rock. Internal TigerSwan documents compared the water protectors to jihadist fighters. TigerSwan operations involved extensive and invasive surveillance. Its agents shared information and coordinated with local, state, and federal law enforcement in a public-private partnership that placed law enforcement at the disposal of corporate interests. TigerSwan's intelligence included a live video feed from a security helicopter, dossiers on activists, a collection of license plate numbers, a counterintelligence campaign, and a "social engagement" strategy to change the narrative around the camps using Facebook postings.[48]

The documents obtained by *The Intercept* included email communications, charts of activists, and daily intelligence updates with activities and analysis. The daily reports were comprised of extensive in-person and social media monitoring. They discussed the major donors bank-rolling environmental causes; analyzed interpersonal dynamics at the camps as operatives sought opportunities for conflict and dissension, particularly among Native Americans and "white allies"; and traced arrivals at camps, frontline actions, tribal leadership meetings, public relations activities, arrests, and even items that water protectors bought at home improvement stores. They discussed LaDonna's Facebook posts about camp expenses and fundraising. The intelligence updates covered activities in North Dakota, Iowa, Illinois, and South Dakota.

One of the most insidious parts of TigerSwan's operations—which were conducted without a license in North Dakota—was a long-term campaign to infiltrate the camps. TigerSwan agents using assumed names and identities tried to build the trust of activists, collecting information on their plans. The information TigerSwan gleaned about life at the camps was essential to its efforts to undermine them: "Exploitation of ongoing native versus non-native rifts, and tribal rifts between peaceful and violent elements is critical in our effort to delegitimize the anti-DAPL movement," one of their internal reports from October read.[49]

LaDonna thought that the infiltrators had tricks to get the crowd to go along with them, including invoking the names of respected elders. She constantly heard people tell her, "LaDonna said they're having a camp meeting" or "LaDonna said they're going to raid the camp." Joye Braun had heard her name used the same way. LaDonna wanted to get a T-shirt that had "LaDonna said" printed on it because she had heard the phrase so many times. People were confused by it, particularly white allies. They had come to camp with the concept of being respectful and listening to the elders, only to have that deference weaponized by the infiltrators.

Jasilyn and Kalen tried to keep surveillance opportunities against them to a minimum. They kept moving around and, as noted, gave information only to the core group who had been there since the beginning. But at times infiltrators put all the camps into distress, spreading the word that someone had drowned or throwing rocks and cursing at the police lines. It could be hard to tell who the infiltrators were at first. Josephine Thundershield, the Standing Rock member who had first called Joye Braun about the pipeline, came up with one way to check: look at the shoes. Water protectors were always working, and their boots got dirty; only infiltrators, she suspected, were walking around with clean boots.

LaDonna started to become wary of anyone entering Sacred Stone. She didn't allow journalists. She had a security escort. She ran camp meetings from 11 p.m. or midnight to 2 or 3 a.m. because security was tighter that way. She asked five security questions of everyone who came into the camp: "Who do you know here? Who are you? Where do you come from? Do you work for the oil company? Do you work for the police department?" LaDonna got a phone that had no sim card in it. She drove her pickup because it didn't have GPS and other electronics that were trackable. She took the new normal in stride: "Native people's lives are automatically chaos, trauma. . . . Crisis is here every day," she decided. She thought they handled crisis better than other Americans because Americans were comfortable.

But another thing was worrying LaDonna as September wore on. She and Dave Archambault, who were actually relatives (he was married to her cousin), had a falling out. LaDonna's job as Tribal Historic Preservation Section 106 Coordinator meant that if there was a federal undertaking—construction, water lines, anything that had federal dollars attached to it—those involved had to consult with the tribe and LaDonna according to the NHPA. But early in the summer she started to realize that she wasn't invited to meetings related to Dakota Access, even when other tribal employees were; other tribal employees were asked to go help with the camps, but she wasn't allowed. She wasn't allowed to speak to the tribe's lawyers. Instead she went in to work at tribal headquarters every day and came to the camp after her work day was over. Finally the tribe eliminated the money for her position with no explanation. She thought the tribe wanted ownership over the camps. September 26 was LaDonna's last day. She resented it but welcomed her newfound freedom. Without a job, at least she was free to post anything she wanted to say on Facebook: "Watch out world," she concluded.[50] It happened so quickly that she didn't even have a chance to process the change or grieve the loss.

LaDonna also hadn't had time to reflect on the loss of her job because managing Sacred Stone Camp was all-consuming. The movement was becoming home to an eclectic mix of supporters: folk singers and rappers, a descendant of oil baron William Rockefeller, and prominent preachers all visited the camp. Charles Rencountre, a Lakota sculptor, arrived at Sacred Stone to create a work titled "Not Afraid to Look," a red figure of a man sitting and gazing forward toward the Cannonball River to the pipeline equipment on the bluffs beyond. It was completed in October.[51] LaDonna loved the sculpture, one of a series of four built by the artist across the country. She saw herself in it—grounded in her home, standing strong. She knew that her descendants would continue to stand on that land for generations to come, honoring its history and protecting it.

When LaDonna talked to people about why they had come, she heard of a disconnect in America. She learned that people could age out of the foster care system and be left in the streets; that elders could work their whole lives and then be cast out of their companies; that young people could buy into careers with no creativity or sense of being. To herself she thought, "What is happening to our world? How did we get into this shape that we're in?" Sacred Stone was a chance to create a different kind of community.

Outside the camps the fall election was underway. Frustrated that candidates didn't seem to be listening to their concerns, at one North Dakota gubernatorial debate, Joye Braun marched down an aisle toward the stage, looking squarely at the candidates and shouting her opposition to the pipeline. "We will never allow this pipeline through!" she called, as one after another of the audience members rose in solidarity, fists raised, chanting, "Water is life!"

Frontline actions were also happening at the camps on a daily or every-other-day basis, some with small groups and some with hundreds. Construction hadn't stopped after the Obama administration had intervened (in fact construction was proceeding seven days a week); it had just moved outside of the twenty-mile buffer zone. By the end of September Dakota Access reported that construction was 87 percent complete.[52]

In early October Sheriff Kirchmeier stood at a podium for a press conference in his khaki uniform. The water protectors had been traveling to sites outside of the twenty-mile stop-work zone to shut down construction, he said. "Not all of the protests have been unlawful," he admitted, but he said that he was looking to be proactive: "Protestors have disdained the rule of law, and that has resulted in a heightened level of fear among our residents."[53]

The neighboring community had been uneasy, with some residents fearing vandalism. The Morton County Sheriff's Department began to respond with "specialized equipment," including armored vehicles and sound cannons. "Reprehensible," local Episcopal priest Rev. John Floberg declared; this was a "militaristic assault."[54] LaDonna too worried as the police stepped up their tactics. She encouraged the young people on the front lines to don masks to avoid facial recognition software.

State and local authorities were on their own in dealing with the water protectors. Federal authorities had denied requests for aid, and the national guard maintained only the Highway 1806 checkpoint. Local frustration with the federal government mounted as state law enforcement was taxed. The Morton County Commission chairman, Cody Schulz, writing in a local newspaper, called Washington's response "disgusting," arguing that it had exacerbated tensions by creating uncertainty.[55] The *Bismarck Tribune* called for the Army Corps to take responsibility for the situation.[56]

Law enforcement officials had set up operations at a base on the campground at Fort Rice, a summer fishing spot eight miles north of Oceti Sakowin, creating a sea of army tents, Humvees, and dirt-moving vehicles. Like at the Oceti Sakowin camp, tents with food, medical equipment, and supplies were mobilized, serving two thousand meals on the site's busiest days. Maps dotted the walls of the operations hub. Radio transmissions called in the latest information.

On October 5 the Court of Appeals held oral arguments on the tribe's emergency motion for an injunction pending appeal; a temporary halt to construction was in place while the court considered. For the lawyers involved, it was another big argument, with pressure and public visibility. On Sunday, October 9, the U.S. Court of Appeals for the DC Circuit issued its decision. The three-judge panel denied the tribe's requested injunction, allowing work to proceed within the twenty-mile radius. Pipeline construction was still halted on Corps land adjacent to Lake Oahe. The court noted, however, that it could only hope that the "spirit of Section 106" of the NHPA might prevail, as the decision was still pending over the permit for the crossing at Lake Oahe.[57]

Jan Hasselman had known that the injunction would be hard to get. In the meanwhile, though, the tribe and its attorneys were engaging in efforts to persuade the administration to conduct a full EIS. Following the court order, the Department of Justice, Department of the Army, and Department of the Interior issued another joint statement. They were hoping to conclude their review soon, but "in the interim, the Army will not authorize constructing the Dakota Access Pipeline on Corps land bordering or under Lake Oahe. We repeat our request that the pipeline company voluntarily pause all construction activity within 20 miles east or west of Lake Oahe."[58] Dakota Access rejected the call for a voluntary pause, and construction resumed near the camps as the company dug trenches and laid pipe.

It began to seem as if the world was watching: a flash mob in a shopping mall in Syracuse, New York; letters of support from over three hundred tribal nations worldwide; at least nineteen cities' resolutions opposing the pipeline or supporting Standing Rock's opposition.[59] A group of U.S. senators, including Bernie Sanders, Patrick Leahy, and Diane Feinstein, wrote a letter to President Obama asking for all permits and easements to be revoked or denied pending full consultation.[60] Behind the scenes Hasselman thought the administration seesawed. There were a lot of conversations between the tribe, its lawyers, and its allies with anyone who would listen.

Some of the most productive conversations were with the Department of the Interior. Hilary Tompkins, the solicitor for the Department of the Interior, had been six months away from wrapping up her eight-year tenure in a demanding, high-level job when the DAPL controversy exploded. It became, she later reflected, a time of challenging internal deliberations. The Obama administration was balancing the Army Corps and its responsibilities with those of the Department of the Interior, whose role was to advise on Indian affairs, and the United States' role as trustee. "It was a complete clash," she concluded.[61]

As Tompkins, who is Navajo, sat at the deliberations table, her role as a Native American federal official was thrown into relief for her. She was the first Native American to serve as solicitor of the Department of the Interior. "I need to voice my perspective," she thought. She explained that the protest wasn't just about this pipeline but about something deeper—"a deep reserve of pain caused by this country's legacy of mistreatment to the tribes," she described it.[62]

Hilary Tompkins saw the issue from both sides. On the one hand, this pipeline fell under a nationwide permit by the Corps that examined only a small crossing, and the pipeline ran alongside preexisting pipe, so it didn't create a lot of new disturbance. The pipeline was 99 percent on private land, and the route had been modified many times upstream to accommodate historical sites. The United States had faced litigation by the tribe and environmental groups and prevailed under the NHPA that there had been adequate consultation and that the impacts were small.[63] But on the other hand, the story read differently from the tribe's perspective: these were the Great Sioux Nation's ancestral lands, and the reservation had been reduced over and over again, including with the Pick-Sloan Plan. The tribe attached religious and cultural significance to the lake bed and had treaty rights on the surface land. Also, the fact that the original proposal to route the pipeline north of Bismarck had been abandoned rankled. "From the tribal perspective, this was an assault on their identities, their homelands, their safety. So that in their minds, the fact that it might not have been a traditional cultural property under the NHPA was meaningless."[64]

There were a lot of tough days, and on some of those Hilary Tompkins felt like an outsider, a minority without a lot of support. But she reminded herself, "This is why I went to college; this is why I went to law school. I need to step up. This is a life-defining moment, to speak truth as a federal official in my formal role but also to explain what was happening on the ground from a Native perspective."

Looking back, Tompkins realized that having powerful non-Native leadership backing her was key. And indeed the Obama administration had been an ally to Native nations, with a record number of Native American appointees in powerful positions. When Hilary Tompkins started in office, there were over one hundred tribes suing the Department of the Interior. President Obama said to settle the cases. They sat in rooms with tribal leaders and their lawyers and settled more than ninety of those cases, with a total of around $6 billion paid out to tribes. She saw her mission in office as trying to rebuild trust with tribes, healing relationships that had been broken.[65]

On Monday, October 10, frontline actions at two construction sites by over two hundred people led to twenty-seven arrests, including actor Shailene Woodley, who was broadcasting a Facebook live feed. (She ultimately pleaded not guilty to the misdemeanor charges of criminal trespass and engaging in a riot. At that point the live video of her arrest on Facebook had been viewed more than 3.6 million times, and she had penned a powerful statement in *Time*.)[66] Law enforcement officers called the demonstrations a "riot," facing water protectors with night sticks and helmets with visors, though there was little violence.[67]

Law enforcement officers were increasingly taking up Kirchmeier's "proactive" approach to handling the water protectors. Preemptive road blocks, an increased number of officers, and more arrests became standard. Police at demonstrations dressed in riot masks, bulletproof vests, and nightsticks; armored vehicles and police cars lined the highway.[68] Jennifer Cook, policy director for the ACLU, called the road block strategy "very concerning": "You shouldn't take preemptive action against a lawful protest," she told journalists.[69] Jasilyn thought that the fear tactics that Morton County was using were reminiscent of strategies that the government had used against Native peoples for centuries to keep them on their reservations.

At camp Jasilyn found that she and fellow IIYC members were increasingly taking on a crucial role: ensuring that the confrontation with law enforcement remained peaceful. After Jasilyn trained in nonviolent direct action, she encouraged all the youth to do so, and they assumed the role of de-escalators. The youth were disciplined and grounded. They organized a silent prayer march, a show of fierce discipline. They stood between the agitators—people who were angry and trying to anger the police—and law enforcement. They talked people down. "We just weren't taking anybody's shit," concluded one IIYC member, Andreanne Catt. They were Indigenous youth on Indigenous land. As Danny Grassrope saw it, he was there to remind everyone else of why they were there.

On October 22 campers went to stand in solidarity with water protectors who had locked themselves to equipment to temporarily halt construction. Law enforcement officers surrounded them. IIYC member Lauren Howland's wrist was fractured, she said, after being beaten by an officer with a baton.[70] The day marked the first mass arrest by the Morton County Sheriff's Department, with eighty-three people arrested.[71]

Reports from the water protectors' scouts suggested that construction was inching closer to the highway and Lake Oahe. Amid the tense standoff some water protectors moved their camp to Cannonball

Ranch, north on Highway 1806 from the reservation—now owned by Dakota Access. The ownership of the land itself was disputed: it had never been ceded by the 1851 and 1868 Fort Laramie Treaties. Joye Braun moved in on October 23, sleeping little amid a constant fear that the camp would be raided. Morton County called on Dave Archambault to halt development of this frontline camp, but it was already growing.[72] By October 24 around two hundred people were settled at the new camp. The barbed wire fences around the property were decorated with flags.

On October 24 Dave Archambault asked the Department of Justice to intervene to investigate abuses by law enforcement.[73] An Oceti Sakowin camp coordinator issued a statement that campers had enacted eminent domain on unceded land, claiming 1851 treaty rights, and would be occupying it peacefully until the pipeline was stopped.[74]

By Tuesday, October 25, the police presence around the new camp was growing as Dakota Access issued a statement: "All trespassers will be prosecuted to the fullest extent of the law and removed from the land."[75] Governor Dalrymple, having declared a state of emergency, had been soliciting assistance under the Emergency Management Assistance compact. With seventy-six law enforcement jurisdictions represented, along with the National Guard and private security, law enforcement deployed its largest presence in the state since 1890.[76]

The Federal Aviation Administration imposed a flight restriction over the camps; only law enforcement flights were allowed, and drones were prohibited. Law enforcement had been targeting drone operators, even shooting at one, in the preceding days. DAPL private security continued to fly over for surveillance purposes, a result of an ongoing partnership with law enforcement.[77]

Pipeline opponents at the camps pinned their hopes to a meeting between Chairman Harold Frazier of Cheyenne River and President Obama, happening in Los Angeles that same day. At the meeting Chairman Frazier later said, President Obama assured him that he would continue the consultation process and review the law.[78] Chairman Frazier admitted he was "a little disappointed." He concluded: "They have their game of politics."[79]

Walking away from negotiations with camp coordinators, Cass County sheriff Paul Laney expressed frustration: "If there's a confrontation, they've chosen to have it," he declared. Water protectors couldn't trespass, Kirchmeier contended, though when it came to their removal, "the last thing we want to do is do it forcefully."[80] A human barricade of around one hundred water protectors, backed by horses, formed across Highway 1806 near the frontline camp. Many wore bandanas across their faces, and some carried goggles in case the police used pepper spray.

Dave Archambault pleaded with Governor Dalrymple by phone, trying to avoid forcible removal. But they couldn't reach an agreement. The governor wanted Archambault to ask the water protectors to leave the land; Archambault wanted the governor to stop construction near the Missouri River.[81]

In the midst of the standoff actor Mark Ruffalo arrived at camp to support the water protectors and deliver solar trailers. Rev. Jesse Jackson also visited, calling the movement of the pipeline route from its original path north of Bismarck "the ripest case of environmental racism I've seen in a long time."[82] Ruffalo and Jackson arrived as negotiations broke down between law enforcement and camp coordinators. Though the presence of famous figures deterred the arrival of law enforcement at the camps, the détente didn't last long.

The next day, October 27, sirens blared. Mark Ruffalo and Jesse Jackson were gone. Helicopters and surveillance planes circled. As police called over a loudspeaker for water protectors at the front line to return to the main camp, between two and three hundred officers surrounded the water protectors. A line of officers in tan shirts and helmets, holding sticks and others in bulletproof vests, moved in along with armored vehicles. Water protectors responded in varying ways, some urging peace and others throwing water bottles, logs, or rocks at the officers. The militarized force advanced, a visible reminder to some water protectors of the centuries-old conflict over land and the U.S. government's failure to honor the 1851 and 1868 Fort Laramie Treaties.[83] As buffalo charged in the distance and eagles circled overhead, it felt to some like the animals had come to support them.

As law enforcement pressured the water protectors relentlessly with pepper spray, tasers, rubber and bean bag bullets, sound cannons, and smoke grenades, the water protectors calmly linked arms and walked backward away from the police. From noon until the evening hours, the police pushed water protectors from the frontline camp south on Highway 1806, arresting water protectors including IIYC members. As the conflict was unfolding, visible over a hill, construction equipment began work on the pipeline a short distance away, in the area the tribe had said contained sacred sites. "They're taunting us," one water protector said.[84] Those who had been arrested had to watch as they were held by the side of the road.

Jasilyn and Kalen were at the frontline camp, along with Kalen's older brother, who had just arrived to visit, hoping for a peaceful day. "You guys are gonna point that gun at me, you better shoot me," Kalen called to the officers. Camp security had been exhorting them not to throw anything, not to give law enforcement any excuse to shoot, but Kalen lobbed a small orange at the police, an act he later regretted. Kalen was shot with rubber bullets and bean bag guns, and Jasilyn was maced four or five times.

That same night, October 27, the standoff between demonstrators and law enforcement continued on the nearby Backwater Bridge, where scores of officers in riot gear lined up.[85] Water protectors were trying to move a burned-out truck from the bridge; law enforcement officers claimed water protectors had attacked them with firebombs and logs and began shooting at the water protectors, later admitting that they used pepper spray, beanbag rounds, and a high-pitched sound device.[86] The conflict escalated.

Dana Yellow Fat was on the bridge that night. An officer recognized him as he was trying to get women and children out of the way of advancing armored vehicles. Yellow Fat thought the officer was trying to antagonize him, to bait him into getting himself into trouble, but Yellow Fat wasn't having it. When he turned around, he remembered, he was blinded by mace, then shot twice in the back with rubber bullets. "I was no threat. I didn't have a weapon. I wasn't even talking to him," he recalled. "But he was trying to get a rise out of me."

Kandi White was there too, on the front line facing the police. A Native man who she believed was working as an infiltrator came up behind her and pointed at the top of her head. She saw the private security officer in front of her nod yes, and then she felt a push, but Kandi fell to the right instead of into the police line. Fortuitously the police grabbed the suspected infiltrator instead. She was sprayed but stayed at the front line. She saw tanks, rubber or bean bag bullets, and sound machines. "It was all the police escalating and escalating because they came and forcibly removed us forcing us back to the reservation line," she wrote that night on Facebook. She felt physically ill after.[87]

Jasilyn and Kalen missed the conflict at Backwater Bridge. They had gone home earlier that day after the conflict at the frontline camp for a few days in Eagle Butte, to rest, heal, and regroup. From afar they heard about the events unfolding on the bridge. "Well dammit," Jasilyn said, wishing they had been there. After that Kalen was determined not to leave. "No more breaks," declared Jasilyn.

Other members of the IIYC were maced, bloodied, and arrested. For many that night was life changing. Teenager Andreanne Catt was lying in the Youth Council's yurt in Sacred Stone that night when she heard her brother knocking at the door. He was having a panic attack. "They're shooting people with rubber bullets," he said. He pulled the rubber bullets he had been shot with out of his pocket, crying and struggling to catch his breath.

LaDonna tried to go up to the bridge, but as she got to the front line, water protectors pushed her back: "Grandma, get back to camp," they said. "We can't afford for you to get hurt." She watched through a telescope. With rubber bullets and bean bags flying, mace hanging in the air, and planes and helicopters circling overhead, it looked how she imagined a war zone would look. As people staggered back to camp, she wrapped them in blankets. Everything she worried about Americans was true, she thought, all her worst fears confirmed. "They walk in blood; they swim in blood; they live in blood," she decided.

**1.** Lisa DeVille. Photo by Jay Brousseau.

2. Jasilyn Charger and Kalen Bald Eagle.
Daniel William Mcknight/Shutterstock.

**3.** LaDonna Brave Bull Allard.
Joel Saget/Getty Images.

**4.** Kandi White. Photo by Dallas Goldtooth.

5. The Pick-Sloan Plan of the Flood Control Act of 1944 authorized the U.S. Army Corps of Engineers to create five large dams along the Missouri River, flooding the fertile bottomlands and devastating Native communities, including those on the Fort Berthold and Standing Rock Reservations. As U.S. secretary of the interior J. A. Krug signed the contract selling reservation land for the dam project, tribal chairman George Gillette of Fort Berthold (*left*) declared: "With a few scratches of the pen, we will sell the best part of our reservation. Right now, the future does not look too good for us." Bettmann/Getty Images.

6. (*above*) In 2008, with most of its population living in poverty, the Mandan, Hidatsa, and Arikara Nation—the three affiliated tribes living on the Fort Berthold Reservation in northwestern North Dakota—opened the reservation to oil development. Tex Hall (pictured in his office in front of a map of reservation oil rigs and wells) was tribal chairman from 2010 to 2014 and took a hard-charging approach to oil development. The tribe has reaped billions in revenues and taxes but faced serious environmental consequences. Linda Davidson/*Washington Post*/Getty Images.

7. (*opposite top*) On April 1, 2016, riders traveled twenty miles north from the Standing Rock Sioux tribal administration building in Fort Yates to inaugurate a spirit camp on LaDonna Allard's land at the confluence of the Cannonball and Missouri Rivers. Lauren Donovan/*Bismarck Tribune*.

8. (*opposite bottom*) On July 15, 2016, twenty youth including Bobbi Jean Three Legs (*second from left*) and Jasilyn Charger (*third from left*) set off on a nearly two-thousand-mile run from Cannon Ball, North Dakota, to Washington DC to deliver a petition to the U.S. Army Corps of Engineers opposing construction of the Dakota Access Pipeline directly upstream from the Standing Rock Reservation. In early August, when the group finally arrived in Washington DC, it included more than eighty runners and their petition had 160,000 signatures. Photo by Indianz.com.

**9.** Joseph White Eyes, one of the first campers at Standing Rock who helped to organize the runs, is shown here in New York for a demonstration against the pipeline after the runners' meeting in Washington. When the runners returned to the camp in August 2016, hundreds of people had begun to flood in. John Lamparski/ WireImage/Getty Images.

**10.** Sacred Stone Camp, September 2016.
Photo by Stan Williams.

**11.** On Saturday, September 3, 2016, the pipeline construction company bulldozed an area that the Standing Rock Sioux Tribe had identified to a federal court only a day before as containing sacred sites. Water protectors at the construction site were pepper sprayed and bitten by dogs handled by private security contractors. Robyn Beck/Getty Images.

**12.** Oceti Sakowin Camp in fall 2016. Buoyed by the youth runs and events, including the dog attack and the arrest of tribal chairman Dave Archambault and Tribal Council member Dana Yellow Fat, the original Sacred Stone Camp swelled to capacity. In this main overflow camp—called Oceti Sakowin after the seven council fires of the Lakota-, Dakota-, and Nakota-speaking peoples—trailers, tipis, and tents soon dotted the landscape. Located within the boundaries of the 1851 Fort Laramie Treaty and unceded by the 1868 Fort Laramie Treaty on land claimed by the Army Corps when it built the Oahe Dam, Oceti Sakowin quickly grew larger than most North Dakota small towns. Photo by Joel Angel Juarez. ZUMA Press, Inc./Alamy Stock Photo.

13. Water protectors pray and sing. Joye Braun (*seated*), the first camper at Sacred Stone, watched in the fall of 2016 as around three hundred tribes planted flags at the camps. Thousands of water protectors found a warm welcome as the camps' populations rose. Joye was in awe. She hadn't expected to see the rising of the Oceti Sakowin—the seven council fires of the Sioux Nation—in her entire lifetime. Photo by Camille Seaman.

**14.** The camps also attracted the attention of celebrities. Actor Shailene Woodley was arrested at the camp in October, and actor Mark Ruffalo arrived at camp in late October to support the water protectors and deliver solar trailers. Rev. Jesse Jackson also visited, calling the movement of the pipeline route from an original path north of Bismarck a case of environmental racism. Pictured (*in foreground, starting second from left*) are Kandi White, Rev. Jesse Jackson, Mark Ruffalo, and Tara Houska of Honor the Earth. Photo by Camille Seaman.

**15.** (*above*) Law enforcement across a roadblock on Highway 1806 at water protectors' new frontline camp. On October 27, 2016, a militarized force of law enforcement officers seized the camp, pressuring water protectors away from it with pepper spray, tasers, and rubber and bean bag bullets. That same night the standoff between demonstrators and law enforcement continued on the nearby Backwater Bridge, where scores of officers in riot gear lined up. Mike McCleary/*Bismarck Tribune*.

**16.** (*opposite top*) The police barricade across Backwater Bridge in November 2016. From late October 2016 through March 2017, law enforcement blocked Highway 1806 at Backwater Bridge. The blockade prevented all pedestrian and vehicle travel, including emergency vehicles, presenting a serious impediment for both water protectors and Standing Rock community residents. Photo by Josué Rivas.

**17.** (*opposite bottom*) On the evening of November 20 water protectors tried to push past the bridge to the pipeline construction site, removing the charred vehicles and concrete barriers blocking their way. A heavily militarized police force assailed the nonviolent water protectors, leading to serious injuries. Cassi Alexandra/*Washington Post*/Getty Images.

**18.** On Thanksgiving Day water protectors crossed the Cantapeta Creek to Turtle Island, a Sioux burial ground, on a makeshift bridge. Law enforcement officers lined the top of the hill. Photo by Josué Rivas.

**19.** (*opposite top*) Police mace water protectors at
Turtle Island. Photo by Josué Rivas.

**20.** (*opposite bottom*) Oceti Sakowin Camp in December 2016. The camps grew to an estimated ten thousand water protectors. Michael Nigro/*Pacific Press*/
LightRocket/Getty Images.

**21.** (*above*) Water protectors celebrate after learning
from Chief Arvol Looking Horse, the spiritual leader
of the Lakota, Dakota, and Nakota people (*right*), on
December 4, 2016, that the Army Corps had denied
the easement necessary for the pipeline to cross
under the Missouri River at Lake Oahe. The Corps
recommended more analysis, tribal participation,
and a full environmental impact statement. Helen H.
Richardson/*Denver Post*/Getty Images.

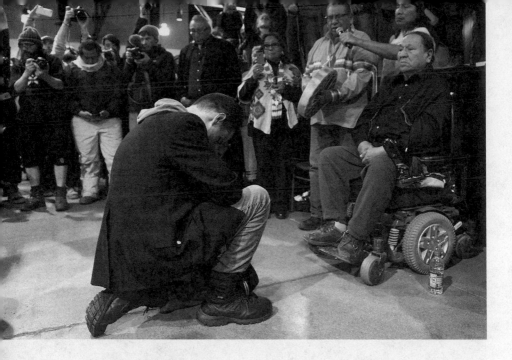

**22.** (*above*) By December 5, 2016, thousands of veterans had arrived at the camp in a blizzard. The veterans took a knee and ceremonially apologized to Native people for centuries of mistreatment at the hands of the U.S. government. Helen H. Richardson/*Denver Post*/Getty Images.

**23.** (*opposite top*) Standing Rock Sioux chairman Dave Archambault speaks with LaDonna Allard after a Tribal Council meeting in January 2017. Following the Army Corps' decision to deny the easement for the pipeline, Archambault asked water protectors to go home. In mid-January the Cannon Ball District passed a resolution declaring that all individuals in the camps needed to leave. The full Tribal Council voted unanimously to approve Cannon Ball's resolution just two days later. Photo by Joel Angel Juarez. ZUMA Press, Inc./Alamy Stock Photo.

**24.** (*opposite bottom*) On February 22, 2017, the deadline for water protectors to vacate Oceti and Rosebud Camps, fires raged as water protectors burned their campsites rather than leave them to be destroyed. Camp residents came together for a ceremony near the site of the Oceti's sacred fire. Water protectors sang, prayed, and waved an American flag high. "Mni wiconi!" they called. Some walked, grim-faced and ankle-deep in the frigid mud, singing and accompanied by drums, out of the camp. The camps were cleared the following day. Stephen Yang/Getty Images.

**25.** Elder Nathan Phillips (*center*), who had been
at the camp since November, leaving Oceti on
February 22, 2017. A confrontation two years later
at the Lincoln Memorial with a high school student
vaulted Nathan Phillips to national prominence.
Photo by Josué Rivas.

**26.** Following the closure of the camps, activists organized the Native Nations March in Washington DC. Thousands joined for four days of events in March 2017, including a tipi encampment on the lawn next to the Washington Monument, and a march from Army Corps headquarters to the White House. Photo by the author.

**27.** The seeds of the movement spread as activists galvanized at Standing Rock returned to communities around the country. One Native leader on the Pine Ridge Reservation in South Dakota provided a groundbreaking model. Nick Tilsen had been working for several years to reimagine how the Lakota people lived, creating the Thunder Valley Community Development Corporation. Their first circle of seven houses was under construction in 2017. Photo by the author.

**28.** Sculptor Charles Rencountre's "Not Afraid to Look," which sits on the site of Sacred Stone Camp. LaDonna Allard sees herself in it—grounded in her home, not backing down. She believes that when she is gone, her daughter will be standing there just the same, and her granddaughter, and all the generations after. Photo by the author.

# Victory on the Heels of Violence 6

We have a legacy that we have to live by: warriors. Our people died for their people, and that has not changed. So I always ask people, "Are you willing to die for this?" And the Native people say, "Yeah." The veterans say, "Yeah." The rest of the people say, "Well, I don't know. Can you bring peace? I'm sure there's a way to compromise." But there's no compromise.

—LaDonna Brave Bull Allard

As the smoke cleared from the October 27, 2016, conflict at Backwater Bridge, a restive peace descended the following morning. Fewer water protectors were on the bridge. Camp residents nursed their wounds— welts from bean bags and rubber bullets, some broken bones. There was a sense that the U.S. government was opposing them.

In the ensuing days, camp leaders criticized law enforcement's response as state officials praised it. U.S. senator Bernie Sanders sent a letter to President Obama, asking him to intervene. "By deploying law enforcement to support DAPL construction, the State of North Dakota is collaborating with Energy Transfer Partners and escalating tensions," Dave Archambault said. "We need our state and federal governments to bring justice and peace to our lands, not the force of armored vehicles." He reported that more than forty people had been injured by the police response. Those who had been arrested had been held in "dog kennels"—small, cold, cage-like temporary holding cells set up in a parking garage.[1] Kandi White, from Fort Berthold, was still in shock: "I went to the frontline in prayer for protection of the Missouri River and found myself in what I can only describe as a war zone."[2]

Bruised and bloodied, the water protectors vowed to continue their frontline actions. But law enforcement was now notorious for the "less than lethal" weapons it used—among them rubber and bean bag bullets, water cannons, and LRAD sound devices.[3]

The state Department of Emergency Services, meanwhile, requested an additional $4 million for law enforcement costs associated with the protests, bringing the department's total line of credit to $10 million. The previous week's operations had involved the largest law enforcement response yet—three hundred officers and one hundred national guard members.[4]

From the events of October 27 came the most serious criminal charges levied against any of the water protectors. As law enforcement had pushed water protectors out of the frontline camp, two sheriff's deputies had tackled and arrested Red Fawn Fallis, a thirty-seven-year-old Lakota woman whose mother had been involved in the American Indian Movement. Fallis had become a camp medic and a mentor figure to some IIYC members.

As the officers attempted to put Fallis in handcuffs, just minutes after she arrived at the front line, gunshots went off; the officers claimed that they recovered a gun from her. She was charged with attempted murder and faced a maximum of twenty years in prison. The gun belonged to a Native man whom she had begun dating in the camp—Heath Harmon. Harmon came from Fort Berthold and, without Fallis's knowledge, was a paid FBI informant.[5] (Ultimately Fallis pleaded guilty to two federal felonies after a year in jail awaiting trial and was sentenced to fifty-seven months in prison.)[6] Most of the 141 people arrested, though, had been charged with the felony of endangering by fire or explosion, punishable by a maximum of five years in prison and a fine of $10,000. A dozen private attorneys—many of them working pro bono—and more than twenty court-appointed lawyers worked to defend over four hundred people arrested in conjunction with the demonstrations.

One of the people who had been arrested at the Backwater Bridge standoff was New York–based freelance journalist Adam Schrader, who said he was arrested after asking officers about the use of pepper spray.[7] His arrest was part of a larger trend of arrests of journalists covering frontline actions, now up to seven. Sara Lafleur-Vetter, a photojournalist providing video coverage for *The Guardian* had been arrested on October 22 and charged with trespass and engaging in a riot. After *The Guardian* warned Morton County of legal repercussions, she received her camera back but not her memory cards. Sheriff Kirchmeier concluded simply, "If a reporter is doing illegal activities while covering protests, they're subject to arrest."[8]

On October 31 a Facebook post asking people to "check in" at Standing Rock to overwhelm the Morton County Sheriff's Department—which it claimed was using check-ins to target water protectors at the camps—went viral. Over a million people checked in at Standing Rock, virtually indicating that they were at the camps, in order to confuse law enforcement and show support for the water protectors. Kandi White told *The Guardian* that while such solidarity was nice, she remained more concerned about on-the-ground surveillance than Facebook monitoring.[9] By the next day the number of check-ins had reached 1.5 million. The Morton County Sheriff's Department claimed that it did not follow Facebook check-ins for the camps or any other location.[10]

Finally, on November 1 President Obama made his first public remarks on the issue. They were equivocal. On the subject of violence against water protectors, he described the situation as "challenging" and urged both sides to forego violence, calling on water protectors to be peaceful and also noting that "there's an obligation for authorities to show restraint." But his words were cause for camp residents to hope. In general, he said, he believed in accommodating "sacred lands of Native Americans," and the Army Corps was considering possible ways in which the pipeline could be rerouted. While the administration was monitoring the situation, it planned to let it "play out for several more weeks."[11] In response Dave Archambault issued a statement, calling on the administration to issue an immediate stop-work order on the pipeline.

Frontline actions were frequently starting to take place at Turtle Island, a site across the Cantapeta Creek from the main camp thought to be a burial ground. On October 31 the State of North Dakota notified the Army Corps "with concerns about individuals who were departing the existing Seven Council Camp encampment and moving by boat up Lake Oahe backwaters to establish new and unauthorized camps on previously unoccupied [Army Corps–]managed federal property on Cantapeta Creek." Colonel Henderson reached out to the "tribal chairman" and then to local law enforcement to remove "unauthorized individuals and structures from the site."[12]

Water protectors complained that law enforcement officers, by patrolling the area, were desecrating it. Indeed cemetery records from Sioux and Morton Counties, obtained by the *Bismarck Tribune*, showed that the remains of at least three people—two of them revered Sioux women—had been buried there but moved by the Corps during construction of Lake Oahe. LaDonna said a number of children who were also buried there had never been moved. Even if all bodies had been moved, the tribal archaeologist determined the land "hallowed ground" because the bodies had originally rested there. LaDonna had visited there with the Army Corps archaeologist in February 2016 and pointed the burial sites out. She was disgusted that law enforcement officers were now parking their armored cars on the site.[13]

On November 1 one of LaDonna's cousins built a wooden bridge across Cantapeta Creek overnight. The next day dozens of water protectors gathered on the banks. They drummed, sang, and burned sage. When law enforcement officers pulled the walkway apart, water protectors swam across and formed a line, standing waist deep in the fifty-degree water, facing a line of uniformed, armed men with helmets and visors. They returned to camp by canoe when they became too cold or were overwhelmed by tear gas and pepper spray. Others took their places. IIYC founder Danny Grassrope was one of them. He swam across to remind water protectors to remain in prayer. "You're here to pray," he called out. Law enforcement shot at least two water protectors with projectiles as they held up tarps and storage bin lids to protect themselves. Back on shore, medics wrapped them in heat blankets. Pepper spray lingered in people's throats.[14] LaDonna watched with binoculars and ran in medical supplies—milk of magnesia for the pepper spray and blankets for the cold.

Meanwhile, Reverend Floberg had been working on a plan to bring a contingent of clergy to Standing Rock. He had two reasons for doing so. First, with such a large Indigenous gathering, he thought that the church needed to be visible in solidarity or risk becoming marginalized in Indian Country. Second, he knew that people in North Dakota respected clergy. After the events of October 27, Reverend Floberg, who was a veteran of the coast guard, became worried that the "less than lethal force" of law enforcement's response would become lethal force. He put out a call for clergy, thinking he needed a hundred people to create a visible presence. The national response was extraordinary: on Thursday, November 3, more than five hundred people from twenty denominations, including Christians, Muslims, Jews, and Buddhists, gathered near the camps, answering the call to join "Clergy for Standing Rock." Some slept on the church floors in Fort Yates or Cannon Ball; others got rooms at the casino. They prepared a booklet that contained a statement repudiating the Doctrine of Discovery.

Reverend Floberg notified the governor's office and sheriff's department of the gathering, but they didn't reply. Indigenous people, though, took note. One Native man who saw the coverage could hardly speak. "I never dreamt that they would come," he observed. One elder told the assembled clergy, "We've been waiting for you." But another had a more practical question: "So, now you going to give us our land back?"

Then on Tuesday, November 8, the world shifted. Donald J. Trump won the presidency. Republicans in North Dakota swept up large majorities in both the state House and Senate, the largest gains they had seen in an election since 2010. Republican Kevin Cramer, reelected to the U.S. House of Representatives, predicted that the Corps would issue the easement before Trump took office.[15] Trump's election even rekindled hopes that the new administration might revive the Keystone XL Pipeline.

The cell service at the camps was erratic, so it took a while for everyone to learn who the next president would be. Polls had strongly favored Hillary Clinton, who had been largely silent or noncommittal on the pipeline.[16] When people finally heard about Trump's victory, many in the camps cried.

Dave Archambault rested his hopes on President Obama's denying the easement pending a full EIS in his last two months in office, but any action taken by Obama would likely be reversed by Trump.[17] TigerSwan cheered the win, noting in internal documents obtained by *The Intercept* water protectors' "despair" and predicting that "the election of President-elect Trump is likely to have a positive effect for the project overall and cooperation from the Federal level will likely improve after 20 Jan," inauguration day.[18] "Protestor morale has deteriorated," TigerSwan concluded.[19]

Dana Yellow Fat was philosophical; he had supported the Green Party. Whether it was Trump or Clinton, he believed, the fight would continue. LaDonna had always voted but concluded of elections: "It's mostly garbage." She didn't know of any good presidents (though she had gotten along with Jimmy Carter while they both worked building Habitat for Humanity houses on the Cheyenne River in the 1990s). Abraham Lincoln, one of American history's most revered presidents, had ordered the hanging of her ancestor. He was among the thirty-eight Dakota men executed on December 26, 1862, as punishment for the Dakota Uprising, still the largest mass execution in U.S. history. LaDonna thought Clinton and Trump were both problematic: "It was one of the times where there was no choice, and I thought, 'This is the beginning of the end of America. Caligula and the fall of Rome is happening.'" She had also voted for the Green Party.

But the election did matter. Just as political will had driven the announcement that the Corps would take a closer look at the pipeline portion under the lake, the change in administration had the potential to shift the landscape.

There was reason for water protectors to be worried. Donald Trump and his party had deep ties to ETP. Trump had once owned $500,000–$1,000,000 in ETP shares according to his candidate disclosures (but according to a spokeswoman had sold them off), and an additional $500,000–$1,000,000 in Phillips 66, which was slated to have a 25 percent stake in the project once completed.[20]

Kelcy Warren, CEO of ETP, had been careful to court political favor as a major Republican donor.[21] In the 2016 election cycle he gave $100,000 to the Trump Victory Fund, $1.53 million to super PACs, and $252,300 to individual campaigns and the Republican party, according to the Center for Responsive Politics.[22] Warren also donated $250,000 to Trump's inauguration celebration.

Two days after Trump's election Warren told investors, "Having a government that actually backs up what they say, that actually says we're going to support infrastructure, we're going to support job creation, we're going to support growth in America, and then actually does it—my God, this is going to be refreshing."[23] He was entirely confident that Trump would help the project to completion.[24]

Some days LaDonna got frustrated. She came from a long line of veterans: her grandfather had been a Lakota code talker in World War I before Native Americans had even been granted citizenship; her uncle served in World War II; her father, in the Korean War; her brother, in Vietnam. Fifteen cousins had fought in Desert Storm, eighteen in Afghanistan. Her family had stood up time and again for the U.S. government. Why were they having to fight it now?

Another frustration: LaDonna was sick with a cough, and so were many of her fellow water protectors. Of course they were living outdoors in cold weather, but some of them thought that more insidious forces might be at work, like chemical sprays. They didn't know for sure. It could have been all of the smoke from campfires. But more and more water protectors were coughing, and they came to call the illness the "DAPL cough."

Water protectors were particularly suspicious because in addition to the more obvious tactics such as constant surveillance by planes and helicopters, more imperceptible changes seemed to suggest nefarious tactics by Dakota Access and TigerSwan. At the camps it felt to many as if the mood had shifted. At frontline actions, things could get chaotic: sometimes people threw things or pushed others into the police or appeared as if they were trying to start fights with the police. Afterward tribal and camp leaders would realize that some of the participants were in fact infiltrators trying to instigate a conflict. But in the midst of multiple camps and thousands of people, the instigators might disappear into the crowd and lay low for a week before resurfacing, even if they had been asked to leave. Many of the infiltrators had Native American heritage, so it wasn't immediately obvious who might be one. On November 1 the Tribal Council, concerned that some camp members' messages were becoming too violent, voted to ask the Red Warrior Camp to leave.[25]

Jasilyn felt protective of the youth council. Everyone was getting paranoid and less willing to trust each other. "The divide between Native and Non-Native groups continues to grow," TigerSwan noted approvingly in its internal report on November 18.[26] Jasilyn and Kalen had seen people they thought were infiltrators throw the camps into distress by spreading rumors, such as that someone had drowned. On the front lines they saw people they thought were infiltrators throwing rocks, cursing, calling the cops names, and riling other people. The IIYC members would spend hours talking in their yurt about things that were suspicious, trying to understand them. They needed to be able to trust each other on the front lines in order to work together.

Both sides knew that an announcement by the Army Corps about the final easement was imminent. Documents filed with the North Dakota PSC showed that construction within North Dakota was nearing 100 percent.

On Monday, November 14, the Department of the Army issued a statement that was heartening for water protectors. "The Army has determined that additional discussion and analysis are warranted in light of the history of the Great Sioux Nation's dispossessions of lands, the importance of Lake Oahe to the tribe, our government-to-government relationship and the statute governing easements through government property," it read.[27] Dave Archambault said the statement showed that the tribe's message had been heard and was an indication that the president was listening.

Pipeline supporters fumed. Frustrated, ETP and Sunoco Logistics filed suit in the U.S. District Court for the District of Columbia on Monday night, charging that the Corps had no right to delay the easement and asking the judge to declare they had a legal right of way to complete the pipeline and begin operations.[28] Jan Hasselman disputed the premise of the lawsuit, arguing that the easement was clearly needed. Dave Archambault suspected that Dakota Access was just rushing to get oil flowing before January 1. The company had previously told the court that if it didn't deliver oil by then, the shipper contracts would expire, costing the company dearly.

On Tuesday, November 15, protest actions were planned in all fifty states and in cities around the world—London, Paris, Kyoto, Marrakech—to show the Obama administration and Army Corps the widespread support for pipeline opponents.[29] In some cities thousands gathered. LaDonna led a march in Washington DC.

The strained relations between water protectors and law enforcement kept worsening as activists' frustration at the barricade of Backwater Bridge mounted. Burned-out trucks and a concrete police barricade now made the bridge entirely impassable, blocking access to the camps from the north, preventing emergency services from passing through and water protectors getting out to demonstrate at nearby construction sites, and burdening the Standing Rock Sioux community and its neighbors. Authorities cited concerns over the bridge's structural integrity.[30] Both sides traded barbs about who was responsible.

On the evening of Sunday, November 20 water protectors tried to push past the bridge to the pipeline construction site, removing the charred vehicles and concrete barriers blocking their way. It was a cold North Dakota night; the temperatures hovered in the twenties Fahrenheit. About four hundred water protectors gathered on the bridge around 6 p.m., and law enforcement lined up opposite them. Then, suddenly, the police began to spray the water protectors—the sheriff later claimed with hoses, but demonstrators saw water cannons—with the effect of blasting water protectors, ironically, with freezing, weaponized water. Rubber bullets, water laced with pepper spray, and tear gas rained down on them. Screams rang out over the misty darkness. The police claimed that the water protectors had thrown rocks and logs toward them. Helicopters flew overhead. Calls of "We need a medic!!" echoed in the darkness, and medics rushed the injured away from the front lines. The whole area quickly became dangerously icy because of the water that law enforcement was shooting in the direction of the water protectors. Hypothermia became a serious concern as water soaked through the water protectors' clothes. Legal observers noted that a number of people lost consciousness after being shot.[31]

That evening Josephine Thundershield had been chopping wood, hauling water, and checking on other campers when, around 6 p.m., she got a call and turned on the radio in time to hear two people saying they needed more people to come to the bridge, where water protectors had been attempting to clear the blockade of Highway 1806. "They're shooting our youth, they're shooting our youth! We need more hands up here," she heard. When she got to the front line, she felt the blast of water cannons. A man escorted by medics walked by clutching his head, blood streaming down his face; he had been shot with a rubber bullet at point blank range. As the injured were evacuated, those who remained collected themselves, praying and singing. Thundershield was angry and sad but also proud of the way the water protectors stood tall together, how they made a line and didn't break it, even though they were injured from the rubber bullets, the cold, and the water—water that burned her skin and afterward left it scarred and rashy.

"Warriors to the front" went the call around camp. Ta'Sina Sapa Win feared the action was doomed for failure; there were just too many law enforcement officers. But she went to the front lines anyway to put her body in front of those who were too naïve to know that they shouldn't be there. Some IIYC members criticized her decision to go to the action, saying they stood for peace—but she was peaceful, she countered, and she wanted to protect her vulnerable relatives in a situation in which she worried they would get annihilated. She tasted tear gas for the first time that night, in the most miserable few minutes of her life. Panic and hopelessness washed over her as she found herself unable to breathe, her face and nose stinging.

Chairman Frazier of Cheyenne River was just getting in a vehicle to leave when one of his tribal members came running over and said, "They're tear gassing our people." He hurried to the front line and it looked like a war zone. Lights crossed the night sky as law enforcement officers shot tear gas. They were also shooting rubber bullets. He could feel the pressure as a concussion grenade landed near him.

Back at Sacred Stone Camp, LaDonna had the fire burning bright deep into the early morning. As people returned from the front lines, she used sticks and rocks to break frozen jackets and clothes off of them, wrapping the water protectors in blankets. LaDonna saw water protectors' knuckles crushed by rubber bullets and others bloodied after being shot directly in the head. One man only had a faint heartbeat. He was in shock and not breathing, in full hypothermia. She got his wet clothes off, got him into a warm car, rubbed his skin, and called an ambulance. LaDonna knew that if she hadn't been there to help, he might easily have died. Camp medics said that at least twenty-six water protectors had been seriously injured and evacuated by ambulance. Three hundred were injured in all. Hypothermia, blunt force trauma, and tear gas contamination were the most common complaints. Other injuries included a seizure, severe eye damage from rubber bullets to the face, and internal bleeding following a rubber bullet to the abdomen.[32]

News quickly spread through the camp: Sophia Wilansky, a twenty-one-year-old from New York who had joined the camp in November, was undergoing surgery and in serious condition after being airlifted to a Minneapolis hospital. According to her father, Sophia Wilansky had been delivering water to water protectors at 4 a.m. when she saw law enforcement officers throw a concussion grenade at her. He said it exploded as it hit her arm.

Law enforcement officers denied the use of any weapons consistent with Sophia Wilansky's injuries, including concussion grenades. The highway patrol released photos of "improvised explosive devices" found near the bridge, including slingshots, rocks, and small propane tanks.[33]

Wayne Wilansky, Sophia's Wilansky's father, called it ridiculous that the Morton County Sheriff's Department denied responsibility for concussion grenades that hit her. "Apparently," he added, "they've changed their story three time since the incident occurred."[34] The muscle was blown off her left hand and arm, from slightly below the elbow to slightly above the wrist. Most of her radius bone was gone, as were the arteries in the arm and medial nerve.[35] Ultimately Sophia Wilansky was able to keep her arm, but even after five surgeries her use of it remained limited.[36] (Wilansky later filed a federal lawsuit, alleging that a law enforcement officer had thrown a flashbang grenade at her, and she was seeking damages.)[37]

"The police did not do this by accident," Wayne Wilansky charged. His pain in seeing his daughter's injuries was immeasurable: "I died a thousand deaths today. . . . I am left without the right words to describe the anguish of watching her look at her now alien arm and hand."[38]

Meanwhile, as activists were dodging weaponized water and rubber bullets, *The Intercept* reported that the FBI, BIA, North Dakota's U.S. Attorney's Office, and local law enforcement were shooting emails to each other as they closely monitored the activists' social media live feeds and calculated how to spin the narrative around the night's events. The email chain revealed that North Dakota officials realized there would be a "massive media backlash."[39] They spread a story from an FBI informant about propane tanks in the camps that were rigged to explode. An attorney representing Sophia Wilansky and her father both claimed that the story about rigged propane tanks was utterly untrue. "Obviously, disinformation is a major component of how they dealt with the protests," Wayne Wilansky told *The Intercept*.[40]

The day after the attacks on the bridge, at a press conference, Sheriff Kirchmeier did damage control. He contended that water protectors had used rocks, burning logs, water bottles, and slingshots against the officers. He claimed that law enforcement had used no water cannons on the water protectors, just a fire hose, and the fire trucks had been called down because of a fire started on the bridge. The field commander decided to keep using them to repel some of the protest activities, a crowd control tactic. He said that there was an explosion in the water protector area that did not come from law enforcement.[41] But water protectors, walking around the area of the conflict, found "Instantaneous Blast" canisters—both exploded and unexploded—manufactured by Defense Technologies in Casper, Wyoming. Instantaneous Blast Grenades, according to their manufacturer, aim to create "pain compliance, temporary discomfort and/or incapacitation" of possibly violent subjects.[42]

The weapons law enforcement officers were using, Dave Archambault allowed, may be considered nonlethal, but they were being used in more and more serious ways so that they effectively constituted lethal force. Projectiles aimed at people's heads, rubber bullets shot into faces, cannons launching tear gas into crowds, water cannons in below-freezing temperatures—"way too much force, way too much aggression, they're putting people's lives at risk now." The force was excessive, Archambault said. "It feels like law enforcement is taking orders from Dakota Access," he concluded.[43] The Water Protector Legal Collective, an initiative of the National Lawyers Guild, filed a lawsuit in U.S. District Court against law enforcement agencies for using excessive force against peaceful demonstrators.[44] The tribe issued a statement calling on President Obama to deny the easement, investigate pipeline safety, and protect tribal sovereignty.[45]

CNN covered the violent turn, airing images of militarized police and Sophia Wilansky's injured arm.[46] The *New York Times* editorial board called Sunday's actions "shameful and bloody." It likened the imbalance of power on display in the conflict to the "brute force against a backdrop of folly" that Native Americans had seen used against them for centuries. The *New York Times* suggested that President Obama could put pressure on local law enforcement to "stand down" for the sake of everyone's safety. "Barring that, resolute protesters, a heavily militarized police force unwilling to budge, a company that refuses to consider an alternate route and an onrushing Great Plains winter—how can this possibly end well?"[47]

The effect of the heightened violence by law enforcement was wearing in camp. Every day when LaDonna thought she had hit rock bottom, she would say to Miles, "I can't do this any more." "You can," he replied. "I'm praying for you. I got you." When she was wound up, he deescalated her. Miles had always taken care of her. He was what she described as "a house person." He cooked all her meals for her; when she got up in the morning, he made her coffee, prepared her eggs. He made sure her clothes were washed and folded. He went out and filled up the car with gas, took care of their lawn, and cared for their animals.

When they were away from the front lines, Jasilyn and Kalen spent a lot of time taking care of the children at the camps. The children were trying to survive, sometimes gathering money from visitors for their families. When adults went to the front lines, the children were left behind. Jasilyn and Kalen wanted to make sure they were fed and that they were safe. They always had tea and coffee at Kalen's family's camp; when Kalen's cousin brought an Xbox and television, all the kids flocked to his tent to play a game or watch a movie. They would make popcorn. "It's like having children live in a war zone where people are getting hurt and giving them a sense of, you know, 'It's okay to be a kid,'" Jasilyn concluded. They wanted the kids to feel like this wasn't the end of the world. Kalen had grown up with lots of kids around—his brothers, his brothers' kids. So he felt like he knew how the kids in the camps felt. But Jasilyn's own childhood had largely been stolen from her. "It gave us a chance to be kids because we didn't get to have that experience," Jasilyn thought.

The kids saw their mothers and fathers come back from the front lines bloodied, in pain, or angry, and they got confused. "Why is this happening?" they asked, or "Why are they hurting us?" Jasilyn knew from experience that children always thought their parents' problems were their own fault. She would tell them, "It's not your fault. Nothing you have done made this happen to our people." But the kids wondered, "What is wrong with us?" or "Why are we so different?" They often didn't understand racism. Jasilyn would say to each one, "You're a child; you shouldn't have to go through this," or simply, "It's okay to be a child; it's okay to have fun."

Jasilyn was in a meeting one day about a frontline action that was being planned; she looked across a field and saw someone peeking into a tent. "That person looks really familiar," Jasilyn thought. "That's your mom," said Kalen. "What? That's my mom? Wait a minute," Jasilyn said. After six months in drug and alcohol treatment, her mom had come to see her daughters. She was looking in every tent for Jasilyn. Kalen went to get her after they spotted her. "At least you saw her before she saw you," Kalen laughed.

After initially being dismissive, Jasilyn's and Kalen's families had joined them at their camp. First Jasilyn's twin sister Jasilea had come, as had Kalen's mother. Finally, that fall all of their family members came and lived with them. After so many months, Jasilyn and Kalen were feeling beaten up mentally and physically, wondering how much more they could take. Seeing their families standing with them helped them to carry on.

Family time alternated with frontline actions that Thanksgiving. On

"flash grenades, high-pressure water cannons in freezing temperatures, dog kennels for temporary human jails, and any harmful weaponry" against the water protectors.[52]

As the snow fell, campers were grateful for their warm yurts. LaDonna embraced it—the first snow was so beautiful as it covered her land, she thought, but she also saw snow as bringing life because it gave the earth time to rest. She was supremely practical, the mother hen to her camp. She cautioned those at Sacred Stone to drive carefully, travel with emergency supplies, check on elders and those who didn't have experience in severe weather, get people into warmer tents, and layer their clothes. Kandi, from Fort Berthold, was one of those who was used to the cold. As the snow started to fall, she walked through the camp watching the snow calmly glide down around her, soaking up the beauty and stillness. The snow lit up the night and crunched under her feet.

On November 30 Governor Dalrymple clarified the emergency evacuation order. The order served as an official notice from the state, he said, signaling that it may not be able to help in an emergency situation. The order advised people to leave the area for health and safety purposes. It was meant to put camp residents on notice, to encourage them to leave.[53] In response, IEN held a press conference. The history of being pushed off treaty lands was being reenacted, one speaker said. LaDonna and Kandi sat shoulder to shoulder. If the governor was so concerned about camp residents' safety, Kandi said, he should clear out Backwater Bridge and open up Highway 1806 to emergency services. LaDonna noted that concern for the campers' safety and refusal to plow the road to camp were contradictory. "Our homelands have always been here; we have always been here," she said. "We know how to live in winter."[54]

With the ground, wood piles, and supplies now covered in a thick blanket of snow, campers were digging in and trying to winterize their tents, tipis, and yurts to weather the snow and predicted single-digit temperatures. Campfires lit the night landscape as snow, icy winds, and freezing temperatures settled in. Bundled in snow pants, campers used shovels to try to clear paths. A few sledded.

Not only were campers hunkering down for the storms, but in fact they were also anticipating that even more people would soon join them. Veterans were planning to gather at Standing Rock December 4–7 in support of the water protectors, defending them from a militarized police force and offering themselves as "human shields." Michael A. Wood Jr., one of the plan's founders, had hoped to bring five hundred veterans but closed sign-ups when they topped two thousand. By December 1 an online fundraiser to cover the veterans' costs had brought in almost $700,000.[55] Facebook posts encouraged the veterans to bring body armor, gas masks, and earplugs but no weapons. Mainstream media were taking notice. A CNN truck arrived at Oceti Sakowin.

Amid everything the IIYC was still working to ease strained relations between the camps and law enforcement. In early December one of the camp elders had seen a list the Morton County Sheriff's Department had put on its website soliciting donations of food and supplies and told the IIYC that the water protectors were going to buy the department everything it wanted except for soda (it would give them water instead, pointedly). The IIYC went to the Morton County offices in Mandan, North Dakota, to deliver the donations—granola, trail mix, batteries, bottled water. Oceti Sakowin was a place of humanity, a place of compassion, despite the aggression with which campers were met, and they wanted to show it. They were also self-sufficient. The Morton County Sheriff's Office thanked them cheerily for their "kindness and support" on Facebook.[56]

That weekend, as December 4 dawned, thousands of veterans began to arrive. Around a thousand of them were planning to camp on the top of the hill at Sacred Stone. The day was cold, but the sun was shining, and the roads were clear.

Then the extraordinary happened. Around 3 p.m. word began to spread through the camps: the Army Corps had denied the easement for the pipeline to cross under Lake Oahe. The Corps recommended more analysis, tribal participation, and a full EIS.

The decision was a triumph for the water protectors. "I feel like I got my future back," thirteen-year-old Tokata Iron Eyes declared to author Naomi Klein.[57] Camp organizer Dallas Goldtooth was jubilant. IIYC members wept with joy.

Joye Braun, the first camper at Sacred Stone back in the slushy April mud, was sitting in her car as word spread, wearing her customary black beret. She knew the news was real but hadn't been able to digest it. In the distance she heard singing and drumming from the camp, car horns blared, and everyone was hugging. Calls of "Water is life!" rang out. A celebratory dance three people deep circled the Seven Councils fire.[58] That evening the news began to sink in. Celebrations were continuing into the night, with fireworks lighting the sky over the tipis. Braun was emotional: despite all the sacrifices involved, the Army Corps' denial was a major victory, she thought. She knew the fight wasn't over, but "This really truly has been an Indigenous rising," she concluded.[59]

Dana Yellow Fat was at the camp when he heard the news. He felt an immediate relief. He had been visiting with some of the veterans as they started to arrive, and he was becoming worried. "This pipeline needs to be stopped. We're here to put a stop to this. We'll be the human shields; we're gonna take that drill pad; we're gonna do what we have to do," he was hearing. He thought a war was beginning. With so many military personnel coming in, he worried that the camps might move toward violence.

Dave Archambault expressed his gratitude in a statement: "In a system that has continuously been stacked against us from every angle, it took tremendous courage to take a new approach to our nation-to-nation relationship, and we will be forever grateful," he said.[60]

Reverend Floberg was preparing for the veterans to arrive when he heard a call to the camp sacred fire. Dave Archambault announced that they had received confirmation from the Corps and the White House that the permit had been denied. Phyllis Young rose and said, "We forgive those who assassinated Sitting Bull and Crazy Horse; we forgive and are at peace with all branches of the United States military." Not in Reverend Floberg's wildest dreams had he ever expected that. He was walking away from the crowd at the fire when his phone rang with an unidentified number. On the line was a staff person for faith-based initiatives from the White House. The person had called to thank him for organizing the church to help keep things peaceful and to arrive at this point without any loss of life. He was stunned—he had no idea how they had even gotten his telephone number.

LaDonna was on media hill (a ridge so called because it had the best signal for journalists to post) when she heard the news. "Bullshit," she declared. "It's not gonna happen." She didn't trust American presidents, and she certainly didn't trust ETP. She would watch the construction crews, she decided, and see if they were still working.

As the other water protectors cried and jumped around her, LaDonna was skeptical. "This is not real, and you know it's not real. You trust no one," she said to herself. Had there ever been a good president in the United States to her people? Abraham Lincoln had been the one to hang her ancestor. Nothing had changed, she thought. All the presidents had been after her resources, her lands, since the day they arrived. Trump soon would be too, LaDonna thought.

# KANDI

# From Victory to Eviction 7

There were so many people that got hurt—they didn't want people to get killed. They didn't want to be responsible for something like that happening. They also had community members telling them, "Look, we're tired of this. We just want it to come to a conclusion." In addition to that, Donald Trump was elected in November, and we knew that he was going to come in and do what he did. So the tribe was at a point where they were like, "This needs to come to an end. We have the power to have it come to an end."

—Kandi White

Late on December 5, 2016, Kandi White stood in the middle of a blizzard, buffeted by winds. The wind chill was negative four degrees at the Oceti Sakowin camp that night, and the campers were expecting ten to thirteen inches of snow.

The last couple of days had been a roller coaster, but when Kandi live-streamed on Facebook that night, she was calm and hopeful. She encouraged everyone to take a deep breath. With the snow they were going to be in camp for a while yet; Standing Rock had opened up gyms and the casino pavilion as warming centers. Tribal Council members were delivering blankets and coordinating housing and meals.

The Army Corps' denial of the easement the day before was a big deal, Kandi emphasized—a really historic moment for treaty rights and tribal sovereignty. She didn't think that ETP would begin to dig illegally, so construction was effectively halted. There was no denying that Donald Trump would be inaugurated in January, but at least this development would create knots the new administration would need to untie before pushing the pipeline through. They had won a brief victory. Kandi wanted to take a moment to celebrate.

Kandi knew Dave Archambault was under a lot of pressure. The bridge and Highway 1806 were barricaded, and law enforcement officers were still protecting the pipeline company. But a blizzard offered a chance to relax. She encouraged her friends to stay inside, stay dry, take care of each other, and do some storytelling. "Drink some hot cocoa or tea; share the love," she laughed. "The world has seen that Indigenous peoples can lead the way," she decided, in pushing for a just transition away from the fossil fuel economy into one based on renewable energy. "The future is looking a little bit brighter every day."[1]

Kandi White's Native American name is Eagle Woman. Her mother, a single mom of four and Head Start teacher for thirty-five years, raised her on Fort Berthold. Kandi spent her summers in the Twin Buttes area on Fort Berthold with her grandparents and her father. She went to school in New Town, now the epicenter of the fracking boom. Her father is Mandan and Hidatsa, her mother Arikara.

When she was young, Kandi played basketball and volleyball and ran track but didn't excel at any of them. Kandi always got in trouble for talking. She wasn't sure what to do with her life. "You have the gift of gab, my dear," her mother advised her. "You're a storyteller."

Kandi had survived cancer at age twenty, a stage four sarcoma tumor, which for many is a death sentence. But Kandi was lucky and tough. She missed only a few weeks of college at the University of North Dakota to have major surgery, still working tirelessly to get good grades. After multiple additional surgeries she was cancer-free.

Kandi became involved in environmental activism after college, returning to school to earn a master's degree in environmental management. She learned about IEN when, beginning in 2000, it helped her community on Fort Berthold fight against a proposed oil refinery that would refine oil from the Alberta tar sands; it still hadn't been built. She had now been with IEN for more than ten years, using her gift for storytelling to speak eloquently against fracking. She had testified before the U.S. Congress and participated in the COP21 United Nations Climate Change Conference in Paris as the coordinator of IEN's delegation. Kandi wasn't born to a family involved in activism, but she had grown into a prominent advocate because of her passion about the environmental injustice she saw all around her.

Before the camps Kandi was already a leading voice on Indigenous environmental issues and fracking, but the camps had given her increased visibility. While she hadn't been particularly active on Facebook before the camps, Kandi had been going live on Facebook a lot; she thought it was a cool new technology. At first she didn't realize how much of an impact her live streams could have, but then she kept meeting people who said, "You're the one I follow for Standing Rock." Over the course of a few months, her live streams on Facebook went from hundreds of views to tens of thousands. Her update on December 5 garnered more than 3,300 reactions and more than 73,000 views. She had gathered more than 10,000 followers on Facebook personally, while Indigenous Rising Media—a media project of IEN that sometimes streamed her videos—amassed more than 200,000; IEN grew to have more than 340,000 followers on Facebook.

Kandi's videos were funny and warm but also forceful, and they revealed her deep knowledge of the issues around fracking and pipelines. While MHA chairman Mark Fox was her stepmom's brother and her sister was his chief assistant, Kandi didn't beat about the bush when it came to her thoughts on the tribe's oil development: she believed that there was no safe fracking, period.

In the winter of 2017 Kandi was thirty-seven. She had been at Standing Rock for the better part of seven months, often with her daughter, Aiyana, who was just three. She stayed alternately at Oceti Sakowin, Sacred Stone, and the casino.

Kandi had first arrived at Sacred Stone Camp in August, and that fall the camps had felt powerful and beautiful to her as tribes arrived and people gathered. In November, though, something changed; Kandi felt a negative energy, and she didn't stay with Aiyana at the camp any more. When Aiyana came down, they stayed at the casino.

Reading *The Intercept* articles, Kandi later realized what she had been sensing: there were infiltrators. They were trying to divide the water protectors, to spread misinformation and rumors. They introduced drugs into the camps; some were even accused of rape. On the front lines they tried unsuccessfully to provoke the water protectors to violence. The camp atmosphere became ugly and twisted. It seemed to Kandi as if the private security preyed on those who were most vulnerable: people with mental health issues or people with pending criminal charges hoping for a deal.

Her experience at the camps had made Kandi mindful of who was watching and listening all the time. She had confronted some of the people she believed to be infiltrators. She saw one Native kid writing down license plate numbers on media hill; he took off running when she asked what he was doing. Another, who always wore an earpiece, was constantly asking Kandi questions. Finally she asked him, "How much do they pay you? Why do you wear earpieces?" He never talked to her again.

Private security and law enforcement were also using increasingly aggressive surveillance tactics, which further poisoned the camp atmosphere: Kandi's phone battery once drained in seconds—a result, she thought, of the Stingrays that law enforcement was using. They were like something out of a movie: machines that could be set up on the prairie to suck the information from a computer or phone, downloading everything and draining the battery in the process. At the casino a friend of Kandi's found a listening device under one of the tables.

Even with the provocation of instigators and constant surveillance, though, the water protectors stood their ground and peace reigned. The crowd at the camps did not turn violent. On December 4 the campers celebrated.

Kandi was not the only one to consider the easement decision momentous. Jan Hasselman was elated; he thought the victory an unprecedented win for Indian Country, a validation not just of the Standing Rock Sioux Tribe's long-held position on the pipeline but also a recognition of the extraordinary tribal unity around this issue, a focal point for a hundred years of mistreatment and dispossession. The Obama administration had listened.

The Army Corps didn't generally view itself as making decisions about right or wrong. Instead it considered regulation criteria and issued permits. And it had been ready to do just that. Back on August 3 Colonel Henderson had recommended the Army Corps immediately issue the permit to avoid delays in construction.[2] As recently as December 3, Colonel Henderson was *still* recommending that the Corps grant the easement.[3] The Corps actually had a draft of the easement prepared.[4] But this time had proved to be different.

Senior White House adviser Brian Deese, in an email to Lowry Crook at Army Corps headquarters, was explicit about the White House's limited role: "I know there have been a number of calls for the President to be directly involved and I know that the White House is receiving periodic updates about the security situation on the ground as events have unfolded. But I don't want there to be any confusion about the White House's engagement here. As you already know—and I just want to make absolutely clear—we expect the Army will make its own independent assessment of decisions related to the project, including when it comes to timing."[5]

But both the White House and the Army Corps had been under extraordinary pressure. On November 28 a coalition of Native Americans who had served as appointees in the Obama administration wrote to the president as private citizens, urging him to immediately block or reroute the pipeline and to protect water protectors from civil rights abuses by local law enforcement. "We believe your Presidency has been the most beneficial for Tribes in perhaps all of United States history," they wrote, "and we want to preserve that legacy. But, as you often say, that work is not yet finished." They cited the dog attack and Army Corps plans to remove water protectors from the camps.[6]

The previous day the National Congress of American Indians had also written to the president, expressing concern that violence would escalate and urging him to deny the easement.[7]

A legal opinion written by Hilary Tompkins (the lead lawyer for the Department of the Interior) and dated December 4 found that "ample legal justification" existed to deny the easement or, alternatively, a decision to issue the easement should not be made without tribal consultation, an EIS, and a more comprehensive analysis of "DAPL's impact on tribal rights, lands, and resources." "Both the Standing Rock and Cheyenne River Sioux Tribes have treaty hunting and fishing rights in Lake Oahe, which is located (at least in part) within the boundaries of both Reservations," Tompkins concluded. "The Tribes additionally retain some proportion of water rights in Lake Oahe. And both Tribes maintain a meaningful historic and cultural connection to the land that was flooded to create the federal floodplains project." The Corps' EA had been inadequate, the legal opinion found.[8] The legal opinion provided a remarkable analysis, laying out where the Army Corps had fallen short, and Jan Hasselman thought it had plainly been influenced by many of the conversations happening in Washington at the time.

The tribes knew the decision came with an asterisk; with Trump's presidency on the horizon, they had no illusions that the victory would last, but the moment was undeniably historic. Tim Purdon agreed that the move was unprecedented, the greatest victory for tribal nations in a century.

Environmentalist Bill McKibben thought that the victory had been inevitable from the moment that the pipeline security company had sicced dogs on the unarmed water protectors, resulting in images that paralleled those from Birmingham during the civil rights movement. The White House understood those pictures and realized that the brutal response had become a human rights issue. The denial of the easement was a vindication of how nonviolence can work effectively, McKibben thought.

Of course Trump had already clinched the presidency. Everyone knew that the easement denial wasn't the last word. Still ETP was furious: "This is nothing new from this Administration," the company complained, "since over the last four months the Administration has demonstrated by its action and inaction that it intended to delay a decision in this matter until President Obama is out of office." It contended that the Obama administration had "abandoned the rule of law in favor of currying favor with a narrow and extreme political constituency."[9]

The day after the Corps' announcement, Dakota Access asked the court to declare that the Corps had already authorized construction of the Lake Oahe crossing. It was unequivocally committed to completing the pipeline along the Lake Oahe route.[10]

In effect the victory was a pause button. The Corps denied the easement and ordered an EIS, which would go forward in three stages: scoping, draft, and final, with an opportunity for public comment in each stage. The main outcome was likely a delay of approval until the Trump administration took office. As Hilary Tompkins later noted, "We reached the position of pausing the pipeline—a super controversial decision. We paused it to look at the impacts to treaty rights and water rights. We knew that was short-lived."[11] There wasn't enough time to finish the EIS before Trump's inauguration.

As Kandi saw the Standing Rock Sioux Tribe win on the issue of the EIS, even temporarily, her own Tribal Business Council's actions on Fort Berthold hurt all the more. Why had the council signed on the dotted line? "MHA Nations Tribal Council, where are you?! The bones of our ancestors have been desecrated and you choose to remain silent. Why?" she asked over Facebook.[12]

One of the great parlor games in the (small) liberal circle in Bismarck was asking whether the involvement of the larger environmental movement, significant resources, and publicity ultimately was a positive for Standing Rock. The answer now seemed to some to be a pretty clear yes. Without the movement the tribes never would have garnered the national attention that allowed them to put pressure on the White House and Army Corps to order the full EIS.

On December 5, as more snow fell, hundreds of veterans, carrying the American flag high, marched from the Oceti Sakowin camp to the barricaded Backwater Bridge. Kandi walked with Wesley Clark Jr., one of the leaders of the veterans' group and son of decorated U.S. Army general Wesley Clark Sr. That day the veterans took a knee and ceremonially apologized to Native people for centuries of mistreatment at the hands of the American government. "We fought you. We took your land. We signed treaties that we broke. We stole minerals from your sacred hills. We blasted the faces of our presidents onto your sacred mountain . . . we've hurt you in so many ways, but we've come to say that we are sorry," said Wesley Clark Jr.[13] The veterans knelt before the elders as those watching wept. For Jasilyn the apology provided a huge step toward healing. This was what her ancestors had wanted, she thought—for the U.S. military to take responsibility for its actions. The apology couldn't erase the historical trauma and the mistreatment her people had suffered, and it certainly didn't restore their lands, but it helped her to move forward.

Dave Archambault made a statement that day, lauding the victory. "There's no need for the water protectors or anybody to be putting ourselves in unsafe environments," he concluded. With winter storms and extreme cold weather coming and law enforcement getting more aggressive, he wanted to keep people out of harm's way. He wanted people to be proud of the victory and go home. "It's time now," he said. "It's OK for you to leave."[14]

At the camps summer tents had given way to tipis, yurts, and wooden structures, insulated with bales of straw and heated with wood stoves. Kandi knew that North Dakota winters were harsh, and December was proving to be cold. Temperatures hovered below zero; twelve degrees Fahrenheit counted as a heat wave. Living conditions could be difficult—one medic had spent months sleeping in a modified doghouse—especially as warm days turned into a frigid winter. Camp medics checked tents after snowfalls to make sure everyone was safe. Lisa and Walter went to visit the camps for their fourth and final time with all of their kids. They brought canned food and blankets.

IEN was in a tough spot, caught between a chairman with legitimate concerns over people's safety in the harsh North Dakota winter and water protectors' conviction that the pipeline was not dead. The organization issued a statement supporting the tribe's decision to ask people not to join the camps.

As questions remained—about the exit strategy, the court battle, the blockage of the bridge—the camps began to clear out on the heels of the temporary victory. The tribe was working with people to help them find transportation and leave if they chose to. Kandi and IEN were trying to help people move too, but the logistics were complicated because so many people needed transportation, and even getting cars started in the bitter cold could be difficult. Kandi thought people would be more willing to leave if the barricade on Highway 1806 were opened by law enforcement. As long as the barricade stood, it left the appearance that construction would continue, despite the Corps' denial.

In early December Jasilyn was in Washington DC and New York City, raising money for the camps, when she learned people were leaving the camps. It hurt her heart, she said. She understood the tribe's decision to ask people to leave, but she didn't believe the decision was the tribe's alone—one generation does not speak for all the generations to come. Jasilyn wasn't going to leave. She had been there from the beginning, had built a community, and considered the camp her home. She put out a call to warriors to stand with her and the original campers. Joseph White Eyes, Joye Braun, and LaDonna agreed, asking people to continue to stand with them at Sacred Stone.[15]

On December 12 Dave Archambault met with Governor Dalrymple to chart a path forward. They laid the groundwork for Backwater Bridge to be reopened following an inspection. Dave Archambault noted that he didn't think frontline actions were helping the cause at this point, but he remarked: "I'm never going to give them a deadline or sweep it out."[16] Mistrust was creeping in between Archambault and the remaining water protectors, though, as unfounded rumors suggested that he had sold out the protest. Small skirmishes continued around Backwater Bridge, despite the fact that police had moved back from it.

Most of those left in camp didn't trust the denial of the easement and knew they would be facing dark times when Trump took office. The Standing Rock Sioux Tribal Council was pressuring the Obama administration to begin the EIS before the end of Obama's term. The prospects under Trump's new administration seemed far worse: Rex Tillerson, the CEO of ExxonMobil, was expected to be named as secretary of state. Trump planned to name Rick Perry, who was on the ETP board of directors, as secretary of energy.

Nearly six hundred water protectors had been arrested by mid-December. As the first of their trials began, it started to become clear that the volume of cases had put a strain on North Dakota's judicial system. The trials were being postponed as Mandan court officials realized they didn't have enough courtrooms and calendar space. North Dakota had just 1,800 lawyers, only 70 of them criminal defense attorneys. Attorneys (including Tim Purdon and the lawyers at the ACLU of North Dakota) petitioned the North Dakota Supreme Court to allow out-of-state lawyers to represent some of the water protectors arrested over the previous months. Finally, in an unprecedented victory, the North Dakota Supreme Court ruled to decrease the requirements for out-of-state lawyers looking to represent DAPL-related arrestees.

Things were changing at the camps. Backwater Bridge (which had been closed since the October 27 conflict) was finally set for inspection on December 22. While frontline actions were still happening, people were also heading home. Much of the youth council left for home around Christmas. By the end of December around one thousand people were left at the Oceti Sakowin camp (which had been renamed Oceti Oyate, the people's camp), another three hundred nearby at Rosebud camp, and one thousand more at Sacred Stone.

Life at the camps was becoming harder during the harsh winter, and the Standing Rock Sioux Tribe was also confronting a significant budget shortfall. While water protectors sought refuge at the casino, some of the casino's usual gambling patrons were boycotting it, and the closure of the bridge and the road were taking a serious toll on the casino's business. The casino employed around 350 people, more than half of whom came from Standing Rock, and many tribal programs depended on casino revenues.

Since early fall donations had been rolling into Sacred Stone, to the tribe, and to countless websites and GoFundMe accounts that claimed affiliation with the camps. The tribe had not set about soliciting donations, but when offered help, it set up a way for organizations or individuals to donate in a way that would be accountable. In late December the Tribal Council decided to use up to $3.2 million of the approximately $6 million it had received in donations to fund tribal government programs adversely impacted by the casino revenue shortfall and reimburse the tribe for costs associated with the NoDAPL campaign and camps—roads, food, shelter, waste, energy, and emergencies.

LaDonna was busy in the lead-up to Christmas, bringing in supplies for Sacred Stone during the short, cold winter days. She thought December was a particularly hard month for Native people because they had always been attacked during the cold and blizzards—the Sand Creek Massacre of 1864, the death of Sitting Bull and the Wounded Knee Massacre of 1890; the list went on. Christmas was also hard for her personally: this year marked forty-nine years since her mother had walked out the door on Christmas Eve, leaving her six children behind. Her mother had long since passed away, but every year LaDonna's mind went back to that day.

The quiet of Christmas itself was a relief. LaDonna was able to properly clean her house for the first time in nine months, to spend time with Miles, and to tell stories and eat chicken and dumpling soup by the wood fire. While her sister cooked a Christmas dinner at Sacred

Stone and they handed out gifts to kids in the camp, on Christmas day LaDonna was preparing a big family meal at home for once—beef brisket, honey ham, pies, and cake.

The new year approached with the camps girding for four to nine inches of snow. In Times Square in New York City, a billboard supporting the fight had gone up in time for the massive New Year's Eve celebrations. "Bring it on 2017!" Kandi cheered on Facebook as she rang in the new year.[17]

In early January Dave Archambault emailed Jo-Ellen Darcy, thanking her for the December 4 decision but expressing a sense of increasing urgency as the Obama administration entered its final weeks. The tribe was "anxiously awaiting" publication of the Notice of Intent for the EIS and was becoming "increasingly nervous" that it had not yet been issued as inauguration day was approaching.[18]

In 2017 the brutal North Dakota winter weather continued. Kandi was thankful for her cozy yurt on nights when the temperature dropped to negative twenty-four degrees Fahrenheit. Winter snowfall totals reached record highs. Everyone at camp and everyone leaving seemed to have the same hacking cough, which they called the DAPL cough. LaDonna still had it, and it just kept getting worse, to the point where she couldn't lie down without endless coughing. A doctor told her she had glass particles in her lungs.

Other disturbing developments also continued: Tribal Council member Dana Yellow Fat still thought he was being followed by two or three white vehicles at all times. In January Yellow Fat's work computer, briefcase, and iPad were stolen out of his truck when he stopped at a gas station in Fort Yates. An iron bar had been thrown through the truck window with the word "TRAITOR" written on it. The briefcase and computer later reappeared, hanging from the mirror of his dad's truck. He blamed TigerSwan.

With the turn of the new year, the Standing Rock Sioux Tribal Council also began to coordinate a massive cleanup and relocation effort with camp organizers. The site of Oceti Sakowin had flooded in 2008 following a similarly heavy winter snowfall. IEN and camp leaders wanted to ensure that the river wasn't polluted by debris in case of spring flooding, and they encouraged people to move out of Oceti to protect lives and the water. (Sacred Stone was on higher ground.) On January 12 the headsmen of Oceti made the decision to let the camp's sacred fire burn down. Cleanup was starting in anticipation of a flood, and they asked people to evacuate.[19]

Also on January 12 state authorities declared Backwater Bridge structurally sound. While some guardrail and surface repairs were necessary, those would take only a few weeks. Nevertheless, the governor's office and Morton County Sheriff's Department agreed to open the road only after an "assurance [that] no criminal activity will take place and federal law enforcement has been introduced into the protest camp to restore law and order."[20] Archambault met with camp leaders to let them know that the bridge would likely remain closed as long as frontline actions occurred. Kandi went live on Facebook in early January, describing her frustration that the bridge was still blocked and that the camp was surrounded by police vehicles and lights. Following the December 4 announcement, the workers shouldn't be working at all, so why, she wondered, was law enforcement still there? She thought that campers would be more willing to leave if law enforcement and private security weren't still there, if the bridge was cleared and the blockade ended.[21]

The blockage of Highway 1806 at Backwater Bridge had, since late October, been a persistent and unwelcome feature of the law enforcement response to the water protectors. The blockade prevented all pedestrian and vehicle travel, including emergency vehicles. The highway was the key north-south thoroughfare through North Dakota and the direct route from the reservation to Bismarck, and its blockade presented a serious impediment for both water protectors and community residents, creating delays and an increased cost of gas for those having to drive around it. (When Highway 1806 was open, a trip from Cannon Ball to Bismarck took around fifty minutes; without it the trip stretched around half an hour longer.) The blockade delayed emergency vehicles reaching injured water protectors on the night of November 20.[22] (Tribal members later filed a class action lawsuit against North Dakota, state and local officials, and TigerSwan related to the road closure.)[23]

Dallas Goldtooth, a camp leader and Kandi's colleague at IEN, had a savvy analysis of the blockade: it had started as a tactical move to keep water protectors away from DAPL construction sites, but as the weeks wore on, North Dakota saw that de facto economic sanctions could help curb the pipeline resistance. Tribal Council members and local leaders complained about the negative impacts of the blockade. It became a method of exerting control over the tribe. Goldtooth concluded that the state "saw that by keeping the police blockade up it was causing turmoil; it was creating tension. It was straining tribal resources and threatening jobs and income. The police barricade was a means to starve the tribe, exert control and coerce Native leaders to make difficult decisions."[24]

By January at least five hundred people remained at Oceti and Rosebud. Youth at the camps lit a new fire, which they called the All Nations Fire. At times Jasilyn felt broken from the macings and the beatings, a kind of PTSD she thought she had been born with from her ancestors' experiences and had been activated. But the fire still burned in her, and she felt her ancestors telling her to continue to fight.[25]

As the clock ran down on Obama's presidency, the Army Corps was starting to move the EIS forward. On January 18 the Federal Register published a notice soliciting public comment on the EIS process for the pipeline. It invited interested parties to comment on potential issues, concerns, and alternatives through February 20.[26] That same day Judge Boasberg denied Dakota Access's request to stop the EIS process from proceeding. Kandi was happy about both events and ready to take any victories the movement could get.[27]

Jo-Ellen Darcy wrote a final letter to Dave Archambault the next day. She referenced the chairman's multiple letters, her own December

4 decision, and the recently published notice of intent that the U.S. Army was gathering the information necessary to prepare an EIS. "I remain mindful of the history of the Great Sioux Nation particularly as it relates to water resources projects in Indian Country," she wrote. "I believe that this history compels us to exercise great caution and an abundance of respect in considering and addressing your concerns regarding the proposed DAPL crossing of Lake Oahe." As her final official act, she shared her gratitude and appreciation for the chairman's leadership and commitment to his people.[28]

Also on January 18 the Cannon Ball district passed a momentous resolution. It declared, "All the individuals at all the camps in and around Cannon Ball need to leave the district." The resolution applied to Oceti, Rosebud, and Sacred Stone Camps. Furthermore, the resolution asked that no new winter camp be built in the area. LaDonna was defiant, but the full Tribal Council voted unanimously to approve Cannon Ball's resolution just two days later.[29]

Cannon Ball had welcomed visitors from the camps' first days. But the Cannon Ball community was poor, with few resources. When the big snowstorm in early December hit, it housed over 1,500 veterans at community facilities. Over time the disruption of the camps to the daily life of the town had begun to chafe. Some community members had also begun to worry about their safety and privacy. The road blockade created a hardship for Standing Rock residents on a day-to-day basis. Even though they knew that the EIS victory was only temporary, local political leaders felt that community members wanted to take a step back, to start to care for themselves again.

There was dissension on the Tribal Council around how to end the camps and what the next step would be. The priority was everyone's safety. "The last thing I wanted was to be picking up bodies of our women and children out of the snow," Dana Yellow Fat concluded. Tribal leaders didn't want people to die for their cause; they wanted them to go home, make change in their own communities, and keep the fight alive.

Kandi understood why the tribe took the action it did. Tribal leaders were under a lot of pressure from the police and from their own people. Not everyone living on Standing Rock was part of the camps. People wanted to be able to get to Bismarck without having to drive a longer and more circuitous route. They didn't want to have to deal with the camps, where there was some drug and alcohol use. The tribe was split, she thought. She knew they were tired. And they didn't want someone to get killed. Dave Archambault found himself in a position where he had to do what he felt was right.

Despite the obvious reasons for ending the camps, conspiracy theories proliferated—including that Dave Archambault was working for the government and enriching himself personally. Even IEN took a hit as conflicting conspiracy theories suggested that it was an organization of paid infiltrators or paid protesters.

Kandi knew people wanted answers. Why didn't the tribe just stand their ground and fight this with the camps? "The answer," she concluded, "is that the tribe *did* fight in court, and was continuing to." The rumors were all false. Dakota Access had built the pipeline even when the camps were there, under law enforcement protection. The tribe had decided to take its fight to Washington DC.

Indeed the eyes of the nation and world were also on Washington. Donald Trump was inaugurated there as president of the United States on January 20, 2017. Kandi was in town to protest the inauguration. The next day she joined the women's march along with hundreds of thousands of others worldwide.

Jasilyn and Kalen were also in Washington DC that week, protesting Trump's inauguration, along with other members of the IIYC. It was Kalen's first time in a big city, and he found seeing thousands of people crowding the streets to be mind-blowing. They led a march that began with a few hundred and combined with other groups until it felt like thousands. "You guys go first," people said when they saw the water protectors. People stretched for blocks and blocks behind them—white, Black, Latino, Asian.

·Jasilyn had grown into a public role in the preceding months. She was a leader for the youth at the camps and had been presented with the sacred staff.[30] An eloquent and moving speaker, she had also become a prominent face of the camps and had received an increasing number of invitations to speak. That fall she had spoken at rallies, attended fundraisers for the camps, and lobbied members of Congress on their behalf. The *New York Times Magazine* published a feature telling her story in late January.[31] She remained humble amid the growing recognition, but she had come to understand the power in her voice: "Coming from not knowing anything, going into a space where people were making change, and then coming back to this place where change is desperately needed . . . was life changing for me," she said. "I understood that I had power, that I had a voice, and that if I used that voice, I could alter everything. I could make a wave of emotion across thousands of people—just me standing up there and saying what I had to say."[32]

After the inauguration, it took only a few days for the other shoe to drop. On Tuesday, January 24, President Trump signed presidential memoranda on the Dakota Access and Keystone XL Pipelines, directing agencies to expedite remaining reviews and approvals.[33] Shares of ETP and TransCanada (which was seeking to build the Keystone XL Pipeline) rose more than 3.5 percent that day in U.S. trading. "I approved two pipelines that were stuck in limbo forever," Trump said. "I don't even think it was controversial. You know, I approved them, I haven't even heard—I haven't had one call from anybody saying 'oh, that was a terrible thing you did.' I haven't had one call." He cited job growth as his impetus. "I think everyone's going to be happy in the end, OK?"[34]

The Standing Rock Sioux Tribe declared that Trump's presidential memorandum violated the law and treaties. "Nothing will deter us from our fight for clean water. We will be taking legal action, and will take this fight head on," the tribe promised.[35] "We are not opposed to energy independence. We are opposed to reckless and politically motivated development projects, like DAPL, that ignore our treaty rights and risk our water. Creating a second Flint does not make America great again," Dave Archambault contended.[36] Archambault was trying to get a meeting with the Trump administration.[37]

Jan Hasselman knew that the law didn't prevent government agencies from changing their minds, but it did require decisions to be based on facts and thorough consideration rather than on the whim of a pipeline-loving president.[38] He vowed to fight the presidential memorandum in court. Earthjustice called Trump's decision "antidemocratic" and raised the possibility of a conflict of interest because of Trump's financial connections to ETP.[39] The question for Hasselman was how effectively the Army Corps would reverse itself, whether it would leave room for legal challenge.

Kandi was frustrated but defiant. She wasn't opposed to jobs, but DAPL and the Keystone XL Pipeline would create only sixty to eighty permanent jobs, she noted in a Facebook live stream on January 24. She encouraged people not to surrender to apathy but to continue to stand with Standing Rock even from afar. "We want a clean energy future, a clean energy economy, and a renewable energy sector," she emphasized. "After five hundred years of work to protect this land, we're not going to give up now."[40] Kandi was still reeling from a traffic accident in the Bakken on January 22 that had claimed the life of a young friend, but she was looking toward the future. Divestment and defunding of the fossil fuel industry were the next big steps as far as she was concerned.

Ta'Sina Sapa Win, returning to the camps in late January after protesting Trump's inauguration in Washington with the IIYC, found the atmosphere to be different. There was no fight left in the movement, she thought, and those who remained seemed sad. But they were working diligently to clean out the camps, sorting items to donate, and clearing trash. Dump trucks, loaders, an excavator, and skid steers buzzed around Oceti, tearing out abandoned camps and structures. Dumpsters ringed the camps' perimeters, while abandoned tents and food, sodden with snow and ice, were loaded into them. Donated items, some only used once, ended up in the trash. Thunder Valley CDC on

Pine Ridge was partnering with Standing Rock on the cleanup effort. The MHA Nation also offered to help, providing a few trucks and some labor. Some camp residents were emotional, but they tried to stay positive. "I don't think the narrative is that this ended up in a trash dump," Thunder Valley CDC founder Nick Tilsen told journalists. "This was like a stone cast in the pond with a ripple effect all throughout the world. The reality is we inspired the world that together we could stand up to a powerful corporation."[41]

On Wednesday, February 1, seventy-six people, including Pueblo journalist Jenni Monet and Chase Iron Eyes, a Standing Rock member and former congressional candidate, were arrested to the west of Highway 1806, at the top of a hill across from the main entrance of Oceti. They had been trying to establish a new resistance camp dubbed "Last Child Camp" on higher ground, but the arrests disbanded the camp. The land itself had not been ceded by the 1851 and 1868 treaties but was currently owned by Dakota Access.[42]

The Army Corps was looking to close down all of the camps on its property too. In early February the Corps issued notices warning that Corps-managed property would be closed as of February 22 because of a potential for flooding. Kandi, warm inside her yurt at Oceti despite the windy fifteen-degree weather outside, knew that the remaining water protectors had a lot of work to do. The snow was piled up high under gray skies. Originally, when people came to the camps, they were asked to leave their tents for the next people that came, a decision that, in retrospect, was complicating cleanup efforts.

Outside her yurt, Kandi could see police—with floodlights and concertina wire—up on the hill where the Last Child Camp had been established for less than a day. Water protectors had recently constructed two other small camps—one named after the Cheyenne River Sioux Tribe and one called the Black Hoop Camp, both up off the floodplain on tribal land. But no matter what happened at the camps, she concluded, a movement had been sparked there that was not going away.

The EIS, though, was looking increasingly unlikely. By the end of January Acting Secretary of the Army Robert Speer had reportedly directed the Corps to proceed with granting the easement. Then in early February, the Department of the Interior withdrew its December 4 analysis, written by Hilary Tompkins, which found "ample legal justification" to deny the easement.

Finally, the water protectors' long-feared moment arrived. On Tuesday, February 7, Deputy Assistant Army Secretary Paul Cramer notified Congress that the Corps would grant the easement for the pipeline. Douglas Lamont, a senior official at Army Corps headquarters, wrote in a letter that he had reviewed the pipeline and concluded that there was no need for additional environmental analysis.[43]

Senators Maria Cantwell and Bernie Sanders immediately wrote to President Trump, expressing their concern: "This decision was made without appropriate tribal consultation, a full environmental review, or sufficient due process. This blatant disregard for federal law and our country's treaty and trust responsibilities to Native American tribes is unacceptable."[44]

Just two weeks after Trump directed the Army Corps to speed its review of the pipeline, on February 8, 2017, the Corps granted an easement to Dakota Access, LLC to install the pipeline under Lake Oahe.[45] ETP announced that it anticipated that the pipeline would be in service in the second quarter of 2017. Drilling immediately resumed near the Missouri River crossing—"a massive blow to the morale of protestors," TigerSwan crowed in its daily report.[46]

Dave Archambault was on a plane to Washington DC when the easement was issued. He had been trying one last time to meet with the Army Corps and the White House. He got the notice when he landed.

Some of those who thought the December 4 victory was meaningless felt grimly vindicated. Tom Goldtooth, executive director of IEN, was incensed, charging that in granting the easement the Army Cops had disregarded legal process, protocol, and over one hundred thousand comments that had been submitted as part of the environmental review that was still under way, "all for the sake of Donald Trump's billionaire big oil cronies." Furthermore, he said, the decision was contrary to the treaty rights of the Seven Council Fires of the Sioux Nation.[47] IEN was urging a call to action across the country, for people to rise up in a mass mobilization of support of Standing Rock. "Think long-term movement building—we are in this for the long haul," Kandi wrote on Facebook.[48] Dave Archambault reiterated his call that supporters not come to Standing Rock, instead taking the fight to their state capitals, members of Congress, and Washington DC.[49]

Around three hundred people were left in the Oceti camp, bundled against the cold wind, when they learned that the easement to drill under Lake Oahe had been granted. They processed the news quietly, continuing their work cleaning up the camps. Many planned to move to higher ground, and others were unsure what their next steps would be.

One person, at least, was celebrating: Kelcy Warren. Since the federal government had shut the company down in December, Warren later said: "Had that not been overturned, we would have been screwed. I mean, in a big way."[50]

Jan Hasselman had been hoping for a short decision by the Army Corps so that it would be vulnerable to legal challenge. But the Army Corps issued two hundred pages of analysis, an extremely detailed memo offering an explanation for the change. Obviously people had been working on this behind the scenes for a while, and the legal team had crafted the memo to withstand judicial review. For the first time in the case Hasselman felt defeated. He hadn't taken a day off in a year, had worked countless all-nighters, had poured his heart and soul into the fight. "We're dead," he said. He put down the decision and went home. His boss, Patti Goldman, took a more sanguine approach, he remembers. She read the decision and came up with a strategy to resume the legal challenge. Together they got back to work.

Judge Boasberg rejected the Standing Rock Sioux Tribe's request for an emergency order stopping construction of the remaining section of the pipeline, concluding that while oil wasn't flowing through the pipeline the tribes faced no immediate harm.[51] The Standing Rock Sioux filed for summary judgment on the Corps' permits, asking the court to overturn the permits before the pipeline could begin operation. It asked the court to rule on some of the essential legal questions in the case that remained unresolved, including whether requirements under NEPA had been met and whether the tribe's treaty rights had been violated.[52]

On February 13 Kandi was at Oceti dismantling her yurt, which she shared with other IEN members. Moving out was bittersweet. Darker elements had appeared—drugs, alcohol, fights—and those who remained were under a cloud of depression. Many people had been volunteering to help clear out abandoned tents, and camp residents and the tribe had worked tirelessly to clean up Oceti. Heavy equipment had been in the camp for the last few days, clearing away the snow. But clusters of tents still remained, interspersed with pools of icy mud. The cleanup was hard going. All the structures were iced into the ground. When the temperature began to rise, the camp turned into thick mud, treacherous for vehicles to traverse. Kandi knew that whatever they left was going to be trashed. She had seen what had happened at the frontline camp after it was shut down at the end of October—confiscated items had been returned soaked in urine.[53]

On February 15 North Dakota's new governor, Doug Burgum, issued an emergency evacuation order for people on Army Corps land in southern Morton County. Citing the risk of floods, he ordered the evacuation of Oceti by 2 p.m. on February 22, coinciding with the Army Corps' notice to vacate.[54]

Even while she cleaned, Kandi was focused on the long game. She still wanted to draw attention to the head of the black snake—the Bakken shale oil formation. One day in February she drove her hybrid car several hours from camp to New Town, where she grew up. She noticed more oil development, new rigs that had sprung up amid the fields. She passed mini man camps, a rail yard where oil tankers came to fill up, an expensive new hotel where oil workers stayed, and huge gas stations filled with trucks that hauled oil or water that had been used in fracking.

As she stood outside her grandfather's house, Kandi could see flares and oil well pumps in every direction; oil trucks buzzed by continuously. She became emotional, thinking about the destruction of her beloved community. She didn't want Aiyana to breathe the air on Fort Berthold, much less swim in Lake Sakakawea. No matter what happened with DAPL, they would still be battling the catastrophic effects of fracking on Fort Berthold. Cancers were on the rise, and she had friends who had died from heroin overdoses and crashes with oil tankers. The MHA Nation experienced death by a thousand cuts, she thought. The pipeline was only a symptom of it.

The racism that had been afflicting water protectors was affecting Fort Berthold too. The previous week, at a high school girls' basketball game in South Prairie, near Minot, one of the teams from Fort Berthold had been called "prairie n——s" from the stands and had heard catcalls supporting DAPL. The team wasn't even from Standing Rock—in fact, it was from the Native nation that had approved the pipeline on its land and was fracking the oil that would run though it—but it was facing discrimination nevertheless.

Back on Standing Rock, trouble was also brewing at Sacred Stone. While the campers had been insulated from the Army Corps' and governor's orders because the camp was on reservation land, on Thursday, February 17, the BIA handed a trespass notice to LaDonna.

The ownership of the land under Sacred Stone was fractured. It had belonged to her father, then had gone in common to his children. In December some of LaDonna's half-brothers and -sisters sold their portion of the property to the tribe; LaDonna said she wasn't brought into any discussions or notified. A BIA title status report in January found LaDonna had just a one-fifteenth interest in the land and that two-thirds of the land was held in trust by the federal government for the tribe, which, the notice said, had not authorized people to live on it.[55]

The BIA gave people ten days to leave or to show why they should not be found to be in trespass. That night LaDonna made a video, reminding the Tribal Council that it had voted 11–0 in favor of the camp on June 8, 2016. But the tribe had more recently voted to endorse the Cannon Ball decision to close the camps. Campers at Sacred Stone began to clean up as well.

On the morning of February 22, the deadline for water protectors to vacate Oceti and Rosebud, fires raged as water protectors burned their campsites rather than leave them to be destroyed. The air was thick with black smoke billowing from the camps. Even the front gate to Oceti was smoking. Jasilyn thought the fires were pretty at first, but then the camp began to look more apocalyptic; everything was on fire.

Chase Iron Eyes spoke in the final moments of the camps to journalists: "History is repeating itself," he said, with Native Americans forced back into the confines of the reservation. Skeletons of burned out tipis harkened back to the Sand Creek Massacre, the Wounded Knee Massacre, forced removal, and ethnic cleansing.[56]

Jasilyn and Kalen remained at Oceti until the bitter end. They understood the tribe's perspective. Jasilyn thought Dave Archambault was looking out for his people, making sure they didn't get hurt, and making sure that the peace wasn't disturbed in Cannon Ball. They respected the decision. But they were also frustrated. Standing Rock had called them there, asked for their help, and they had asked others to come. People had left their jobs, their families, everything, to come. "And you're gonna just say it's over? 'Go home now; we don't need you anymore?'" They couldn't just go about their lives again. They felt that their duty was to be there on the last day, to stand and witness.

Rain and snow fell while the camps burned. Deep mud ran with icy cold rivulets of water as the remaining water protectors squished through in heavy boots. At 1 p.m. the camp residents came together for a ceremony near the site of the camp's sacred fire. Water protectors sang, prayed, and waved an American flag high. "Mni wiconi!" they called. Some—including elder Nathan Phillips, who had been at the camp since November—walked, grim-faced and ankle-deep in the frigid mud, singing and accompanied by drums, out of the camp.[57] Their signs read "Honor the Treaty," "Water Is Life," and "Generosity." Campers from Sacred Stone stood on the hills along the river, giving support to the leaders at Oceti. LaDonna believed this was not the end but the beginning.

On Highway 1806 journalists gathered in what they thought was a safe zone. A line of law enforcement officers wearing black uniforms and face shields stood on the road. Journalists had been expecting a camp raid, but none had materialized. Unicorn Riot journalists, who had followed the camps closely from their inception, concluded that law enforcement officers were focusing most of their attention on the road, pushing media to the reservation border before they moved into the camp. After 4 p.m., with just a bit of daylight left, the police started to advance, targeting on their way both water protectors and journalists. They had allowed a few chosen media behind their line but began chasing the journalists in front of them, arresting at least two.[58]

Law enforcement officers retreated with the waning of daylight, returning the following day. The governor declared that the few dozen people remaining in the camp would have the chance to leave peacefully without arrest again on Thursday, February 23.

When February 23 dawned, Kalen and Jasilyn were ripped from their sleep. A convoy of dozens of law enforcement vehicles rolled in: an MRAP military vehicle (which some journalists believed was responsible for some of the more violent acts in the standoff, including the incident in which Sophia Wilansky's arm was injured) with a sniper, a long line of more than a dozen tan Humvees, several BearCat armored vehicles, police cruisers, excavators and a Bobcat, and more than two hundred policemen and national guard soldiers in riot gear, armed with automatic rifles. Law enforcement officers were dressed like soldiers in a war zone—helmets, camo, automatic weapons. They advanced alongside Humvees, gunners in their turrets, trying to avoid falling in the snow. They locked down the entrances. "This is my home, this is my mother!" Jasilyn called.

SWAT teams cleared the tipis, barrels of the guns poking into them first, making sure they weren't occupied. Everyone who refused to leave was arrested and escorted out. A helicopter with U.S. Customs and Border Protection emblazoned on the side circled low overhead.

Waniya Locke, a Standing Rock member who had helped to organize the first relay runs, was on the banks of the Cannonball River watching them come in full force and realized: "This is what my grandmother saw; this is what my great grandfather saw—they saw the U.S. Army charging across their lands and displacing Indigenous people."

In *The Guardian* on February 23, Julian Brave NoiseCat, an Indigenous writer, concluded that colonialism was alive and well while impoverished residents of Standing Rock were forced to live in proximity to the pipeline: "The most expensive piece of infrastructure in their community will not be the schools, homes or hospitals they desperately need. Instead it will be a pipeline that they have vehemently opposed."[59]

Kandi and Aiyana watched the events on a television from the nearby casino, alternately crying and laughing, as the police stumbled in the snow. No one wanted to get shot as law enforcement rolled in, so people put their hands up or ran. "Thank God," she thought; they didn't shoot anybody who was running. Forty-six people were arrested, including seventy-six-year-old Regina Brave, a veteran of the standoff at Wounded Knee.[60]

Kandi agonized with the advantage of hindsight: if Fort Berthold had taken a strong stance against DAPL, could the MHA Nation and the Standing Rock Sioux Tribe together have stopped the pipeline? She thought maybe they could have.

# The Standing Rock Legacy

Whatever happens with this pipeline, I don't think that
the world is ever going to look the same. This case and this
movement have expanded the narrative in which we talk about
these issues. This is a fight over a big crude oil pipeline—but
it hasn't been primarily a fight about "keep it in the ground" or
climate. It's about justice and sovereignty.

And it has forced people to grapple with some of our
history—our very awful history on how we treat Native
people—and recognize that it's not all in the past. When
we think about the mistreatment of Native nations, we have
this image of black-and-white photographs—but it's not. It's
happening today.

—Jan Hasselman

The *Bismarck Tribune* lauded the evacuation of the camps. State and law enforcement officials offered water protectors food vouchers, a night's stay at a hotel, taxi vouchers to the bus terminal, and a free bus trip home, though it was unclear how many actually took them up on it.[1]

The Army Corps planned to spend more than a $1 million in the cleanup effort for Oceti and Rosebud Camps. Bulldozers and large vehicles worked in the melting snow, stacking remaining donations and tents. The Rosebud cleanup was completed quickly. Oceti was cleaned up a week later. A Corps spokesman said that more than two thousand cubic yards of material had been removed in all, filling more than six hundred dumpsters.

Dana Yellow Fat thought that the camps had been as clean as possible by the time of the evacuation under the circumstances—after all, there had been ten thousand people there at one time, preparing for winter and trying to make semi-permanent shelters. But a lot of donated materials, including lumber, were left at the end, and the state simply discarded them. It seemed like a terrible waste. With just a few more weeks, Joye Braun thought, they could have cleaned the camps out. They had moved as quickly as they could after the Cannon Ball resolution, but it took hours to dig a tipi out of frozen ground, and vehicles kept getting stuck in the mud.

When Sheriff Kirchmeier admitted that no weapons were found at Oceti, Kandi was incensed. "Of course there were no weapons. It's what we've been saying all along," she fumed on Facebook. Law enforcement and private security were the ones trying to force war against unarmed, nonviolent water protectors, not the other way around.[2]

Most of the remaining water protectors trickled home. Some established small camps near Wakpala, South Dakota (on the Standing Rock Reservation) and Eagle Butte, on Cheyenne River. Chairman Harold Frazier of the Cheyenne River Sioux Tribe, using Joye Braun as an intermediary, had offered the pow wow grounds in Eagle Butte as a transitory place where water protectors could have a meal and a shower and camp. He provided the land to honor and thank the water protectors. Braun, sick with pneumonia, loaded up her truck and hauled supplies to the new camp. They named it Wakpa Wasté—Good River—or, as Joye Braun affectionately called it, "Black Sheep Camp." Between twenty and thirty water protectors rotated through.

Even a move to this new camp was a tough transition for some water protectors. One resident, a camp medic, struggled with drugs and alcohol and even contemplated suicide. After the camps closed, he concluded, "There's days I just really want to grab a big bottle of Jack Daniels and just go off and just do my thing, but that helps nobody. It doesn't even help me. The only person that helps is the white man who's trying to destroy us."

Joye Braun herself was in the hospital for a few days after the camps closed. She had been sick with the DAPL cough for months and had coughed up pumice during a sputum test in January. She also bore scars from rubber bullets that had ripped through her shirt and flesh. The tear gas and pepper spray from the front lines had permanently burnt her vocal cords, exacerbating her gravelly voice.

An hour after law enforcement cleared the main camp on February 22, a series of protest-related bills were signed into law by North Dakota governor Doug Burgum. The bills were North Dakota legislators' response to the water protectors. Even the right-leaning *Bismarck Tribune* had opposed some of the bills that had been initially proposed, warning that they could harm individual rights.[3] One proposed bill would have removed driver liability for unintentionally hitting or killing someone obstructing a public roadway, allowing motorists to run over protestors without charge. (It did not pass.) House majority leader Al Carlson, a Republican, had proposed opening six state-operated casinos, claiming that they were necessary to raise money for the state; the state's former lieutenant governor called the proposal "the most vindictive piece of legislation I have seen in 60 years of legislative tracking . . . obviously a thinly-disguised effort to punish Native Americans for their resistance to the Dakota Access Pipeline construction."[4]

The laws that passed in February covered a wide array of protest-related offenses: increasing the penalty for a riot conviction, criminalizing the wearing of a mask while protesting, expanding the definition of criminal trespass. The legislation was part of a larger conservative backlash against direct actions that only continued to grow. In 2018 the International Center for Not-for-Profit Law had found that thirty states had introduced 56 bills aimed at restricting the right to peaceful assembly since Trump's election.[5] By October 2020 forty states had considered 135 bills, with 25 enacted.[6]

TigerSwan, in its February internal situation reports, followed the North Dakota bills' progress, lauding "the ND State Legislature's willingness to work together and pass bills aimed at increasing penalties during protest actions."[7] It had also watched cleanup efforts. TigerSwan was hopeful that "the internal Standing Rock Sioux affairs will most likely self-destruct from within due to the turbulence between leaders (or lack of). A special mention to all of the LE [law enforcement] Men & Women who made this possible." Fortunately, TigerSwan concluded, the clearing of the main camp, along with the passage of the new laws stemming from the camps, "gave a detrimental blow to overall protester movement in ND."[8]

Soon almost all of the remaining water protectors were swept away. The small Seventh Generation and Eagles Nest Camps were cleared out by the BIA a few days after Oceti closed.

On February 28 the BIA blocked the way to Sacred Stone. Campers' faces glistened with tears as they left, but there was no loss of life and just two arrests. LaDonna put up about sixty people in her house and yard because they had nowhere else to go. They loaded up a truck with the food they could gather and dropped it at every home in Cannon Ball. They also watched surreptitiously to see what happened to their things left behind at Sacred Stone—generators, yurts, tents, tipis, trailers, boats. All were gathered and carried away, she said.

Jasilyn, among the first and last at the camps, found herself back in Cheyenne River. The transition home was hard for Jasilyn and Kalen. For months they had made the camps their home. They had lived without currency, listening to the songs of their people echo through the night. They had slept outside but were not homeless. They preferred that way of life, with so much pride and togetherness. Coming back to Cheyenne River, everyone seemed to fall apart. They saw their friends from camp turning to drugs and alcohol, saying, "I don't want to live with this; I don't want to live in this environment."

Jasilyn and Kalen went in different directions, each with their own struggle. It was one of Jasilyn's toughest years. The reservation was the same dreary place as ever. Jasilyn worried that any change they had achieved wasn't for her own community. She and Kalen had inspired people and brought them together—but all to help another tribe. They felt out of place, like their home was gone. Kalen was angry, Jasilyn depressed. They couldn't uplift and heal each other.

Then Jasilyn discovered she was pregnant. When she found out, she was even more depressed. "I'm not ready for this," she worried. She didn't know what to do. She didn't know anyone she could turn to. She didn't want to tell her mom, who she thought would judge her.

After the camps were disbanded, public and media interest in the pipeline seemed to plummet. Jan Hasselman had been used to walking into his office every day to find thirty voice mails—everyone from CNN and the *Washington Post* to the *Wichita Eagle* wanted to talk to him—but a month later he wasn't getting those calls any more. The litigation was soldiering on, but the Trump administration was creating a whiplash of new events that kept public attention occupied elsewhere.

Not everyone was struggling in the aftermath of the camps: Kelcy Warren had made out quite well. In fact, as ETP shares rose 200 percent between February 2016 and 2017, his net worth nearly tripled. His personal fortune reached $4.5 billion.[9]

TigerSwan was triumphant and determined. One TigerSwan situation report to ETP, by Chief of Security John Porter, warned not to become complacent in the face of the camp closures, as lone wolf activities were always possible. Porter was more determined than ever in his commitment to watching the water protectors: "The movement continues, and We/I will not stop. That's not in my vocabulary. We will always over-watch as the protectors what is in the best interest for ETP, as we are the guardians."[10]

The weeks following the closure of the camps were difficult for Kandi as she tried to navigate the responses of those in the movement. Along with IEN, she began gearing up for a big march in Washington DC in March 2017; they were calling it the Native Nations March. The planning was bittersweet, but they didn't want the camps to end and the movement to fade without a clear next step. They planned four days of events, including tipis on the lawn next to the Washington Monument, panel discussions, and a march from Army Corps headquarters to the White House. Trying to organize the logistics was difficult and hectic, but Kandi thought it showed that they would not go quietly, that they would continue the fight.

The Native Nations March was thrilling for Kandi. On March 9 Reverend Floberg and the Episcopal presiding bishop, Michael Curry, held a service at the National Cathedral. Kandi met with Senator Bernie Sanders. Buses came from all over the country in solidarity—the Dakotas, Los Angeles, Albuquerque, New York, Chicago, Minnesota. Many people from Standing Rock were there, as were people from the camp. When Kandi finally made it to the tipi encampment under the Washington Monument a few days before the march, rain was falling in the dark sky. The sight was beautiful, she thought, with the tipis against the backdrop of the illuminated monument.

On March 10, despite a cold rain that verged into sleet, the crowd outside the Army Corps headquarters grew steadily. The smell of sage smoke hung in the wet air, throbbing with a persistent drumbeat. Intrigued, employees of the Army Corps peered down from their windows as the crowd swelled to thousands. Meanwhile, a sixty-foot-long inflatable black snake bearing the words "No pipeline, no consent" began to slither its way around the crowd.

The crowd began as predominantly Native—an estimated 150 different tribes were represented. "Make way for the youth!" "Let the youth go in front!" the calls came, as the water protectors moved forward. When the march gathered steam, it began to encompass a diverse array of allies. College students mingled with Indigenous water protectors, aging hippies, Black Lives Matter activists, and environmentalists. Some had slept in their cars the night before. Signs abounded: "Protect the water," "Keep it in the ground," "Mni wiconi—Water is life," and, everywhere, "We exist, we resist, we rise."

The march halted as the Trump International Hotel came into view, and some of the marchers swiftly erected the long poles they had been carrying into a large, white tipi. A teenage boy looked out from the hotel wearing a Trump/Pence shirt, pointing at it in triumph before retreating behind the curtains. People in the crowd burned sage and began to pray. "Deport Trump!" rang out a voice in the crowd.

As an organizer, Kandi was rushing around making sure everyone was where he or she was supposed to be, doing interviews, dropping people off, trying to find a place to park, making sure all the buses arrived smoothly. She met up with the march as it progressed, finding Aiyana and Aiyana's father, Loren White, who were already in the crowd. Kandi thought the crowd of thousands sailing by was beautiful, live-streaming parts of the day for followers who couldn't be there.

LaDonna wasn't in the crowd that day, though she wished she could have been. She was still sick with a terrible cough. It had grown worse and worse, and she was constantly wracked by coughs. She was at home in Fort Yates, trying to recover.

Kandi and IEN had invited Lisa and Walter DeVille's teenage daughter, Maria, to Washington to speak at the rally after the march. Lisa and Walter joined her. They also met with Bernie Sanders, Lisa sharing her story of life on Fort Berthold. Dana Yellow Fat's daughter, just seventeen years old, was there too, holding a corner of the Standing Rock flag. She had traveled by airplane for the first time.

At the rally speakers and performers spoke warmly about human rights and climate justice. "Standing Rock changed everything," Judith LeBlanc, director of the Native Organizers Alliance, concluded. "We interrupted and disrupted the colonial race-based narrative of what American Indians are, and it will never, ever, ever be changed back." Kandi was on the stage, helping everything to flow smoothly. It all did, until Dave Archambault stepped up to the mic.

As he spoke, Archambault got boos from some in the crowd. "You know we're here in unity," Kandi said, encouraging people to listen to him; she reminded the crowd that the tribe had filed the lawsuits against the pipeline. (TigerSwan, following the march, noted in its reports approvingly: "The protests in Washington DC once again demonstrated a growing discord between native American protestors and non-Native protestors. . . . This growing divide will continue to weaken the protest movement in North Dakota.")[11]

"We're not defeated, and we're not going to be the victims," Archambault declared. "You know I love you guys," he said. "It's okay for you to be upset." He was dismayed by unfounded accusations that he had sold out. He lived a simple life in Cannon Ball, earning his own living and not taking money from anyone. But he had been faced with the responsibility of the safety of thousands in the face of militarized law enforcement, bitter cold, and even "unlawful acts" within the camps themselves.[12] It had been an impossible situation.

As the rally wore on, the mood shifted. Prolific the rapper performed, as did Taboo from the Black Eyed Peas. Kandi danced and sang along to "Where Is the Love."

On Standing Rock the physical traces of the camps began to disappear. Highway 1806 finally reopened in late March. By the end of the month LaDonna was allowed back into Sacred Stone. The land was dry; the snow was gone, but the flood hadn't materialized. There was nothing left except the red man statue. "He is still watching," she wrote on Facebook.[13]

LaDonna was still processing what had happened. Everyone's emotions were raw. She was grieving the loss of Sacred Stone, the school and kitchen, the homes, and the scattering of all of the brave and strong relatives who had stood with her. LaDonna had dreams of honoring the water protectors for their sacrifices—for standing against rubber bullets, pepper spray, water cannons. For withstanding lies, rumor, and gossip. She honored them in her heart. She was also resolute: "Those who are afraid of this movement should know that we have just begun."[14]

In April 2017 LaDonna submitted a report to the Standing Rock Sioux Tribe on her camp-related expenditures. Sacred Stone's GoFundMe had received over $3 million in donations, and she had been accused of using the money for houses, vacations, and new vehicles, but she was adamant that the accusations weren't true. In fact, she said, she was struggling to pay her bills. When people asked her to travel, she didn't even have money for breakfast at the conference hotel. And she was angry about all of the property from Sacred Stone that had been removed by the tribe: trailers, yurts, tipis, stoves.

In early April Kandi went back to visit Standing Rock. She was happy to see LaDonna again, and she felt like exciting things were on the horizon. But when she drove past the site of the camps and saw the empty land at Oceti, sadness washed over her. The former area of the camp was covered by little blue signs saying, "No Trespassing, U.S. Government Property." It didn't appear that anyone was around, but as she stood in front of the camp, a yellow helicopter buzzed over the hill. They were still watching, she thought.

Kandi was also busy further north, back on Fort Berthold. She was working with IEN to get a project off the ground aimed at creating a healthy, sustainable Indigenous community using renewable energy.[15] She planned to use solar panels to power the reservation's senior center. She called it Just Transition.

Kandi had been involved in renewable energy in Indian Country since 2005, when she was still working on her master's degree. She had done a year-long study on wind energy using Fort Berthold's one turbine, located across the road from the casino. Now she had come full circle with the Just Transition project, looking at small-scale wind and solar energy use to create a sustainable community. They were putting up an earth lodge, the kind her Mandan ancestors might have lived in.

She held listening sessions in the community. "What do you actually want to see?" she asked. "What do you think is achievable?" People asked how a just transition would take place, and Kandi answered: "It's already happening. We are either going to be forced into it, unprepared, or we will be prepared." Like it or not, the climate was changing. Trump could deny it all he wanted, she thought; his children and grandchildren would have to deal with the consequences.

A just transition, for Kandi, meant not just a switch to renewable energy sources. It meant teaching her own people to return to the ways of their ancestors. Her ancestors—Mandan, Hidatsa, Arikara—were farming tribes, growing corn, squash, beans, and tobacco along the Missouri River. They traded produce for supplies from other tribes. The Mandan controlled a vast trading network before they were decimated by smallpox. A just transition meant going back to how they had been living before colonization, before they had been put on a reservation and told how to live. They were strong and resilient people. When they were forced onto the reservations, they had formed communities, roads, a hospital; after the dam was built and pushed them from the bottomlands, they learned to become ranchers on the dry, windswept plains. She believed they could learn again.

Returning to the old ways could be a challenge. Like so many others, Kandi's own grandmother had been taken away and put into the boarding school system as a child; it had taught her not to be Hidatsa, and she was beaten if she spoke her language. For Kandi a just transition was partly about healing—returning to her culture and the importance of family. She found it sickening how competitive the U.S. economy could be, how many hours people worked away from their families. She didn't want to take away jobs but did want to offer alternative solutions—hemp farms, small-scale wind and solar farms, sustainable homes. She was teaching Aiyana how to garden and how to find water if someday the tap didn't turn on. She wanted her to know how to live on the land.

One visionary leader on the Pine Ridge Reservation in South Dakota provided a groundbreaking model. Nick Tilsen had been working for several years to reimagine how the Lakota people lived, creating the Thunder Valley CDC. Tilsen had been deeply involved in the Standing Rock camps from the early days. He had been arrested in September 2016 for locking down to construction equipment, garnering one of the first felony charges of the movement. Thunder Valley and Tilsen had a major stake in the game: the Mni Wiconi (Water Is Life) pipeline from the Missouri River to Pine Ridge is the water source for Tilsen's new sustainable community.

Pine Ridge is one of the poorest places in the nation. Spread over roughly three million acres in South Dakota, it is a checkerboard of ownership, like Standing Rock and Fort Berthold. Unemployment hovers around 80 percent; addiction and suicide rates are high. Driving across the reservation, one sees a picture of rural poverty: boarded trailers, junkyards, rez dogs, dirt roads, broken down cars. But it is a place with a proud and poignant history. In 1890 the U.S. government murdered hundreds of Native Americans at Wounded Knee on the Pine Ridge Reservation in the last battle of the Indian wars; in 1973 several hundred members of AIM and community members occupied Wounded Knee for seventy-one days as the federal government blockaded food and supplies and met them with a militarized force. They demanded a change in the conditions on the reservation, land, and rights.[16]

When the camps at Standing Rock closed, some water protectors moved south to Pine Ridge, where a (successful) fight was brewing to shutter the liquor stores in White Clay, Nebraska, which preyed upon Native customers on nearby Pine Ridge.[17] For years the tiny town—population fourteen—of four liquor stores had profited off of alcohol sales to the twenty thousand tribal members on Pine Ridge, where the tribal government banned alcohol sale and possession. White Clay sold four million cans of beer a year, eleven thousand a day. Up to two-thirds of the adults on Pine Ridge, meanwhile, lived with alcoholism.[18]

One of Nick Tilsen's grandfathers was Ken Tilsen, a Jewish civil rights lawyer and activist who had been an attorney for AIM. Nick Tilsen was also Lakota and liked to joke that he was either Sioux-ish or Jew-kota. In consultation with community members on Pine Ridge, he had developed a vision.

Founding Thunder Valley CDC, Tilsen began working to build a "regenerative" community—one that was regrown from a foundation that had been damaged or lost. The Lakota had never made the full transition from being nomadic to living in a built environment, he thought; all of their communities were established through the colonization process. Tilsen wanted to start from scratch. To do that, he was building homes that took Lakota culture into account in the design and planning of the whole community. The first circle of seven houses was under way in spring 2017: high quality, three- or four-bedroom mixed-income housing that would accommodate large Lakota families and provide for community spaces. They were built to withstand the strong winds and powered by solar panels. Thunder Valley had a host of other initiatives in its multifaceted approach to creating systemic change on Pine Ridge: incorporating the Lakota language into street signs and nursery schools; creating community centers; rethinking the reservation food supply with sustainable agriculture; providing early childhood education; and developing a construction workforce, jobs for teenagers, and kids' sports programs.

Even beyond the fact that the Missouri River was Thunder Valley's water source, Tilsen felt a strong motivation to help the NoDAPL campaign. As someone who had devoted his professional life to building the future of Indian Country and building community wealth, the DAPL project represented to him the opposite. Dakota Access generated wealth on the backs of those less fortunate, Tilsen thought. But he saw this as a time in history when his people were rising up, smart and organized. What had happened to Indigenous peoples in America—from the decimation of the buffalo to being forced into boarding schools to losing their language—these were an assault on the spirit of Indigenous people. The low life expectancy on Pine Ridge and the multigenerational poverty were human rights issues. For Tilsen disrupting the status quo and dismantling systems of poverty and oppression that perpetuated the problems of his community were types of activism.

The seeds planted by the movement were also starting to flourish at Standing Rock. Cody Two Bears, who had been the Tribal Council member for Cannon Ball during the camps, wanted Indian Country to show how the reservation could transition away from fossil fuels.

Leaving politics, he started a nonprofit solar farm just outside of the Cannon Ball community along Highway 1806. The solar farm planned to offset electricity in communities on Standing Rock, starting with Cannon Ball. Two Bears thought it fitting that the solar farm was just three miles from the pipeline. For him capitalizing on solar power came down to sovereignty also, to the tribe's controlling its own fate. Solar energy provided a way for the tribe to become self-sustaining and secure in the next seven generations. He thought that the tribe was in a healing phase and that the solar farm was part of that process. He thought it time for Native Americans to show the world how to live again, as they had when they had taught Europeans how to live on the land when they arrived. He called it Indigenized Energy.[19]

LaDonna was also turning the momentum of the camps into a longer-term movement for change on Standing Rock. When Sacred Stone closed, people turned to her. "What do we do?" they asked her. "Plant something," she replied. She and supporters helped to clean up the Cannonball River. They began holding prayer ceremonies. They went into the communities to remove dead trees and pick up garbage. They held youth media training sessions where they taught young people to develop their own voices, editing and producing video, learning to control the story. They also created Sacred Stone Village, a long-term version of the camp, which aimed to create sustainable, eco-friendly communities. A remaining water protector who was also an architect designed a solar trailer that could be pulled in and hooked up to houses. Along with AIM veteran and former Standing Rock Tribal Council member Phyllis Young and the Lakota People's Law Project, LaDonna was working on a green energy project with the Massachusetts Institute of Technology that aimed to transition the reservation to renewable energy sources.

Kandi was also involved in efforts by Native activists to divest major banks from the company behind the DAPL. In the fall of 2016 the Standing Rock Sioux Tribal Council passed a resolution to divest from financial entities invested in the DAPL.[20] All together thirty-eight banks had provided $10.25 billion in loans and credit facilities to finance the companies building the pipeline (ETP, Sunoco Logistics, Energy Transfer Equity, and Dakota Access, LLC), with $2.5 billion to Dakota Access for the pipeline itself. These included some of the biggest banks in the world: Barclays, J. P. Morgan Chase, Bank of America, Deutsche Bank, Credit Suisse, UBS, Goldman Sachs, Morgan Stanley, Wells Fargo, BNP Paribas, Citibank, ING Bank, and others.[21]

Kandi was pleased to see Norwegian bank DNB announce on March 26 that it would sell its loans related to the pipeline—a total of $340 million, almost 10 percent of the total project. The bank's senior executive, Harald Serck-Hanssen, said the sale was a reflection of the importance of involving the Indigenous population in these types of projects, involvement that in this case seemed to have been inadequate. Dutch bank ING sold its $120 million shares, and Citizens Bank ended its financing of ETP. The city of San Francisco began to divest $1.2 billion from the companies that had financed the pipeline. In early April the Standing Rock Sioux Tribe cheered BNP Paribas' decision to divest from the pipeline.[22] Wells Fargo actually reached out to the Standing Rock Sioux Tribe, requesting a meeting, and they had several. Ultimately the bank created a grant to give Native communities $50 million over five years (though activists were not satisfied, as Wells Fargo was still financing the Keystone XL Pipeline).[23]

In late April 2017 Kandi was in New York City for the United Nations Permanent Forum on Indigenous Issues. While in New York, Kandi had the chance to attend the Citigroup shareholders annual meeting, to speak about the pipeline, and to urge Citibank to divest. Citibank was one of four lead banks that had provided financing for the DAPL. Kandi and fellow activist Casey Camp-Horinek, a council member for the Ponca Nation, spoke with Chairman Mike O'Neill and CEO Mike Corbat. Kandi felt the response was lukewarm. "We wish we could have a do-over on this," Mike O'Neill said at the meeting. Mike Corbat acknowledged that Citigroup hadn't given enough consideration to Indigenous concerns but argued that it could do more to protect the environment by maintaining its investment.[24] The looks on their faces were priceless, Kandi thought, when she said she would see them at the next meeting.

Kandi, her family, LaDonna, and Miles also went to the premiere of *Awake: A Dream from Standing Rock*, a documentary about the camps by filmmakers Josh Fox, James Spione, and Myron Dewey, at the Tribeca Film Festival. "We've only just begun; we continue to stand," LaDonna said. "That's right; right now we're standing in line," Kandi quipped. In its daily situation reports, TigerSwan noted both the premiere and the United Nations' permanent forum that Kandi was attending.[25]

On April 29, the one hundredth day of the Trump administration, Kandi was back in Washington for the Peoples' Climate March, along with Joye Braun and LaDonna. The temperature reached a sweltering ninety-one degrees, a heat record—for Kandi, a sticky reminder of what they were fighting for. More than two hundred thousand people were at the march in Washington, with tens of thousands more taking part in sister marches around the world. It felt like the beginning of a new movement. They met with Bernie Sanders again, as well as with Senator Jeff Merkley of Oregon and actor Leonardo DiCaprio. Kandi told them about her home in North Dakota and the destruction of the MHA Nation homeland from fracking.

There was still no oil running through the DAPL—pipeline workers had had some mishaps and damaged sections of pipe—but it undoubtedly soon would be. Kandi was in Washington to prove that the water protectors weren't alone in the movement for climate justice.[26]

Banners filled the streets during the march. "Keep it in the soil, can't drink oil!" marchers chanted as they surrounded the White House. They demanded a government response to climate change. A large group was getting energized.[27] Indigenous peoples from around the world were at the forefront. "I believe that we will win!" marchers chanted. "Mni wiconi! Water is life!" As part of the events, hundreds of Indigenous people also held a round dance in front of the Trump hotel. Kandi was there, and Joye Braun spoke. She told the crowd that they were gearing up for the fight over Keystone XL.

IEN had an outstanding federal lawsuit against the Keystone XL in Montana. Kandi saw the movement around her growing, from hippies and tree huggers, she thought, to include everyone. A lot of times it started as a "Not in My Backyard" (NIMBY) issue, but that was okay, she decided. The devastation wrought by fracking and oil development was in so many backyards now that it had created a global problem.

As spring turned to summer on Standing Rock, revenues were still down at the casino, contributing to an ongoing financial crisis for the tribe. Dave Archambault had decided to seek reelection to the chairmanship. He was one of ten candidates, with a primary vote coming up in July.

On Fort Berthold Lisa DeVille was working harder than ever. As the Trump administration and Republican lawmakers set about rolling back Obama-era environmental regulations, Lisa was fighting against repeal of the Methane and Natural Gas Waste Rule, which was designed to prevent loss of natural gas through flaring, venting, and leaks on public land.[28]

North Dakota's oil production was on the rise, increasing 2.4 percent in April. The pipeline was expected to increase the state's oil revenues as transportation costs fell.

Spills were also continuing. Between January 1 and May 1, 2017, the North Dakota Department of Health reported 539 spills related to the oil and gas industry in the state, including 287 oil spills and 176 saltwater spills.[29] The DAPL had already experienced three leaks before even officially entering service. Two leaks—of eighty-four gallons and twenty gallons—had been in early March, then another eighty-four gallons in early April. The spills were small, but activists felt grimly vindicated.[30]

Kandi was frustrated by the leaks. Her commitment to a full EIS was as strong as ever. But by late March, the pipeline under Lake Oahe was loaded with oil in preparation for the beginning of operation.

The Standing Rock and Cheyenne River Sioux Tribes were asking the court for summary judgment, arguing that President Trump had improperly overturned the Obama administration's directive to the Corps to conduct a full EIS. They knew that oil would likely soon be flowing. In April filings with the U.S. Federal Energy Regulatory Commission suggested that the pipeline would begin to transport oil across state lines in mid-May.[31]

Kandi understood the stakes of her work; a record two hundred brave environmental and land defenders had died fighting for their cause in 2016.[32] But Kandi took the long view. "Are we going to win?" she asked herself. "I'm not entirely sure." Despite the challenges of her work, Kandi was fundamentally an optimist. She believed that knowledge really was power. And she had seen progress: five years ago people hadn't been talking about climate change in the context that they were doing so now. The change was a result of what activists like Kandi were doing as well as the visible effects of a warming planet.

TigerSwan intelligence updates on DAPL continued through the spring, mentioning IIYC chapters as well as ongoing activities in North Dakota, Illinois, Iowa, and South Dakota.[33] TigerSwan monitored social media, watched prominent activists who returned to Standing Rock for brief visits, photographed "suspicious vehicles" in the vicinity of the pipeline, tracked additional camps to which water protectors had gone, and followed the divestment campaign actions.[34] It cheered disagreements among the activists on social media and followed internal tribal divisions.[35] It also had an eye to the future, watching water protectors going to Eagle Butte under the direction of Joye Braun: "Eagle butte is the sustainment hub and central coordination point for protestor activities against the Keystone XL," the reports warned.[36]

Down on Cheyenne River, Jasilyn and Kalen were back together and happy; in fact Jasilyn asked Kalen to marry her. They had mourned the loss of camp and had reached the other side.

But even after they had grieved the loss of their camp community, there was a separate grief to work through. Jasilyn had miscarried.

She had been about three months along. As mixed as her emotions had been on learning about the pregnancy, with the miscarriage Jasilyn was devastated. She cut her hair short. She was in a delirious state of mourning and crying. "I lost my mind. I wasn't there," Jasilyn remembers. They buried their baby near Kalen's grandmother's ranch, alongside a creek.

On Memorial Day, May 30, 2017, LaDonna went with Miles to her family cemetery on the hill at Sacred Stone. That day the graves at the cemetery were heavily decorated with American flags honoring her family members who had been veterans. The day before, the water at her house hadn't been working, so she had heated water to wash her hair in the sink. She thought about her grandma, when all the grandkids lined up at the wash basin, hauling water from the Cannonball River and later from the well.

As she walked around the hillside that day, where Sacred Stone had stood, LaDonna was reminded of how the earth can heal itself. Only a few months after the campers had left, the grass was reemerging, the area clear. Purple and yellow wildflowers dotted the hillside. Few signs remained of the small town that had sprung up on the prairie a year earlier and disbanded only a few months since.

A week later, on June 7, Donald Trump announced that the pipeline was open for business. He joked about how he had approved the final section of it: "Nobody thought any politician would have the guts to approve the final leg. I just closed my eyes and said, 'Do it.'" He concluded: "It's up, it's running, it's beautiful, and it's great. Everybody is happy. The sun is still shining, the water is clean. But you know, when I approved it, I thought I would take a lot of heat. And I took none. Actually none. People respected that I approved it."[37]

The DAPL was in service. Oil began to flow through it, wending its way from the Bakken south, past the wildflowers of Standing Rock, below the water of Lake Oahe. The black snake had come alive.

# Epilogue

If you think about the planet being 4.6 billion years old and
the human life span, even if you live for a century, it's a blink of
an eye. And if it takes this long to change the policies to save
ourselves as humanity then that's what it takes. Are we going to
win? I'm not entirely sure. You know we have prophecies that
talk about that fork in the road where we're either going to take
the right road or the wrong road, and that's going to decide our
fate. I don't know if we're going to go down the right one. But
I'm going to fight like hell to make sure we do.

—Kandi White

On a chilly, overcast weekend in late September 2018 Kandi White
was on one of her last trips for the foreseeable future. She planned to
take a break from her frenetic travel schedule speaking about climate
change and fracking. The fall was full of changes for Kandi, and she was
anticipating slowing down. Her daughter Aiyana was starting school;
Kandi and her long-time partner Loren, Aiyana's father, had recently
gotten married; and they had a baby boy on the way in the spring.

Kandi drove six hours from her Billings, Montana, home with Aiyana
in the back seat to convene at a hotel in Bismarck with her mother,
sisters, nieces, and nephews. They were celebrating a walk for children
with Down Syndrome, a condition with which her young niece had
been born.

By nature sunny and warm, Kandi had been growing increasingly
frustrated. She had been in California the previous week, protesting at
the Global Climate Action Summit. The summit had brought together

high-profile climate champions, like California governor Jerry Brown and former New York mayor Michael Bloomberg. But Kandi thought the summit attendees just wanted to use carbon trading and offsets to shuffle around the problems associated with fossil fuels while still extracting oil and making money. Kandi was indignant. They were in positions of power; they had health and wealth. They weren't in the trenches, living with the effects of fracking like Kandi's family on Fort Berthold was.

On Saturday night in Bismarck, Kandi ran into Mark Fox; he had come down from Fort Berthold to support MHA Nation members with Down Syndrome. Kandi was still reeling from the chairman's primary contest, which had left Mark Fox alone with former chairman Tex Hall on the November ballot. (Fox ultimately prevailed.) "Why are we always stuck with the lesser of two evils?" she wondered. Not that she considered Mark Fox evil, but she thought he could be doing more. Why was he continuing to sign leases for more oil production?

She was frustrated also with her fellow activists on Fort Berthold. She was tired of people saying, "We wish we could stop oil development, but it's here" and asking only for more regulation. Kandi didn't think fracking could ever be regulated enough because there was nowhere safe to put the wastewater. Landowners on the reservation—even a few of whom, like Lisa, were speaking out against fracking's devastating effects—were making money from oil leases. Sadly, though, Kandi recognized that there was some measure of truth to the argument that oil development couldn't be stopped on Fort Berthold.

Kandi heard about the tribe spending money on tribal appreciation days and people getting expensive gifts like televisions. She thought the money just pacified them. "What good is your TV when you're dead in five years from cancer?" she wondered. When that happened, though, she knew proving causality would be difficult: "They're just bumping us off slowly, and nobody can really prove it, especially with the industries' proprietary information. Even if people's cattle get sick or people get sick and you look in their blood and you see all the toxins that are in there that are used in fracking, you still can't tie it back to any one company."

Kandi had always loved being in the Mandan-Bismarck area because of the history there. Her ancestors had lived along the Missouri River, and she could almost feel the ancient villages. But after her experience at Standing Rock, new memories crowded in when she came to visit. Bismarck had turned for her into a place filled with racism and hate that she hadn't seen as clearly before.

While her family was in Bismarck, Kandi took Aiyana to the Heritage Center, next to the State Capitol buildings. Her daughter was captivated by the mastodon replica and fascinated by dinosaurs. But Kandi also wanted Aiyana to see the exhibits on Native history, which were carefully segregated from another part of the museum—a display on the oil industry, which had provided generous funding.

When Kandi and Aiyana went to the First Peoples Gallery and saw the pictures of Native history, she had flashbacks to Standing Rock. Images appeared in her mind of unarmed water protectors facing militarized law enforcement. She relived the attacks and the desecration and destruction of sacred sites on treaty land.

Kandi wondered how many people were content to visit the Heritage Center and look at the images of Native peoples facing the military as long as they believed what they were seeing was in the past. She hoped that someday in North Dakota there would be a place that told the whole truth. She also hoped that one day North Dakota would be known for its renewable energy, that its political leaders would care about climate change, and that she would be proud to say she was a North Dakotan. In the meantime she would keep teaching her daughter the importance of little things like recycling, gardening, and reducing energy consumption. She prayed that goodness would prevail over evil in the world and that people would have the wisdom to know the difference.

Kandi's Just Transition work on Fort Berthold had been moving slowly, stalled by the uncertainties of a tribal election year. Loren had been working on the project also, planning a class on solar energy. They had come out with a Just Transition pamphlet and were beginning to move forward.

Kandi was ready to get home and wait for the arrival of the new baby. She needed to harvest her garden, till the soil, and can vegetables. She recalled going out with her grandmother to pick chokecherries, juneberries, bull berries, turnips, ground berries, and sand cherries; she wanted to teach Aiyana how to do that too.

Kandi's connection to the land had shifted because of pollution. She was scared to go to certain chokecherry patches because the oil industry was so close. But she knew in her blood what science was still discovering: that a forest makes you feel good, that there is medicine in bark. She still went outside—lying in the grass, looking at the stars—to reconnect to the land. It made her mind, body, and spirit better.

Kandi's work had taken her to many cities where she saw how people could become disconnected from nature. She could understand why people gave up or got stuck in apathy. They become separated from their place in the world, she thought.

At times Kandi hated having a phone, a computer. They were necessary for her work, but in dark moments she wondered how much of a difference her work was making. She saw that she was having an influence in her own family at least—particularly on her uncles and father, who used to work in the oil industry until they realized it could damage their health—but there were moments of uncertainty and frustration. Setbacks in the movement, especially because of the Trump administration, which had steadily worked to dismantle half a century of environmental protections, left her discouraged.[1]

Despite living in challenging times, Hilary Tompkins, former solicitor of the Department of the Interior saw opportunities for Indigenous people in the United States. "We're protectors of tradition," she said, "but we make decisions for future generations and are guided by that. We welcome outsiders to our homelands, but we are the true first

Americans. . . . We are here to stay in our original homelands, no matter where the political winds may blow."[2] Tompkins saw the effect that the DAPL had already had for other industry projects; it had created a "really big disruption." "There is a sense of 'Oh, we don't want another Dakota Access on her hands,'" she had noticed.[3]

Was her activism going to be enough, Kandi wondered? "I don't really have the answer," Kandi concluded, "but we still have to keep trying."

In August 2017 ETP had sued the NGOs BankTrack and Greenpeace and the EarthFirst! movement in federal court (among others), claiming that their actions against the DAPL constituted racketeering under the Racketeer Influenced and Corrupt Organizations (RICO) Act. "What happened to us was tragic," company chairman Kelcy Warren complained to CNBC shortly after the suit was filed. "We were greatly harmed."[4]

The lawsuit was wide-ranging, and TigerSwan had been gathering information for it for months.[5] It alleged that environmental groups had instigated protests against DAPL to increase donations. The suit sought $300 million in damages for ETP.

ETP's suit was an example of a tactic known as Strategic Litigation against Public Participation (SLAPP), aimed at miring nonprofits in costly litigation that would suck their time and resources, distracting and frightening people so that even if the suit were ultimately dismissed, others might think twice about future activism. ETP was represented by the New York City–based law firm Kasowitz Benson Torres LLP, a frequent defender of President Trump.

Marco Simmons, an attorney with EarthRights International, defended some of the targets—BankTrack and Krystal Two Bulls, one of the former media spokespeople for Red Warrior Camp. "On the one hand," he concluded, "it says something about the power of the NGOs and activists and their actions against the pipeline. ETP wouldn't be doing this if it were inconsequential. But it is also a fairly alarming tactic." In July 2018 a federal judge dismissed the claims against BankTrack entirely, rebuking ETP and its lawyers; the suit against Greenpeace was dismissed in February 2019.

Even in the face of scare tactics, Kandi saw people coming together. What happened at Standing Rock was still a big deal in her community. Kandi had been involved in the legal battle against the Keystone XL Pipeline through IEN. She had heard from people in Cheyenne River that the pipeline company was starting to build. The DAPL battle had already brought together a broad coalition of Native and non-Native allies. She thought people were ready for another.

As summer 2018 turned to fall on the Fort Berthold reservation and the trees nestled among the clay buttes and grassy hills changed from green to yellow and red, Lisa and Walter drove in their red pickup down the rocky, rutted red clay roads to the site of the Crestwood million-gallon brine spill, now more than four years past.

As soon as they opened the car doors, they heard it: the rushing, all-consuming sound of a jet engine racing to the end of the runway. A pair of flares on the next hill over, perhaps half a mile away, was making the sound. Their grinding noise filled the air twenty-four hours a day, seven days a week. The noise reminded them of President Trump's efforts to rescind Obama-era regulations governing methane emissions from fracked wells.[6] (In August 2020 the EPA issued two final rules that would "make it simpler and less burdensome for the oil and natural gas industry" to comply with the New Source Performance Standards controlling methane emissions.[7] The rules formally weakened the Obama-era regulation, eliminating oil and gas companies' obligations to find and repair methane leaks.[8] The move was one of many by the Trump administration to roll back Obama-era attempts to combat climate change and unburden energy companies of regulation.)[9]

In a little valley near the Missouri River lay the path of the spill: some low grasses grew there but none of the scrubby vegetation of trees that rolled down the surrounding hills. Those had all been burned away by the brine and had never returned. The soil hadn't been removed. All of the giant trees had been chopped, mulched, and put back down on top of it.

Walter pulled out his phone, remembering the video by the MHA *Times* showing the "cleanup effort" of the spill—hoses spraying water, washing the brine down the muddy hill and toward the tribe's water intake. In the video Tex Hall looked on in a cowboy hat.

The specter of a chairman Tex Hall was more than a distant memory, and, like Kandi, Lisa and Walter were following his new campaign for tribal chairman closely. "He *literally* got away with murder," Walter grumbled. Fort Berthold POWER was planning a candidates' forum, and Lisa was reluctant to openly take sides. Mark Fox seemed to talk a better game to Lisa—she had heard him calling for transparency, saying, "If I had to pick between oil and water, I'd pick water"—but when it came down to it, he was often voting to side with the oil industry. And not all of the tribe's investments seemed logical: a new outdoor water park sat disused on this September day—as indeed it did for most of the year—with temperatures already in the thirties and forties and flurries of snow in the air.

At his office forty-five minutes away in New Town, Mark Fox was five weeks from the election; his platform was for the MHA Nation to continue to make progress. His signature program, health insurance for the tribe, was by his count serving over six thousand people, around 35 percent of the membership. The program was expensive and infuriatingly necessary only because of the failures of the federal government to make good on its treaty obligation to provide adequate health care. "Some people couldn't afford to wait until some distant date for the federal government to fix [the program]," Fox concluded. They had no choice, he thought; the government had failed in its treaty obligations.

Mark Fox, like Lisa, was continuing to fight the constant flaring, because of both the waste and the environmental impact. He wanted the federal government to require oil companies to capture the gas.

He was also frustrated with what he saw as a constant battle with the state and federal governments to acknowledge the primacy of MHA Nation law within the reservation borders. He found himself repeatedly dealing with the issue of waste disposal—landowners within the reservation borders were disposing of fracking waste because they claimed that since they had permits from the state and the EPA, the tribe had no jurisdiction over them. Trying to assert primary authority was a constant headache, stretching into lawsuits and administrative appeals that the tribe often did not win.

Roads were also a constant problem; fixing the damage done by oil trucks was expensive, and the government gave only paltry sums to help with it. Fox believed that the majority on the reservation supported oil and gas development and thought that the positives outweighed the negatives. But there was a price to pay. Lisa and Walter had seen a partial EA of the impacts of oil and gas on Fort Berthold that was finally completed in 2017, but many of the impacts were simply listed as "Unknown."

Oil development continued to be a complex issue, both for the tribe and for Lisa personally. She still threaded the needle by calling for better regulation rather than an end to fracking, hoping that that would save Fort Berthold's water. "There's leases already signed," she argued. "Right now, what we want is regulation and environmental law enforcement." She was not against oil production per se, but "There's a right way to do it," she contended.[10]

Lisa's sons Thomas and Michael had gone into environmental science too. Lisa was always telling them, "If you guys are gonna stay here, you're gonna stay to fight." The fight had been tough and often unpopular. They were asking for better regulation of an industry that was providing people with opportunities in a place where options were limited. And, of course, oil development had helped them: Lisa's grandmother had passed away, and her oil leases transferred to Lisa's mother; someday Lisa will own a portion of them. One oil well had been drilled on the property, and more may come. Lisa's mother helped them out financially, and the oil money on Walter's family's land had helped see the family through for years. Walter had oil and gas prices a tap away on his phone.

The money that Lisa and Walter had received in royalties had enabled her to work on these issues as a volunteer for the previous ten years. In 2020 Lisa launched a bid for North Dakota's state legislature.

The stunning beauty of Fort Berthold's grassy, tree-studded hills, red clay soil, and striped buttes shone in the evening light as Walter and Lisa drove through Independence. Lisa's family had buried her grandmother in Independence, on the low, hilly site of Lisa's family's land, near where they picked juneberries when Lisa was growing up. But the lake nearby was lined with megapads, some with twelve oil-well pump jacks a piece, dipping relentlessly to extract oil from underneath the lake. Cows grazed on the pasture land around them. Pipelines ran under the smooth water of shimmering Lake Sakakawea. Flames leapt over the land as methane flared bright orange.

As Walter and Lisa drove home, they passed Mandaree's convenience store, where stray dogs played outside; they passed rows of houses put up in tracts following the flooding of the reservation, some now dilapidated or even boarded and abandoned. They pulled up next to a new, large, bluish-gray building under construction. It had a prominent sign outside: "Future Home of the Crestwood Mahgiddashda Center, a Head Start Facility." "A one-million-dollar Head Start Center for a one-million-gallon brine spill," sighed Lisa. Actual compensation for the spill, though, had been slower to come; Mark Fox was still in the process of resolving a settlement with Crestwood. In February 2018 Crestwood Equity Partners had paid a fine of $49,000 to the EPA for the spill and provided spill response equipment to the MHA Nation.[11]

A glance around the town showed a few signs of the change brought by fracking. One house, with spattered pickups in front of it, belonged to someone working in the oil fields. Another, Lisa and Walter knew, belonged to someone consumed by drug addiction. A truck weigh station—which Walter said cost the tribe $70,000—lay just outside of town. No one ever used the weigh station, he reported, because no one was ever trained to operate it. Nearby, trucks rattled by, damaging the reservation's new roads.

Lisa took heart in slivers of good news: she had heard that her work and studies had helped in approving a recently passed ban on fracking in New York State. Also she was looking to the future. At the moment she had her eye on the Keystone XL Pipeline. That pipeline was planned to run near Spirit Lake, where the Hidatsa people's origin stories lay. If the Keystone XL Pipeline was built, any oil spills would flow downstream to Fort Berthold. Lisa was planning to file a public comment. She thought she would share the Duke University study about the residual effects of fracking pipeline spills, just as she had when she had commented on the DAPL. She would warn them of the dangers of spills. Maybe this time it would make a difference.

What would happen to Fort Berthold when the oil dries up and the fracking waste remains, the tribe left with ruined land? Lisa worried about that day. "When the oil runs out," she warned, "we're all going to be pitiful again. But then we're not going to have clean air, we're not going to have clean water, [and] we're not going to have clean land."

Mark Fox saw the gamble on oil development as a calculated risk. "The tribe made a deliberate decision to allow oil and gas development on the reservation, the tribe as a whole," he concluded. He hoped there was still time to protect the land for generations to come. This was the tribe's chance, he believed, to increase the quality of life for all of its members. He hoped the oil boom provided an opportunity through health care and education to help eradicate the historical trauma, the social and economic problems the tribe had suffered for the last 150 years—alcoholism, suicide, poor health. "If you think the federal government someday is going to ever wake up and say, 'You know what we did to those tribes is really bad; let's go ahead and give a $50 billion budget and get back in and repair these reservations and undo what we did,'" Mark Fox said, "you are making a sad mistake. That's never going to happen, so we have to do these things on our own. We have to fix what has been done to us, and here's an opportunity to do that." He hoped that the tribe would be ready when the oil ran out.

LaDonna sat in her house in Fort Yates in September 2018, trying to work. Her son, Freedom, stopped by, as did the mayor of Fort Yates, a water protector from Boston who had stayed on after the camps closed. LaDonna's house was cozy, with three overstuffed brown sofas packed into a living room decorated with family photos, a television, and a tray table where she held court with her laptop. Her kitchen had a large basket of freshly picked tomatoes, some of the last of the season, and a list of house rules, which included no drugs or alcohol. There was a small shed in the yard where Sacred Stone's official offices were housed, and across the street in a grassy lot sat solar trailers. An additional home where water protectors could stay (she had had many in her house ever since the camps closed) lay directly beyond.

LaDonna was keeping busy, surrounded by work and water protectors, but the year had been filled with unimaginable loss: her beloved husband, Miles, had passed away on February 8, 2018, at home in Fort Yates. It had happened so quickly. LaDonna was talking to him one evening, and two hours later he was gone. The doctor said he had had a heart attack; a blood clot had entered his heart.

Despite the difficult year, LaDonna and former Tribal Council member Phyllis Young were hard at work on their renewable energy project, trying to transfer the reservation to hydro, thermal, geothermal, and wind power. LaDonna's mission now was "reeducating people about how to live on the land with respect. Reeducating people [on] how to respect water. Reeducating people [on] how to live on the land instead of consuming resources." She was writing and working on projects to give back to the reservation community. She was part of a global movement called Defend the Sacred, which brought Indigenous people from around the world to stand together in the face of threats.

LaDonna and Phyllis Young had also been regulars at the court hearings for water protectors still facing charges. In all, 832 cases came out of Standing Rock; while some had been dismissed, more than 100 were pending in the summer of 2018.[12]

From camp mother and organizer, LaDonna had become an icon, a symbol of the movement for many. Sacred Stone Camp had more than 389,000 followers on Facebook, and LaDonna was invited all over the world to speak about standing up to environmental dangers. She also still received constant death threats.

Dave Archambault had been ousted from the tribal chairmanship in the election the previous fall. Reverend Floberg's analysis was that his loss had nothing to do with the camps but rather was a result of pushback against belt-tightening of the tribal budget following a previous bookkeeping error that was discovered when Archambault came into office. "He provided some of the steadiest leadership that I've seen anywhere during those months," Floberg concluded. Some tribal members speculated that dissatisfaction with Archambault handling of the camps could have been a factor. Dave Archambault himself was philosophical about the loss. He wanted to give back, to keep the movement alive. He was getting involved with Nick Tilsen in a new organization called the NDN Collective, which would provide assistance to Indigenous peoples looking to defend their rights and their lands or to build their nation.

Dana Yellow Fat was still on the Tribal Council. He had a new grand-baby and was amazed, while cooking fry bread in his Fort Yates kitchen, to reflect on the role that he and the tribe had played in the fight against the pipeline and the opposition they had faced. "In my wildest dreams, did I ever think that I would be entangled in such a web—lies, deceit, lawsuits, you name it? No, I didn't. I never foresaw this."

The pipeline was still a constant topic of discussion. The North Dakota Pipeline Authority reported that DAPL had increased tax revenues in the state by $19 million between June and August 2017. Ron Ness, president of the North Dakota Petroleum Council, reported the pipeline had been a game changer, raising oil production in the state to close to record levels in 2017. State tax revenues for the first five months of operations had increased to around $43.5 million.[13] One year in, Kelcy Warren of ETP reported that the pipeline was running near capacity, providing the Bakken with a competitive edge. By June 2019 ETP was looking to nearly double capacity of the pipeline so that it could transport up to 1.1 million barrels per day to meet growing demand, a plan hotly contested by activists and by the Standing Rock Sioux Tribe. (In October 2020 ETP received approval from Illinois, the final state necessary, clearing the way for the expansion.)[14]

Meanwhile, ETP was spreading money around in North Dakota. The company gave $5 million to the University of Mary's capital campaign for the engineering school, the campaign's single largest donation. State officials continued to try to recover costs associated with the pipeline and camps, particularly from the federal government. All together the state had spent around $38 million on its pipeline security response.[15] In August 2017 the Department of Justice awarded North Dakota $10 million to cover costs associated with the protests. Dakota Access, for its part, gave $15 million out of "generosity" to the state to help defer the cost of the response to the protests; a top Republican legislator admitted that the arrangement was unusual but still a boon to taxpayers.[16]

Spills, though, were a constant in the state: the counties that included Fort Berthold and Standing Rock were regularly seeing new spills of oil and hydraulic fuel, some of which were reportedly contained and some of which weren't. North Dakota still did not have meaningful standards for detecting and repairing leaks. (Instead it relied on federal standards: the EPA's New Source Performance Standards and similar standards by the Bureau of Land Management, which the Trump administration had fought.) As the months ticked by, spills continued to mount. In January 2018 cold temperatures helped contribute to a spill of 29,400 gallons of saltwater and 1,050 gallons of oil following a line freeze north of Killdeer; later that month there was a spill of more than 23,000 gallons of produced water and oil at a saltwater disposal well north of Killdeer. The DAPL itself experienced its first spill—a

placed each stone on Miles's grave. "To honor the dead," she explained, "you place rocks on the grave because they communicate with each other. Because another rock knows every heartache and pain a human being has ever suffered." Miles had collected the rocks himself from everywhere he had traveled, and she thought it appropriate to bring the rocks back to him. These rocks had history, and Sacred Stone itself was a place with a long history with rocks. The grave was also covered with offerings from visitors from around the world.

LaDonna took out a dish of red paint and spread it carefully on Miles' headstone. She used a sacred paint, made from red rocks from the Big Horn Mountains, part of the Sioux treaty territory. She dreamed, she said, that she had painted his headstone and so had come to follow the dream. "I'm a bad painter, Miles," she lamented. She felt him speaking to her as she painted.

The road that had once run through Sacred Stone Camp was so craggy and overgrown with prairie grasses and sage that it seemed impossible LaDonna's truck would make it through until the moment that it did. She passed the former epicenter of Sacred Stone, where the cooking fire had burned, the kitchen, the sacred fire, the temporary structures where the medics had worked—all now just memories whistling through the prairie grasses. She chuckled as she drove, remembering that the government had said the land was irreparably damaged, when in fact it had quickly regenerated, full of plants and other life.

The blue truck stopped at the former entrance to Oceti Sakowin, where "We are still here" was carved into wooden fence posts. A large blue and white "U.S. government property: No Trespassing" sign had been tacked onto another. LaDonna began to paint one post with her mixture of red rocks. Immediately she heard a noise above: a small plane was flying in circles over the site. In an area where seeing another car would have been remarkable, the sudden presence of a plane was almost unthinkable. But LaDonna was unfazed: "DAPL plane," she remarked dismissively. "They are always watching us." She returned to her truck, and it skidded in the rocks as she sped away, making haste for the reservation borders.

In January 2020 LaDonna underwent emergency brain surgery for stage 5 cancer—glioblastoma—followed by chemotherapy. She suspected that those who had been at the camps at Standing Rock were still suffering the aftereffects of poisoning. "Many people got sick with the DAPL cough. Many dogs and other animals died at camp. Then we had those who had miscarriage[s] and [babies that] died at birth. I know that it was DAPL that did this to us and I know people who came to camp suffered and still are with illnesses now. The glioblastoma brain tumor, stage 5 cancer, is not normal. We must not let DAPL get away with poison[ing] our people," she wrote on Facebook. She called on others to help her gather evidence.[21]

In May 2018 the IIYC was awarded the Robert F. Kennedy Human Rights Award, along with youth activist groups March for Our Lives, Color of Change, and United We Dream. On Monday, June 4, IIYC members boarded planes around the country to converge on the U.S. Capitol for the awards ceremony. They stayed in an Airbnb together.

The day of the awards ceremony was warm and sunny in Washington. President Trump had disinvited the Philadelphia Eagles football team from a White House visit that day, and that and new developments in the Mueller investigation of Russian interference into the 2016 U.S. elections dominated the news cycle. Inside the Russell Senate Building, through the marble halls, past offices with senators' names outside the doors, the award recipients were giddy as they were shepherded around. The Parkland, Florida, students who had arranged March for Our Lives had become overnight celebrities, and their familiar faces passed through the corridors.

The room in which the awards ceremony was held was stately—large chandeliers, colorful banners celebrating past awards recipients, a gilded ceiling. Some of the IIYC members milled around in the front before the ceremony with other recipients and Kennedy family members. Sage burned on the podium as an IIYC member presented a blessing, beating a drum and singing. When their turn came to speak, "We are living now," one IIYC member declared, "in the seventh generation. We will no longer follow our elders off of a cliff." They called on the adults in the room to clean up their own messes.

Jasilyn wasn't in Washington DC that day; she was home in Eagle Butte, gearing up for the fight over the Keystone XL Pipeline. She no longer considered herself a part of IIYC by the time the news of the award came in. She hadn't created it to have power, and she had stepped back after seeing that the members disagreed about money. She just wanted to focus on the pipelines. "You know, we don't need a trophy for us to understand what we did was real and awesome," she concluded. But she was proud of the IIYC.

"Birthing a movement is really hard; it takes a tremendous amount of energy," Jasilyn concluded. "I think that's the closest thing men can get to understanding childbirth. It gives them insight into how beautiful creation can be and also that it takes suffering and pain and work and dedication to really make that dream come true."

The pain of the closure of the camps at Standing Rock was still raw though. Recently Jasilyn had gone back to Standing Rock for the first time in months. She found it difficult to even get out of the car. She just sat inside and cried.

In addition to the lingering pain, the camp had changed Jasilyn fundamentally. In addition to becoming a well-known frontline activist, she was confident and determined. "I will never be the same girl I was when I first came to camp. I'll never be that person again because I'm not scared. I used to be, but then I found courage. My people gave me courage," she told journalists a few months after the camps closed. "I'm going to continue this fight, and I'm probably going to continue fighting for the rest of my life."[22]

The Keystone XL Pipeline was in "preconstruction." Jasilyn and Kalen had been talking to people about a possible camp—what, where, when, or who was going to be there first. They were enjoying the calm before the storm. The pipeline would be running near their home, a place they knew well, and they wanted to be prepared.

In late September 2018 Jasilyn and Kalen set out from Eagle Butte for a place just over the southern border of the reservation where "preconstruction" on the Keystone XL was taking place. The day was a bright Tuesday, warm and windy. The fields of sunflowers and corn glowed yellow as they drove out of town. They passed Bridger, a small valley community on the reservation where a resistance camp had been set up to fight Keystone XL back in 2015. The community wasn't keen to be proximate to a camp again, so Jasilyn, Kalen, and their friends were planning for it to be about twenty miles away on tribally owned land. They stopped briefly in Faith, a community just past the reservation line in South Dakota, to buy some snacks for the road. The white convenience store worker was chilly. "Not very friendly to Natives here. An old KKK town," Kalen remarked.

Jasilyn and Kalen pulled over as they approached a spot on the long, straight road. A small trailer was positioned next to mounds of earth and what appeared to be the beginnings of construction. Two pickup trucks with North Dakota plates were parked at the site. The landscape was one of wide sky, dramatic clouds, and windswept grass. "Minimum Maintenance: Travel at Your Own Risk" a yellow sign at the entrance read.

Jasilyn and Kalen scampered over the cattle guard that separated the site from the road. The visit was quick: they took a few pictures and turned around. Still, in the five minutes they were stopped, a silver SUV with South Dakota plates, driven by an older white man, did a quick U-turn on the road. He pulled up behind the car, taking photos of the license plates and of Jasilyn and Kalen before pulling off down the dirt road across from the site. Jasilyn and Kalen took it in stride.

On their way back to Eagle Butte, they stopped first at Kalen's aunt and uncle's house in the small community of Takini. Everyone there was a relative of Kalen's, and Kalen went back to Takini after camp closed. Kalen's father's house nearby existed off the grid, without running water or electricity.

Visiting Takini was always special to Jasilyn and Kalen. When Jasilyn miscarried, they buried their son nearby, in land that was now sacred to them. "I think about him sometimes," Jasilyn said. "I go visit him. I keep him in my mind. I know he'll come back to me when I'm ready."

Their son's grave was also not far from the prospective Keystone XL site, a fact that compounded their commitment to protecting the land. "We couldn't protect him when he was alive, but we can protect him now," Jasilyn said of her baby. "In our belief, he's part of the earth now. He's with his grandmother, the Mother Earth, and he's a part of her. And so we have to protect him and the water and the earth."

Chairman Harold Frazier knew that things were heating up with Keystone that fall. Conservatives were not pleased that almost two years after Trump had ordered the administration to proceed with the pipeline, it still had not been laid. There was a recent court decision out of Montana requiring that an EIS be conducted on the entire route, but Frazier saw a lot of movement on the construction sites in South Dakota. The tribe's opposition to the pipeline centered around the contamination of water. To him DAPL and Keystone XL weren't movements in and of themselves. They were just more battles to protect the tribe's way of life.

The tribe was still struggling, even without the pipeline to worry about. Part of the ceiling in Frazier's office had fallen down a few days earlier; there were twenty leaks at the school. Worse, tribal members were still attempting suicide. Frazier said that usually there were over twelve suicide attempts a month. In the past fourteen months there had been ten completions. Why? "Hopelessness, despair, nobody cares," he concluded.

Frazier thought reeducating people about their culture would help. He had met with groups of young people when he was first elected who said they wanted their culture back. He reflected: "That was one good thing about that camp up there [at Standing Rock]. I've seen a lot of these guys; they sobered up; they got away from drugs; they had a purpose. Now that it's over, what is there to do? You know, up there they were somebody, and now they're not, and that's kind of a hopeless feeling."

Jasilyn was continuing to work with the youth on the reservation. "I give them opportunities," she said, "and sometimes they take it, and sometimes they don't." She was preparing the youth for the Keystone xl fight and future battles.

The state also was preparing for a fight over the Keystone xl. In the wake of the Standing Rock standoff, pipeline camps sprang up around the country: in Minnesota around the Enbridge Line 3 Pipeline; in Louisiana around the Bayou Bridge Pipeline; and in numerous other places. Anti-protest bills like the ones in North Dakota had also been introduced into legislation around the country—some criminalizing the wearing of masks, others increasing penalties for riot offenses. In South Dakota legislators passed a vague law in March 2019 that would allow the state to sue people who encouraged violence at multi-person gatherings—"riot boosting" (a lawsuit by the aclu later led to a settlement in which South Dakota governor Kristi Noem agreed not to enforce parts of it). The legislation was a blatant attempt to ward off Indigenous protests against the Keystone xl, and in 2020 Noem signed a new law against "riot boosting."[23]

Jasilyn tried to motivate the youth, but it could be an uphill battle: "Working with Native American youth on the reservation and getting them motivated and inspired when they have an environment that was designed to keep them down and keep them oppressed is really hard; it's a struggle," she sighed. But for Jasilyn the struggle was for the very survival of her people, one that had to pull people out of their daily battles to live on the reservation: "We think to our rez lines; we don't think about the whole world; we're so trapped in our own little prison that we don't think about those things. But when something interrupts that cycle and it adds more bad shit, like drugs, human trafficking, and everything that comes up with man camps, it's going to make it even harder, and our youth are going to feel threatened." Jasilyn wanted her people and the youth to survive. "There are so many things the government has done to really eradicate us, and this is just another attempt to kill us off."

Jasilyn and Kalen were trying their best to watch over all of their loved ones. "Sometimes it feels like our best isn't good enough," she feared, "but you have to keep trying." Youth came to Jasilyn and Kalen for emotional support or if they needed to eat. It could be hard, and they needed space to breathe sometimes—from the drama and the death. Four of their friends had killed themselves in the last year.

Jasilyn continued to care deeply for her mother, though their relationship could be troubled. Her mother had a new boyfriend who worked doing day labor and helped to support her mother on the $80 a day he made, enough that they could have food or a decent beer. It gave Jasilyn a sense of relief that he was providing for her. Her own experience with addiction made her understand her mother's alcoholism better. "I can tell her I know it's hard; I know you're going through a really bad day and you just want a beer. But go for a walk; go visit people; have some coffee." She knew that if her mother was impatient or angry, her addiction was responsible. "When she is sober, she's a nice person. She's so loving and caring."

Kalen had been there for Jasilyn almost since she had gotten out of state care, as long as she had been free. He and his family had supported her in ways her own family couldn't. They weren't a couple any more, but they still spent every minute of every day together. The relationship was challenging to navigate. They had grown apart and become different people as they had grown older. Now they were getting to know each other again.

Jasilyn had been able to travel the country: California, Georgia, New York, Washington, Florida. She had traveled with a bus of youth to the Bayou Bridge Pipeline protest camp, the tail of the black snake in Louisiana. She had been to Hawaii to see where Indigenous groups were fighting the building of a thirty-meter telescope at Mauna Kea. She had visited other camps too, including one in the Black Hills that was taking a stand against uranium mining and gold exploration. She had tried fried frog legs in New Orleans (they tasted like chicken; she liked them) and a small piece of alligator burger. She and LaDonna had gotten tattoos together in Hawaii. Her life had taken an unexpected turn; she got emails from Shailene Woodley's mom. But Jasilyn remained humble and focused.

Jasilyn feared for her safety all the time, but weighing the risks and the threat to her future children, she decided that her work was more important than the fear. "Our ancestors went through a lot to make sure we were here today. They went through tremendous atrocities, but they stood up for what they thought was right and was in the best interest of their people," she concluded. Their struggles inspired her, gave her strength to live a life of activism, even when it was mentally and physically wearing. Wanikiya Win Loud Hawk, another water protector from Cheyenne River, agreed: "Every generation has to do something for their next seven generations to survive, you know? And I'm doing all I can do so that the next seven generations will still be here. If I don't try, then what's the purpose of living? What's the purpose of being Lakota?"

The specter of future pipelines haunted Jasilyn. She knew that the fights ahead would be hard and stressful. But she also knew that the man camp for the Keystone XL Pipeline construction was planned right near the rural community she knew so well in Takini—no gas station, no police, no hospital, just unprotected communities, with kids playing outside. She wanted her community to be safe.

The urgency of the climate change movement was also growing around her. As environmentalist Bill McKibben has written, "The momentum of the heating, and the momentum of the economy that powers it, can't be turned off quickly enough to prevent hideous damage. But we will keep fighting, in the hope that we can limit that damage. And in the process, with many others fighting similar battles, we'll help build the architecture for the world that comes next, the dispersed and localized societies that can survive the damage we can no longer prevent."[24] For many in the United States and worldwide, coming to terms with the crisis involved an altering of worldviews requiring radical changes.[25] For Jasilyn it meant being true to her ancestors.

Night had fallen by the time Jasilyn returned to Eagle Butte. A huge orange moon loomed over the horizon. She was tired, but she was still planning to have a talk with two local youths who had taken some money the previous night from her trusting and kind sister. And she was texting and calling other activists in her network, letting them know what they had seen and preparing for a meeting on Keystone XL the next day. Jasilyn was quiet for the first time all day.

Whether the next battle was over the Keystone XL or another pipeline in the future, Jasilyn, LaDonna, Lisa, and Kandi all knew that their fight would go on.

TransCanada, the company seeking to build the Keystone XL Pipeline, had recently written to Harold Frazier notifying him that it was preparing for construction. Frazier's reply was simple and spoke for many: "We will be waiting."[26]

# Afterword

It is a great victory, but we are not quite there yet. Not until every pipeline is shut down across the world.

—LaDonna Brave Bull Allard

We are all Indigenous; we all came from somewhere across this world. We all have a home that we need to protect. Educate yourself, find a water fight, find a fight near you—no matter what it is. Whether it be Black Lives Matter, whether it be DACA, whether it be fighting for water—join the fight. No person is so insignificant that their voice doesn't matter. Your voice matters and it's powerful. . . . If you do speak up and if your words fall on deaf ears, [they] will bounce into open hearts across the world because that's what happened at Standing Rock.

—Jasilyn Charger

The summer of 2020 was a time of deep unrest in America. The Covid-19 pandemic, which had led to lockdowns around the world and ravaged New York City in the spring, was still running rampant across the United States as case counts spiked in the South and West. Protests calling for racial justice following the killing of George Floyd by the Minneapolis police on May 26 had swept the country, forcing a national reckoning on race. On July 3 President Trump came to Mount Rushmore, in the Lakota heartland of the Black Hills—land that had been stolen from the Lakota. Jasilyn peacefully protested on the road to Mount Rushmore with the Cheyenne River Sioux Tribe. "Land back!" rang the calls of the protestors.[1] Nick Tilsen was arrested.

The faces of the four American presidents carved into the Black Hills looked down on Trump as he delivered a dark speech laced with fear and divisiveness. He declared that the monument would stand forever. "USA! USA!" the crowd chanted. America, Trump proclaimed, was "the most just and exceptional nation ever to exist on Earth."[2]

A few days later a federal court did indeed serve the water protectors with a stunning measure of justice. Judge Boasberg had in March struck down the DAPL's permits, determining that the Army Corps had not adequately considered the risks of the pipeline route under NEPA and ordering the Corps to conduct a full environmental review.[3] On Monday, July 6, Judge Boasberg ordered the pipeline shut down and emptied of oil while the Corps prepared its EIS. "Fearing severe environmental consequences, American Indian Tribes on nearby reservations have sought for several years to invalidate federal permits allowing the Dakota Access Pipeline to carry oil under the lake. Today they finally achieve that goal—at least for the time being," Judge Boasberg acknowledged in his opinion.[4]

The shutdown order was an unprecedented, hard-fought victory for the Standing Rock Sioux Tribe; additional tribes, including the Cheyenne River Sioux Tribe, that were involved in the legal battle; Indigenous organizers; and their attorneys. (The tribes had also received support from prominent members of Congress, including then-senator Kamala Harris, who had signed an amicus brief urging the shutdown of the pipeline during the EIS.)[5] The Standing Rock Sioux Tribe had voted every year since the camps closed to continue its fight against the pipeline.[6] "At any point along the process they truly could have reached accommodation that in exchange for funding [by Dakota Access of] some terrific new daycare center or health-care center or something, they would have dropped their opposition. There was never once any discussion of that," said Earthjustice attorney Jan Hasselman, who represented the tribe.[7] Their determination was inspiring to him. "It took four long years, but today justice has been served at Standing Rock," Hasselman concluded in a press release.[8]

ETP vowed to fight the DAPL ruling and expressed confidence that "oil will continue to flow."[9] Dakota Access immediately sought a stay of the order and filed an emergency motion asking to continue pipeline operations while it appealed the shutdown.[10] Ultimately it was successful in preventing the shutdown pending further litigation.

Still, some climate activists began to sense a turning point in their long fight against a fossil fuel–based infrastructure.[11] The Atlantic Coast Pipeline had also recently been canceled, and it seemed as if the combination of frontline action and legal strategy was proving successful in stalling pipelines and changing the national conversation.[12]

Kandi, LaDonna, Jasilyn, and Joye Braun joined together to celebrate the judge's shutdown order. They reminisced about the beginning of the camps. Kandi in particular was overjoyed. Her daughter Aiyana, now almost seven, joined the celebratory call for a moment, a visible reminder of the years that had passed since, as a three-year-old, she had marked Halloween in a tiny bumblebee costume at the camp. Kandi's young son was already walking. "It only took four years," Kandi laughed, "but here we are." Finally, they all began to see, their sacrifices on the front lines at Standing Rock had not been in vain.

While the water protectors had taken the cry of "Mni wiconi" to the world, the events of four years earlier continued to scar many lives. Some, including Red Fawn Fallis, were still in prison, where Covid-19 was running rampant. (Fallis was released to a reentry program in September 2020.) Other activists still felt as though they were under surveillance. LaDonna recognized that law enforcement officers' violent reaction to the water protectors had, in the years since, become a sort of playbook to attack other groups standing up for their rights across America. The "nonlethal" force that law enforcement officers used at Standing Rock had continued to gain traction as a means of crowd control, particularly in response to protests decrying police brutality and demanding racial justice.[13]

In a colorful headscarf following her recent chemotherapy treatments for brain cancer, LaDonna smiled. She thought back to the early days of 2016, when the water protectors were unsure of what would happen, and marveled at how theirs had become a global movement. The camp had created a new, enormous family around her; she had become a grandmother to everyone who had come to Sacred Stone. When she looked back on the camp, she thought, "It made me feel like, as a Native person, I am no longer invisible."

Jasilyn, in Takini, kept the story of the youth who came to Standing Rock alive in her heart. She had matured in the four years it had taken the pipeline case to wend its way through the courts. She had been almost a child when Sacred Stone Camp started. LaDonna, Joye Braun, and other mentors had changed her life. "I was on a bad road before," she acknowledged, but they helped her to a better one. "I have been walking ever since."

They all recognized that the pipeline battles would continue. "We are not quite there yet," LaDonna concluded. "Not until every pipeline is shut down across the world." "There's no stopping us," declared Kandi. This victory, though ephemeral, proved their collective strength. "It's for the next seven generations," Kandi said.[14]

On January 20, 2021, Joe Biden was inaugurated as the forty-sixth president of the United States. His first day in office, President Biden canceled the federal permit for the Keystone XL Pipeline to cross the Canada-U.S. border. He also quickly signed a series of executive orders related to the environment, including ones reviewing the Trump administration's actions on methane emissions and prioritizing an ambitious approach to environmental justice.[15]

Native voters were important in Biden's victories in the swing states of Arizona and Wisconsin.[16] He took early steps to honor that support, nominating Deb Haaland for the post of secretary of the interior and signing a presidential memorandum emphasizing tribal sovereignty.[17] If confirmed, Haaland, who is Laguna Pueblo, would be the first Native American secretary of the interior and the first Native American cabinet member. Haaland had visited the camps at Standing Rock, and many environmental groups and tribes supported her nomination.

"It's profound to think about the history of this country's policies to exterminate Native Americans and the resilience of our ancestors that gave me a place here today," Haaland said upon being nominated.[18] President Biden's administration had the potential to be a new era when Indigenous voices demanding full recognition of their treaty and land rights, climate justice, and a just transition might be heard.

Dallas Goldtooth of IEN called the Keystone XL cancelation "a vindication of 10 years defending our waters and treaty rights from this tar sands carbon bomb."[19] Kandi thought there was no question activists were seeing a sea change on pipelines, and that the movement against the DAPL had contributed to Biden shutting down the Keystone XL. Politicians were recognizing that large numbers of people believed in a transition away from fossil fuels and cared deeply about protecting the land. "People are still out there willing to put themselves on the line to fight and defend the planet and the future," she observed. Indeed, Jasilyn was facing a possible year of incarceration following her arrest for locking down in opposition to Keystone XL construction in November.

But even as this great environmental battle was settled, other crucial ones remained, notably over the DAPL and the Line 3 Pipeline, an expansion of which was planned to cross from Canada to Minnesota. The water protectors knew that a final decision on the DAPL would likely be a political one. Judge Boasberg's July order closing the pipeline, even if it had gone into effect, had never been intended by the court to be permanent. It had been intended to last while the Army Corps was preparing a full environmental review and deciding whether the pipeline should cross under the Missouri River at Lake Oahe; the Corps would do so during the Biden-Harris administration.

President Biden was under pressure from all sides. Moderate Democratic senator Joe Manchin, the chairman of the Senate Energy Committee, criticized Biden's decision on Keystone XL, arguing that pipelines were the safest way to bring oil to market. Some union leaders also opposed shutting down the pipeline.[20]

The winter had been a brutal one. The Covid-19 pandemic had taken a terrible toll on Native nations as it surged across the country, with the death toll especially devastating on reservations in North and South Dakota; Standing Rock suffered severe losses.[21]

But Native American activists were again rallying for a fight around the DAPL. A group of seventy-five Indigenous women leaders—including LaDonna and Kandi—signed a letter in the days preceding Biden's inauguration calling on him to shut down the Keystone XL, DAPL, and Line 3 pipeline projects.[22] Calls to shut down the DAPL had come from the Standing Rock, Cheyenne River, and Oglala Sioux Tribes, supported by additional tribal organizations, Indigenous advocates, prominent actors, and members of Congress.[23]

On February 9, 2021—the day Trump's second impeachment trial commenced in the U.S. Senate—a group of twenty runners from the Cheyenne River and Standing Rock Sioux Tribes set out on the ninety-three-mile run from Cheyenne River to Cannon Ball to again raise awareness about the pipeline battle. Many of the faces, slightly older, were familiar from the youth runs four years earlier—Joseph White Eyes led off the run at the Cheyenne River border, followed by Bobbi Jean Three Legs. The temperature that morning was negative eighteen degrees Fahrenheit, and their eyelashes frosted over from the cold. They held the staff they had carried on their run to Washington DC in summer 2016.

At the time of this writing, the DAPL was operating without a permit, pending further litigation and assessment. On January 26, 2021, a federal appeals court held that the pipeline required a full EIS to consider the risks the pipeline posed to the tribe and to evaluate alternate routes. The court declined to shut down the pipeline while the environmental review took place, but it speculated that the Army Corps might need to consider doing so to "vindicate its property rights."[24] U.S. district judge James Boasberg gave the Army Corps until February 10 to explain how it would deal with the pipeline given that it now lacked a permit for the essential river crossing. The Army Corps requested more time to consider and to brief new administration officials, and the judge granted its request.[25] The Army Corps could choose to shut down the pipeline while the environmental review was underway; when the EIS was complete, it would decide anew whether to permit the pipeline to cross under Lake Oahe.

Water protectors were confident that one day the pipeline would be ripped from the ground.

# Acknowledgments

First and foremost, my thanks go to all the individuals who visited and generously shared their stories with me: Trey Adcock, Dave Archambault, Kalen Bald Eagle, Joye Braun, LaDonna Brave Bull Allard, Andreanne Catt, Jasilyn Charger, Jordan Daniel, Lisa DeVille, Walter DeVille, Nicole Donaghy, Kathy Eagle, John Floberg, Mark Fox, Harold Frazier, Carol Gallagher, Emily Gallagher, Francis Joseph Giles, Danny Grassrope, Jan Hasselman, Simone Johnson, Waniya Locke, Wanikiya Win Loud Hawk, Bill McKibben, Sheldon Nez, Alethea Phillips, Nathan Phillips, Tim Purdon, Ta'Sina Sapa Win, Marco Simmons, Josephine Thundershield, Nick Tilsen, Cody Two Bears, Donald Warne, Kandi (Mossett) White, Joseph White Eyes, Dave Williams, Dana Yellow Fat, Phyllis Young, and others who wished to remain unnamed. Without all of your guidance and wisdom, this book would have been impossible.

To the four women on whose lives I focus in this work—Lisa DeVille, Jasilyn Charger, LaDonna Brave Bull Allard, and Kandi White—I cannot tell you how much I admire you. I am immensely grateful to you for sharing your stories; for opening your homes; for generously responding to my calls, emails, and questions; and, above all, for devoting your lives to this important work. I hope that these pages do justice to this small part of each of your incredible stories. Thank you for fighting every day for water, for health, for sovereignty, and for human rights.

To the water protectors, past and present, named in this book and unnamed, who have faced unimaginable hardships to fight for the water—thank you all. I hope that this book is a small contribution to remembering your courageous fight.

Huge thanks to my tireless agent, Gail Hochman, for believing in the importance of this project and fighting to see it in print. Many thanks also to the entire University of Nebraska Press team. This book benefited immeasurably from exceptional feedback from my editor at the press, Bridget Barry, and from the thoughtful comments of Dina Gilio-Whitaker and Madonna Thunder Hawk. I deeply appreciate all of your guidance. Sara Springsteen and Heather Stauffer at the University of Nebraska Press expertly guided the manuscript into production. I am very grateful to Bojana Ristich for stellar copyediting. It was a pleasure to work with Erin Greb on the map, and I am grateful to all of the exceptional photographers whose work is included here and brings to life the stories the book tells.

Thank you to all of my wonderful friends and extended family in Brooklyn and beyond for being so supportive of my work and for always being ready for another conversation about fracking. Special thanks to Joe Amon for helping to guide me to this topic.

I could never have written this book without my indefatigable mother, Candace O'Connor. She accompanied me on two extended research trips to North and South Dakota, ferrying me in our little Prius from one interview to another, only to be thanked by my endless requests for advice and editing. I can't thank you enough. My father, Bob Wiltenburg, was also an invaluable reader of drafts. More than anything, though, thank you both for always teaching me to speak out against injustice. My huge thanks also to Mary, Karol, Steve, and Mark for all of your support over the years.

To Alex and Eliza, my inspiration and my loves: this book is for you. You understand already what it has taken many of us decades to learn: the importance of caring for this fragile world. Everything I do is to try to make it a better one for you.

And finally to Eric: you make everything possible with your support, your encouragement, and your love.

# Notes

INTRODUCTION

Research for this book included dozens of interviews over a period of several years. For purposes of readability, these interviews are not individually cited in the text. Individual interviews (in some cases multiple interviews) were conducted with the following: Trey Adcock, Chairman Dave Archambault, Kalen Bald Eagle, Joye Braun, LaDonna Brave Bull Allard, Andreanne Catt, Jasilyn Charger, Jordan Daniel, Lisa DeVille, Walter DeVille, Nicole Donaghy, Dr. Kathy Eagle, Rev. John Floberg, Chairman Mark Fox, Chairman Harold Frazier, Dr. Carol Gallagher, Emily Gallagher, Francis Joseph Giles, Danny Grassrope, Jan Hasselman, Simone Johnson, Waniya Locke, Wanikiya Win Loud Hawk, Bill McKibben, Sheldon Nez, Alethea Phillips, Nathan Phillips, Tim Purdon, Ta'Sina Sapa Win, Marco Simmons, Josephine Thundershield, Nick Tilsen, Cody Two Bears, Dr. Donald Warne, Kandi (Mossett) White, Joseph White Eyes, Dave Williams, Dana Yellow Fat, Phyllis Young, and others who wished their comments to remain on background.

Epigraph: "White House Meeting with County Sheriffs," C-SPAN, February 7, 2017, https://www.c-span.org/video/?423663-1/president-trump-holds -listening-session-county-sheriffs. See also "Trump: 'Haven't Had One Call' Complaining about Dakota Pipeline," ABC News, https://abcnews.go.com /Politics/video/trump-havent-call-complaining-dakota-pipeline-45331538 (accessed October 2020).

1. North Dakota Census Office, *Growing ND by the Numbers*, February 2017, https:// commerce.nd.gov/uploads/8/CensusNewsletterFeb2015.pdf.
2. Debra Utacia Krol, "Life Expectancy Falling in U.S.—But in Tribal Communities, Not So Much," *Indian Country Today*, May 11, 2017, https://newsmaven .io/indiancountrytoday/archive/life-expectancy-falling-in-us-but-in-tribal -communities-not-so-much-nh_16pV-I0i_cY8vNKmGgA.
3. United States v. Sioux Nation of Indians, 448 U.S. 371, 388 (1980).

4. Edward Lazarus, *Black Hills White Justice: The Sioux Nation versus the United States 1775 to the Present* (New York: HarperCollins, 1991).

5. As scholar Nick Estes has explained, the Sioux Nation did not cede 1851 Fort Laramie Treaty lands under the 1868 Fort Laramie Treaty (or other treaties), and it also retained water rights from the 1851 treaty that gave it jurisdiction over the proposed crossing at the Missouri River. Nick Estes, "'The Supreme Law of the Land': Standing Rock and the Dakota Access Pipeline," *Indian Country Today*, January 16, 2017, https://indiancountrytoday.com/archive /the-supreme-law-of-the-land-standing-rock-and-the-dakota-access-pipeline -25phRkIJB0GmipEDLvPLPw.

6. U.S. Department of Transportation Pipeline and Hazardous Materials Safety Administration, *Pipeline Basics*, https://primis.phmsa.dot.gov/comm /PipelineBasics.htm (accessed October 2020).

7. Pipeline and Hazardous Materials Safety Administration, *Data and Statistics Overview*, https://www.phmsa.dot.gov/data-and-statistics/pipeline/data-and -statistics-overview (accessed February 2021).

8. Dakota Access, LLC, "Dakota Access Pipeline Project: North Dakota Public Service Commission Combined Application for Certificate of Corridor Compatibility and Route Permit," December 2014, https://psc.nd.gov/database /documents/14-0842/001-030.pdf.

9. Naomi Klein, *This Changes Everything: Capitalism vs. the Climate* (New York: Simon and Schuster Paperbacks, 2014).

10. Quoted in Devin Leonard, "The Billionaire behind the Dakota Access Pipeline Is a Little Lonely," *Bloomberg Businessweek*, March 27, 2019, https://www .bloomberg.com/news/features/2019-03-27/the-billionaire-behind-the-dakota -access-pipeline-is-a-little-lonely.

11. Energy Transfer LP, "Dakota Access Pipeline," https://daplpipelinefacts.com (accessed October 2020).

12. U.S. Environmental Protection Agency, "Environmental Justice," https://www .epa.gov/environmentaljustice (accessed October 2020).

13. Winona LaDuke, *All Our Relations: Native Struggles for Land and Life* (Cambridge MA: South End Press, 1999).

14. Dina Gilio-Whitaker has argued that settler colonialism is itself a structure of environmental injustice, and the mainstream environmental movement participates in settler colonialism when excluding Indigenous people. Gilio-Whitaker identifies Indigenous approaches to environmental justice in Indian Country and posits that "Indigenous peoples' pursuit of environmental justice (EJ) requires the use of a different lens, one with a scope that can accommodate the full weight

of the history of settler colonialism, on one hand, and embrace differences in the ways Indigenous peoples view land and nature, on the other." *As Long as Grass Grows: The Indigenous Fight for Environmental Justice, from Colonization to Standing Rock* (Boston: Beacon Press, 2019). Additional scholars have also grappled with Indigenous environmental justice. See, for example, Traci Brynne Voyles, *Wastlanding: Legacies of Uranium Mining in Navajo Country* (Minneapolis: University of Minnesota Press, 2015); Elizabeth Hoover, *The River Is in Us: Fighting Toxics in a Mohawk Community*, 3rd ed. (Minneapolis: University of Minnesota Press, 2017); Beth Rose Middleton, *Trust in the Land: New Directions in Tribal Conservation* (Tucson: University of Arizona Press, 2011); and Kari Marie Norgaard, *Salmon and Acorns Feed Our People: Colonialism, Nature, and Social Action* (New Brunswick NJ: Rutgers University Press, 2019).

15. Quoted in Earthjustice, "In Conversation: Standing with Standing Rock," March 22, 2017, https://earthjustice.org/features/teleconference-standing-rock.

16. Barack Obama, "How to Make This Moment the Turning Point for Real Change," *Medium*, June 1, 2020, https://medium.com/@BarackObama/how-to-make -this-moment-the-turning-point-for-real-change-9fa209806067.

17. Obama, "How to Make This Moment the Turning Point for Real Change"; emphasis in original.

18. Nick Estes, *Our History Is the Future: Standing Rock Versus the Dakota Access Pipeline, and the Long Tradition of Indigenous Resistance* (London and New York: Verso, 2019).

19. Rebecca Solnit, "Standing Rock Inspired Ocasio-Cortez to Run. That's the Power of Protest," *The Guardian*, January 14, 2019, https://www.theguardian .com/commentisfree/2019/jan/14/standing-rock-ocasio-cortez-protest-climate -activism.

20. Roxanne Dunbar-Ortiz, *An Indigenous Peoples' History of the United States* (Boston: Beacon Press, 2014).

21. Dunbar-Ortiz, *An Indigenous Peoples' History of the United States.*

22. Energy Transfer LP, "Dakota Access Pipeline."

23. Reuters Staff, "Energy Transfer Projects Expanded Dakota Access Pipeline to Operate Late Next Year," Reuters, September 8, 2020, https://www.reuters .com/article/us-usa-pipeline-dakota-access/energy-transfer-projects-expanded -dakota-access-pipeline-to-operate-late-next-year-idUSKBN26000P; Adam Willis, "With a Green Light in Illinois, Dakota Access Pipeline Clears Final Barrier to Double Its Capacity," *Grand Forks Herald*, October 15, 2020, https:// www.grandforksherald.com/business/energy-and-mining/6718963-With-a

-green-light-in-Illinois-Dakota-Access-Pipeline-clears-final-barrier-to-double
-its-capacity.

24. Lisa Coleman, PR and Communications, Energy Transfer, email to Katherine Todrys, June 10, 2020.

25. Jan Hasselman, "DAPL Update: Tribe Asks Court to Shut Down DAPL Due to Failed Remand; Massive Pipeline Expansion Planned," Earthjustice, March 18, 2020, https://earthjustice.org/features/dakota-access-pipeline-legal-explainer -remand.

26. See, for example, David Abel, "Legacy of Seabrook Nuclear Protest Debated," *Boston Globe*, April 28, 2017, https://www.bostonglobe.com/metro/2017 /04/28/forty-years-later-nuclear-power-opponents-mull-results-their-fight /fsBR6Hokv8Pfs8yTvvJuIL/story.html.

27. Quoted in Joe Whittle, "'We Opened Eyes': At Standing Rock, My Fellow Native Americans Make History," *The Guardian*, November 30, 2016, https://www .theguardian.com/us-news/2016/nov/30/standing-rock-indigenous-people -history-north-dakota-access-pipeline-protest.

28. Throughout this book Lisa DeVille, Jasilyn Charger, LaDonna Allard, Kandi White, and their immediate family members are referred to by first names for clarity.

## 1. OIL PRODUCTION IN THE BAKKEN

Epigraph: MHA Nation Energy Division, "Keepers of the Bakken—Sovereignty by the Barrel," July 2013, https://docplayer.net/39752136-July-2013-three -affiliated-tribes-fort-berthold-reservation-keepers-of-the-bakken-sovereignty -by-the-barrel.html.

1. U.S. Energy Information Administration, "Oil: Crude and Petroleum Products Explained," May 29, 2018, https://www.eia.gov/energyexplained/index.cfm.

2. North Dakota Department of Mineral Resources, "ND Monthly Bak-ken Oil Production Statistics," https://www.dmr.nd.gov/oilgas/stats /historicalbakkenoilstats.pdf (accessed January 2020).

3. Dee DePass, "North Dakota Oil Production Has Record May," *Minnesota Star Tribune*, July 13, 2018, http://www.startribune.com/north-dakota-oil-production -has-record-may/488144051.

4. Robert Krulwich, "A Mysterious Patch of Light Shows Up in the North Dakota Dark," NPR, January 16, 2013, https://www.npr.org/sections/krulwich/2013/01 /16/169511949/a-mysterious-patch-of-light-shows-up-in-the-north-dakota-dark.

5. Deborah Sontag and Robert Gebeloff, "The Downside of the Boom," *New York Times*, November 22, 2014, https://www.nytimes.com/interactive/2014/11/23/us/north-dakota-oil-boom-downside.html.

6. Stephen Moore, "How North Dakota Became Saudi Arabia," *Wall Street Journal*, October 1, 2011, https://www.wsj.com/articles/SB10001424052970204226204576602524023932438.

7. North Dakota Department of Mineral Resources, "North Dakota Historical Monthly Oil Production," https://www.dmr.nd.gov/oilgas/stats/stateoilchart.pdf (accessed January 2020).

8. James MacPherson, "Burgum: Higher Revenue Doesn't Wipe Away Budget Challenges," *U.S. News and World Report*, September 5, 2018, https://www.usnews.com/news/best-states/north-dakota/articles/2018-09-05/burgum-higher-revenue-doesnt-wipe-away-budget-challenges.

9. Curt Brown, "While North Dakota Embraces the Oil Boom, Tribal Members Ask Environmental Questions," *Minnesota Star Tribune*, February 25, 2014, http://www.startribune.com/n-d-tribal-members-question-oil-boom-s-effects-on-sacred-land/233854981.

10. Emily Arasim and Osprey Orielle Lake, "Women on the Front Lines Fighting Fracking in the Bakken Oil Shale Formations," *EcoWatch*, March 12, 2016, https://www.ecowatch.com/women-on-the-front-lines-fighting-fracking-in-the-bakken-oil-shale-for-1882188778.html.

11. David Treuer, *The Heartbeat of Wounded Knee: Native America from 1890 to Present* (New York: Riverhead Books, 2019); Mandan, Hidatsa and Arikara Nation, "MHA Nation History," https://www.mhanation.com/history (accessed January 2020).

12. State Historical Society of North Dakota, "Section 2: Mandan, Hidatsa, Arikara," *North Dakota Studies*, 2018, http://www.ndstudies.org/resources/IndianStudies/threeaffiliated/historical_laws.html.

13. Vine Deloria, *Custer Died for Your Sins: An Indian Manifesto* (Norman: University of Oklahoma Press, 1969); Russell Means and Marvin J. Wolf, *Where White Men Fear to Tread: The Autobiography of Russell Means* (New York: St. Martin's Griffin, 1995).

14. *Flood Control Act of 1944*, Pub. L. 78-534, 58 Stat. 887, 1944.

15. Estes, *Our History Is the Future*.

16. Hearing before the Committee on Indian Affairs, U.S. Senate, "Rural Health Care Facility on the Fort Berthold Indian Reservation," S. Hrg. 108-164, June 11, 2003, https://www.gpo.gov/fdsys/pkg/CHRG-108shrg87959/pdf/CHRG

-108shrg87959.pdf. The tribe initially received $12.6 million in compensation for its flooded lands, with an additional $149.2 million in the 1990s. "Impact of the Flood Control Act of 1944 on Indian Tribes along the Missouri River before the S. Comm. on Indian Affairs," 110th Cong. 4, November 1, 2007, https://www .indian.senate.gov/sites/default/files/upload/files/November12007.pdf.

17. Curt Brown, "While North Dakota Embraces the Oil Boom, Tribal Members Ask Environmental Questions."

18. U.S. Senate, "Final Report and Recommendations of the Garrison Unit Joint Tribal Advisory Committee, Joint Hearing before the Select Committee on Indian Affairs," March 30, 1987, https://babel.hathitrust.org/cgi/pt?id=pur1 .32754074491261;view=1up;seq=12.

19. Hearing before the Committee on Indian Affairs, U.S. Senate, "Rural Health Care Facility on the Fort Berthold Indian Reservation."

20. MHA Nation, "A Resolution Entitled, 'Approval of Oil and Gas Tax Agreement between the Three Affiliated Tribes and the State of North Dakota,'" Resolution No. 08-88-VJB, May 29, 2008, https://static1.squarespace.com/static /5a5fab0832601e33d9f68fde/t/5b1acd2e2b6a282a6136fb5a/1528483119422 /08-088-VJB.pdf.

21. Sierra Crane-Murdoch, "The Other Bakken Boom: America's Biggest Oil Rush Brings Tribal Conflict," *High Country News*, April 23, 2012, https://www.hcn .org/issues/44.6/on-the-fort-berthold-reservation-the-bakken-boom-brings -conflict.

22. Abrahm Lustgarten, "Land Grab Cheats North Dakota Tribes Out of $1 Billion, Suits Allege," *ProPublica*, February 23, 2013, https://www.propublica.org /article/land-grab-cheats-north-dakota-tribes-out-of-1-billion-suits-allege; George Lerner and Christof Putzel, "Tribal Environmental Director: 'We Are Not Equipped' for N.D. Oil Boom," Al Jazeera America, May 16, 2015, http:// america.aljazeera.com/watch/shows/america-tonight/articles/2015/5/16 /tribal-environmental-director-we-are-not-equipped-for-nd-oil-boom.html.

23. The U.S. government administers its obligations to Native peoples through the BIA, once a part of the War Department and now part of the Department of the Interior.

24. Two Shields v. United States, U.S. Court of Appeals for the Federal Circuit, April 27, 2016, http://www.cafc.uscourts.gov/sites/default/files/opinions-orders/15 -5069.Opinion.4-25-2016.1.PDF.

25. Quoted in MHA Nation Energy Division, "Keepers of the Bakken."

26. Tallsalt Advisors, "NDIC FBIR Well Production for 959 Active Horizontal Wells on *FBIR* Based on Enerdeq 4/3/2014," April 8, 2014, https://static1.squarespace

.com/static/5a5fab0832601e33d9f68fde/t/5b86ae42898583f96a0bda58
/1535553092370/NDIC+FBIR+Well+Production+2014-08-04+A.pdf.

27. Eloise Ogden, "North Dakota's Oil Production Remains High," *Minot Daily News*, April 8, 2017, http://www.minotdailynews.com/special-sections/progress /2017/energy-industry/2017/04/north-dakotas-oil-production-remains-high.

28. U.S. Energy Information Administration, *Crude Oil Production*, October 31, 2018, https://www.eia.gov/dnav/pet/pet_crd_crpdn_adc_mbblpd_m.htm.

29. Three Affiliated Tribes, Mandan, Hidatsa, and Arikara Nation Office of Tribal Enrollment, "Three Affiliated Tribes Enrollment Report," November 9, 2018, https://static1.squarespace.com/static/5a5fab0832601e33d9f68fde /t/5beae9be88251b70dd9523e5/1542121919906/TAT+Census+Summary +-+November+9+2018.pdf.

30. Mark N. Fox, "Strategic Highway Safety Plan," http://chairmanfox.com/2017 /11/17/strategic-highway-safety-plan (accessed June 2020).

31. Dakota Access, LLC, "Dakota Access Pipeline Project"; U.S. Department of Transportation, "Pocket Guide to Large Truck and Bus Statistics," October 1, 2014, https://rosap.ntl.bts.gov/view/dot/170.

32. MHA Nation, "Strategic Highway Safety Plan," http://fortbertholdplan.org /safety (accessed June 2020).

33. Carol A. Archbold, "'Policing the Patch': An Examination of the Impact of the Oil Boom on Small Town Policing and Crime in Western North Dakota," August 2013, https://www.google.com/url?sa=t&rct=j&q=&esrc=s&source= web&cd=&ved=2ahUKEwi43a-8cDsAhU_lXIEHZuoA7cQFjAAegQIBBAC &url=https%3A%2F%2Fwww.aamva.org%2FWorkArea%2FDownloadAsset .aspx%3Fid%3D5533&usg=AOvVaw0FFGDBbcGoUHNjyvdk_ByN.

34. "Episode 4: Native American Boomtown," *America by the Numbers with Maria Hinojosa*, PBS, October 23, 2014, https://www.pbs.org/wgbh/america-by-the -numbers/episodes/episode-104.

35. Kandi Mossett, "Kandi Mossett: Standing against Big Oil to Defend the Earth, Water and Indigenous Communities," Bioneers Conference, 2017, https:// bioneers.org/kandi-mossett-standing-big-oil-defend-earth-water-indigenous -communities-ztvz1801.

36. Sari Horwitz, "Dark Side of the Boom," *Washington Post*, September 28, 2014, http://www.washingtonpost.com/sf/national/2014/09/28/dark-side-of-the -boom.

37. State of North Dakota Office of the Attorney General, "Statewide Crime Statistics," November 16, 2018, http://crimestats.nd.gov/public/View/dispview .aspx?ReportId=3.

38. Nikke Alex, "Dark Side of Oil Development: Bakken Oil Boom Pumping Sexual Violence into Fort Berthold Reservation," *Last Real Indians*, January 20, 2015, https://lastrealindians.com/news/2015/1/20/jan-20-2015-dark-side-of-oil -development-bakken-oil-boom-pumping-sexual-violence-into-fort-berthold -reservation-by-nikke-alex.

39. "Episode 4: Native American Boomtown."

40. Damon Buckley, "Firsthand Account of Man Camp in North Dakota from Local Tribal Cop," *Lakota Country Today*, May 5, 2014, lakotacountrytimes.com.

41. "Episode 4: Native American Boomtown."

42. "Episode 4: Native American Boomtown."

43. Amy Dalrymple, "Enerplus Lets School Adopt-A-Well," *Dickinson Press*, March 8, 2013, https://www.thedickinsonpress.com/business/1823551-enerplus-lets -school-adopt-well.

44. Shelley Lenz, "Homegrown Stories Episode 10 with Lisa Finley DeVille," June 4, 2020, https://www.youtube.com/watch?v=9Pzsjea6JnU.

45. Lisa Finley-DeVille, "Letters to the Editor: Tribal Workers Lose Their Jobs," *Bismarck Tribune*, December 7, 2010, https://bismarcktribune.com/news/opinion /mailbag/article_f27844ce-018a-11e0-adb7-001cc4c002e0.html.

46. A. Dalrymple, "Tribes Collect Millions in Oil Revenue: Three Affiliated Tribes Set to Collect $184 Million in Revenue; Money to Be Used for Infrastructure," Bakken.com, April 24, 2014, http://bakken.com/news/id/148702/tribes-collect -millions-oil-revenue-three-affiliated-tribes-set-collect-184-million-revenue -money-used-infrastructure.

47. Deborah Sontag and Brent McDonald, "In North Dakota, a Tale of Oil, Corruption and Death," *New York Times*, December 28, 2014, https://www.nytimes.com /2014/12/29/us/in-north-dakota-where-oil-corruption-and-bodies-surface .html.

48. Stephen Hill, "Investigative Report on Tex Hall," 2014. See also "Episode 4: Native American Boomtown."

49. Quoted in Sontag and McDonald, "In North Dakota, a Tale of Oil, Corruption and Death."

50. Three Affiliated Tribes, "Resolution of the Governing Body of the Three Affiliated Tribes of the Fort Berthold Indian Reservation: 'Establishment of Ethics Committee Budget, Clerk, and Submission of Pending Ethics Complaints,'" Resolution No. 15-009-LKH, February 11, 2015, https://static1.squarespace.com/static /5a5fab0832601e33d9f68fde/t/5b05b0d91ae6cf654a57023f/1527099618475 /15-009-LKH.pdf.

51. Hill, "Investigative Report on Tex Hall."

38. Nikke Alex, "Dark Side of Oil Development: Bakken Oil Boom Pumping Sexual Violence into Fort Berthold Reservation," *Last Real Indians*, January 20, 2015, https://lastrealindians.com/news/2015/1/20/jan-20-2015-dark-side-of-oil -development-bakken-oil-boom-pumping-sexual-violence-into-fort-berthold -reservation-by-nikke-alex.

39. "Episode 4: Native American Boomtown."

40. Damon Buckley, "Firsthand Account of Man Camp in North Dakota from Local Tribal Cop," *Lakota Country Today*, May 5, 2014, lakotacountrytimes.com.

41. "Episode 4: Native American Boomtown."

42. "Episode 4: Native American Boomtown."

43. Amy Dalrymple, "Enerplus Lets School Adopt-A-Well," *Dickinson Press*, March 8, 2013, https://www.thedickinsonpress.com/business/1823551-enerplus-lets -school-adopt-well.

44. Shelley Lenz, "Homegrown Stories Episode 10 with Lisa Finley DeVille," June 4, 2020, https://www.youtube.com/watch?v=9Pzsjea6JnU.

45. Lisa Finley-DeVille, "Letters to the Editor: Tribal Workers Lose Their Jobs," *Bismarck Tribune*, December 7, 2010, https://bismarcktribune.com/news/opinion /mailbag/article_f27844ce-018a-11e0-adb7-001cc4c002e0.html.

46. A. Dalrymple, "Tribes Collect Millions in Oil Revenue: Three Affiliated Tribes Set to Collect $184 Million in Revenue; Money to Be Used for Infrastructure," Bakken.com, April 24, 2014, http://bakken.com/news/id/148702/tribes-collect -millions-oil-revenue-three-affiliated-tribes-set-collect-184-million-revenue -money-used-infrastructure.

47. Deborah Sontag and Brent McDonald, "In North Dakota, a Tale of Oil, Corruption and Death," *New York Times*, December 28, 2014, https://www.nytimes.com /2014/12/29/us/in-north-dakota-where-oil-corruption-and-bodies-surface .html.

48. Stephen Hill, "Investigative Report on Tex Hall," 2014. See also "Episode 4: Native American Boomtown."

49. Quoted in Sontag and McDonald, "In North Dakota, a Tale of Oil, Corruption and Death."

50. Three Affiliated Tribes, "Resolution of the Governing Body of the Three Affiliated Tribes of the Fort Berthold Indian Reservation: 'Establishment of Ethics Committee Budget, Clerk, and Submission of Pending Ethics Complaints,'" Resolution No. 15-009-LKH, February 11, 2015, https://static1.squarespace.com/static /5a5fab0832601e33d9f68fde/t/5b05b0d91ae6cf654a57023f/1527099618475 /15-009-LKH.pdf.

51. Hill, "Investigative Report on Tex Hall."

52. Sontag and McDonald, "In North Dakota, a Tale of Oil, Corruption and Death."

53. Sontag and McDonald, "In North Dakota, a Tale of Oil, Corruption and Death."

54. Tracy Simmons, "North Dakota Oil Truck Operator Gets Life Term for Two Contract Killings," Reuters, May 24, 2016, https://www.reuters.com/article/us -northdakota-murders/north-dakota-oil-truck-operator-gets-life-term-for-two -contract-killings-idUSKCN0YF1AJ.

55. Amy Dalrymple, "No Jail Time for Woman Connected to Bakken Murder-for-Hire Plot," *Dickinson Press*, June 6, 2017, http://www.thedickinsonpress.com /news/crime-and-courts/4278836-no-jail-time-woman-connected-bakken -murder-hire-plot.

56. Hill, "Investigative Report on Tex Hall."

57. Jenni Monet, "The Crisis in Covering Indian Country," *Columbia Journalism Review*, March 29, 2019, https://www.cjr.org/opinion/indigenous-journalism -erasure.php.

58. *Four Bears Segment December 2013 Newsletter*, December 2013.

59. Sontag and McDonald, "In North Dakota, a Tale of Oil, Corruption and Death."

60. Quoted in Sontag and McDonald, "In North Dakota, a Tale of Oil, Corruption and Death."

61. Brad Plumer, "The Battle over the Dakota Access Pipeline, Explained," *Vox*, November 29, 2016, https://www.vox.com/2016/9/9/12862958/dakota-access -pipeline-fight.

62. Dakota Access, LLC, "Dakota Access Pipeline Project."

2. PIPELINES AND POWER

1. Sontag and McDonald, "In North Dakota, a Tale of Oil, Corruption and Death."

2. Quoted in Sontag and McDonald, "In North Dakota, a Tale of Oil, Corruption and Death."

3. Antonia Juhasz, "From North Dakota to Paris with Love," *Newsweek Magazine*, November 25, 2015, http://www.newsweek.com/2015/12/04/north-dakota -paris-love-397895.html.

4. *MHA Times* channel, "Saltwater Spill Clean Up Near Mandaree, ND," July 15, 2014, https://www.youtube.com/watch?v=RDHdnWhU874.

5. Quoted in Lerner and Putzel, "Tribal Environmental Director: 'We Are Not Equipped' for N.D. Oil Boom."

6. Amy Sisk, "Upstream from Standing Rock, Tribes Balance Benefits, Risks of Oil Industry," NPR, November 24, 2016, https://www.npr.org/2016/11/24 /503212965/upstream-from-standing-rock-tribes-balance-benefits-risks-of -oil-industry.

7. Lisa Coleman, PR and Communications, Energy Transfer, email to Katherine Todrys.

8. See, for example, Energy Transfer LP, "Dakota Access Pipeline"; Energy Transfer, *Energy Transfer's Fact Checker Blog*, https://energytransferfacts.com (accessed June 2020).

9. Dakota Access, LLC, "Dakota Access Pipeline Project."

10. Energy Transfer LP, "Corporate Overview," http://www.energytransfer.com /company_overview.aspx (accessed December 2019).

11. "#159 Kelcy Warren," *Forbes*, https://www.forbes.com/profile/kelcy-warren (accessed January 2020).

12. Devin Leonard, "The Billionaire behind the Dakota Access Pipeline Is a Little Lonely," *Bloomberg Businessweek*, March 27, 2019, https://www.bloomberg.com /news/features/2019-03-27/the-billionaire-behind-the-dakota-access-pipeline -is-a-little-lonely.

13. Brian Gehring, "7 Oil Companies Charged with Killing Migratory Birds," *Bismarck Tribune*, August 25, 2011, https://bismarcktribune.com/news/local /d13fa46e-cf66-11e0-a0b4-001cc4c03286.html.

14. Quoted in Deborah Sontag, "Where Oil and Politics Mix," *New York Times*, November 23, 2014, https://www.nytimes.com/interactive/2014/11/24/us /north-dakota-oil-boom-politics.html.

15. Associated Press, "Judge Says Bird Law Doesn't Apply to Oil Pits," *Denver Post*, January 17, 2012, https://www.denverpost.com/2012/01/17/judge-says-bird -law-doesnt-apply-to-oil-pits.

16. "Transcript and Audio: Second Presidential Debate," NPR, October 16, 2012, https://www.npr.org/2012/10/16/163050988/transcript-obama-romney-2nd -presidential-debate.

17. Andrew Restuccia and Elana Schor, "Trump's Energy Whisperer," *Politico*, July 20, 2016, https://www.politico.com/story/2016/07/trumps-energy-whisperer -225877; Steven Mufson, "How a North Dakota Oil Billionaire Is Helping Shape Trump's Views on Energy," *Washington Post*, June 6, 2016, https://www .washingtonpost.com/business/economy/how-a-north-dakota-oil-billionaire -is-helping-shape-trumps-views-on-energy/2016/06/06/e6f101d0-2822-11e6 -ae4a-3cdd5fe74204_story.html.

18. Darryl Fears and Dino Grandoni, "The Trump Administration Has Officially Clipped the Wings of the Migratory Bird Treaty Act," *Washington Post*, April 13, 2018, https://www.washingtonpost.com/news/energy-environment/wp /2018/04/13/the-trump-administration-officially-clipped-the-wings-of-the -migratory-bird-treaty-act.

19. U.S. Department of Health and Human Services, "Toxicological Profile for Toluene," June 2017, http://atsdr.cdc.gov/toxprofiles/tp56.pdf.

20. Thomas Jemielita et al., "Unconventional Gas and Oil Drilling Is Associated with Increased Hospital Utilization Rates," *PLOS ONE*, July 2015, http://journals.plos .org/plosone/article?id=10.1371/journal.pone.0131093; Lisa M. McKenzie et al., "Childhood Hematologic Cancer and Residential Proximity to Oil and Gas Development," *PLOS ONE*, February 2017, http://journals.plos.org/plosone /article?id=10.1371/journal.pone.0170423; Elise G. Elliott et al., "Unconventional Oil and Gas Development and Risk of Childhood Leukemia: Assessing the Evidence," *Science of the Total Environment* 576 (January 2017): 138–47, http:// www.sciencedirect.com/science/article/pii/s0048969716322392; Physicians for Social Responsibility, "Too Dirty, Too Dangerous: Why Health Professionals Reject Natural Gas," February 2017, https://www.psr.org/wp-content/uploads /2018/05/too-dirty-too-dangerous.pdf.

21. Elyse Caron-Beaudoin et al., "Gestational Exposure to Volatile Organic Compounds (VOCs) in Northeastern British Columbia, Canada: A Pilot Study," *Environment International* 100 (January 2018): 131–38, https://www.sciencedirect .com/science/article/pii/S0160412017310309.

22. U.S. Environmental Protection Agency, "Hydraulic Fracturing for Oil and Gas: Impacts from the Hydraulic Fracturing Water Cycle on Drinking Water Resources in the United States," December 2016, https://www.epa.gov/sites /production/files/2016-12/documents/hfdwa_executive_summary.pdf.

23. Elliott et al., "Unconventional Oil and Gas Development and Risk of Childhood Leukemia."

24. N. E. Lauer et al., "Brine Spills Associated with Unconventional Oil Development in North Dakota," *Environmental Science and Technology* 50, no. 10 (May 2016): 5389–97, https://www.ncbi.nlm.nih.gov/pubmed/27119384.

25. I. M. Cozzarelli et al., "Environmental Signatures and Effects of an Oil and Gas Wastewater Spill in the Williston Basin, North Dakota," *Science of the Total Environment* 579 (February 2017): 1781–93, https://www.ncbi.nlm.nih.gov/pubmed /27939081.

26. Michelle Bamberger and Robert Oswald, "Impacts of Gas Drilling on Human and Animal Health," *New Solutions: A Journal of Environmental and Occupational Health Policy* 22, no. 1 (2012): 51–77, https://www.ncbi.nlm.nih.gov/pubmed /22446060; Physicians for Social Responsibility, "Too Dirty, Too Dangerous"; Elizabeth Royte, "Fracking Our Food Supply," *The Nation*, November 28, 2012, https://www.thenation.com/article/fracking-our-food-supply.

27. North Dakota Department of Health, "North Dakota 2016 Integrated Section 305(b) Water Quality Assessment Report and Section 303(d) List of Waters Needing Total Maximum Daily Loads," February 21, 2017, https://deq.nd.gov /publications/WQ/3_WM/TMDL/1_IntegratedReports/2016_Final_ND _Integrated_Report_20170222.pdf.

28. North Dakota Department of Health, "North Dakota 2014 Integrated Section 305(b) Water Quality Assessment Report and Section 303(d) List of Waters Needing Total Maximum Daily Loads," February 12, 2015, https://deq.nd.gov /publications/WQ/3_WM/TMDL/1_IntegratedReports/2014_Final_ND _Integrated_Report_20150428.pdf; "North Dakota 2012 Integrated Section 305(b) Water Quality Assessment Report and Section 303(d) List of Waters Needing Total Maximum Daily Loads," October 29, 2012, https://deq.nd.gov /publications/WQ/3_WM/TMDL/1_IntegratedReports/2012_Final_ND _Integrated_Report_20121029.pdf; "North Dakota 2010 Integrated Section 305(b) Water Quality Assessment Report and Section 303(d) List of Waters Needing Total Maximum Daily Loads," April 23, 2010, https://deq.nd.gov /publications/WQ/3_WM/TMDL/1_IntegratedReports/2010_Final_ND _Integrated_Report_20100423.pdf; and "North Dakota 2008 Integrated Section 305(b) Water Quality Assessment Report and Section 303(d) List of Waters Needing Total Maximum Daily Loads," September 29, 2008, https://deq.nd .gov/publications/WQ/3_WM/TMDL/1_IntegratedReports/2008_Final _ND_Integrated_Report_20080929.pdf.

29. U.S. Environmental Protection Agency, "Draft Plan to Study the Potential Impacts of Hydraulic Fracturing on Drinking Water Resources," February 7, 2011, https://www.epa.gov/sites/production/files/documents/HFStudyPlanDraft _SAB_020711.pdf.

30. Juhasz, "From North Dakota to Paris with Love."

31. Lerner and Putzel, "Tribal Environmental Director: 'We Are Not Equipped' for N.D. Oil Boom."

32. Lerner and Putzel, "Tribal Environmental Director: 'We Are Not Equipped' for N.D. Oil Boom."

33. Raymond Cross, "Development's Victim or Its Beneficiary?: The Impact of Oil and Gas Development on the Fort Berthold Indian Reservation," *North Dakota Law Review* 87 (2011): 535–69, https://www.narf.org/nill/bulletins/lawreviews /articles/cross.pdf.

34. Timothy Cama, "Clinton Wants to End 'Halliburton Loophole' on Fracking, Adviser Says," *The Hill*, July 27, 2016, http://thehill.com/policy/energy

-environment/289475-clinton-wants-to-end-halliburton-loophole-on-fracking
-adviser-says.

35. Michelle Bamberger and Robert Oswald, *The Real Cost of Fracking: How America's Shale Gas Boom Is Threatening Our Families, Pets, and Food* (Boston: Beacon Press, 2014).

36. Bamberger and Oswald, *The Real Cost of Fracking.*

37. N. E. Lauer, J. S. Harkness, and A. Vengosh, "Brine Spills Associated with Unconventional Oil Development in North Dakota," *Environmental Science and Technology* 50, no. 10 (May 2016): 5389–97, https://www.ncbi.nlm.nih.gov /pubmed/27119384.

38. Sarah Jane Keller, "North Dakota Wrestles with Radioactive Oilfield Waste," *High Country News,* July 14, 2014, http://www.hcn.org/articles/north-dakota -wrestles-with-radioactive-oilfield-waste.

39. Neela Banerjee, "Oil Drilling in North Dakota Raises Concerns about Radioactive Waste," *Los Angeles Times,* July 26, 2014, http://beta.latimes.com/nation /la-na-oil-drilling-radioactive-20140727-story.html.

40. Lauren Donovan, "Potentially Radioactive Material Spilling out of Trailers near Watford City," *Bismarck Tribune,* February 22, 2014, https://bismarcktribune .com/bakken/potentially-radioactive-material-spilling-out-of-trailers-near -watford-city/article_dbc501c6-9bd4-11e3-b001-0019bb2963f4.html; Western Organization of Resource Councils (worc), "No Time to Waste: Effective Management of Oil and Gas Field Radioactive Waste," November 24, 2015, http://www.worc.org/media/notimetowaste1.pdf.

41. Keller, "North Dakota Wrestles with Radioactive Oilfield Waste."

42. Arasim and Lake, "Women on the Front Lines Fighting Fracking in the Bakken Oil Shale Formations."

43. Sontag and McDonald, "In North Dakota, a Tale of Oil, Corruption and Death."

44. Elliott et al., "Unconventional Oil and Gas Development and Risk of Childhood Leukemia."

45. Natural Resources Defense Council (nrdc), "Fracking Fumes: Air Pollution from Hydraulic Fracturing Threatens Public Health and Communities," December 16, 2014, https://www.nrdc.org/sites/default/files/fracking-air-pollution -IB.pdf; Gregg P. Macey et al., "Air Concentrations of Volatile Compounds Near Oil and Gas Production," *Environmental Health* 13, no. 82 (October 2014), https://ehjournal.biomedcentral.com/articles/10.1186/1476-069X-13-82.

46. S. G. Rasmussen et al., "Association between Unconventional Natural Gas Development in the Marcellus Shale and Asthma Exacerbations," *jama Internal*

*Medicine* 176, no. 9 (September 2016): 1334–43, https://www.ncbi.nlm.nih.gov /pubmed/27428612.

47. Lara J. Cushing, Kate Vavra-Musser, Khang Chau, Meredith Franklin, and Jill E. Johnston, "Flaring from Unconventional Oil and Gas Development and Birth Outcomes in the Eagle Ford Shale in South Texas," *Environmental Health Perspectives* 128, no. 7 (July 2020), https://ehp.niehs.nih.gov/doi/10.1289/EHP6394. See also Julia Rosen and Lisa Friedman, "Gas Flaring and Preterm Births," *New York Times*, July 22, 2020, https://www.nytimes.com/2020/07/22/climate/nyt -climate-newsletter-premature-babies.html.

48. Bamberger and Oswald, *The Real Cost of Fracking*.

49. Hearing before the Committee on Indian Affairs, U.S. Senate, "Rural Health Care Facility on the Fort Berthold Indian Reservation."

50. "Fort Berthold Health Center to Open," *Bismarck Tribune*, October 11, 2011, http://bismarcktribune.com/news/state-and-regional/fort-berthold-health -center-to-open/article_b0b58c56-f421-11e0-b466-001cc4c03286.html.

51. Nick Martin, "Congress Is Still Breaking Treaties and Cheating Indian Country," *New Republic*, September 26, 2019, https://newrepublic.com/article/155180 /congress-still-breaking-treaties-cheating-indian-country; Dana Ferguson, "Violated: How the Indian Health Service Betrays Patient Trust and Treaties in the Great Plains," *Sioux Falls Argus Leader*, February 6, 2019, https://www .argusleader.com/in-depth/news/2018/12/05/south-dakota-health-care-ihs -hospital-native-american-trust-violated/1728819002.

52. Sierra Club, "Community Members Say Missouri River at Risk from Coal's Mercury Pollution," October 1, 2014, https://content.sierraclub.org/press -releases/2014/10/community-members-say-missouri-river-risk-coal-s-mercury -pollution.

53. U.S. Department of Labor, "Health Hazards Associated with Oil and Gas Extraction Activities," https://www.osha.gov/SLTC/oilgaswelldrilling /healthhazards.html (accessed January 2020); National Institute for Occupational Safety and Health, "Worker Exposure to Silica during Hydraulic Fracturing," June 2012, https://www.osha.gov/dts/hazardalerts/hydraulic_frac _hazard_alert.pdf.

54. John Eligon, "An Oil Boom Takes a Toll on Health Care," *New York Times*, January 27, 2013, http://www.nytimes.com/2013/01/28/us/boom-in-north -dakota-weighs-heavily-on-health-care.html.

55. Quoted in Curt Brown, "Test: 'Keepers of the Earth' Struggle to Come to Terms with North Dakota's Growing Oil Industry," *Star Tribune*, March 3, 2014, http://

www.startribune.com/n-d-tribal-members-question-oil-boom-s-effects-on
-sacred-land/235656621.

56. Dakota Access, LLC, "Application for Corridor Compatibility and Route Permit," December 22, 2014, https://psc.nd.gov/database/documents/14-0842
/001-010.pdf.

57. North Dakota Department of Health, letter to Public Service Commission,
May 18, 2015, https://psc.nd.gov/database/documents/14-0842/055-010.pdf.

58. Erin Jordan, "Man Alleges Company Offered Prostitute for Pipeline Right-of-
Way," *Bismarck Tribune*, May 14, 2015, http://bismarcktribune.com/bakken
/man-alleges-company-offered-prostitute-for-pipeline-right-of-way/article
_3a0ccfeb-4388-53ec-915c-b88491eba789.html.

59. North Dakota Public Service Commission, "Electronic Record of June 15, 2015,
Formal Hearing," June 15, 2015, https://psc.nd.gov/database/docket_file_list
.php?s_dept=PU&s_company_name=Dakota+Access%2C+LLC&s_year_case
=14&s_seq_num=842&s_doc=78.

60. Lisa DeVille, "Written Testimony to the North Dakota Public Service Commission," June 15, 2015, https://psc.nd.gov/database/documents/14-0842/082
-010.pdf.

61. Quoted in North Dakota Public Service Commission, "Electronic Record of
June 15, 2015, Formal Hearing."

62. North Dakota Public Service Commission, "Electronic Record of June 15, 2015,
Formal Hearing."

63. "'Sovereignty by the Barrel': Tribe Takes Control of Oil Production," *Indian
Country Today*, June 6, 2016.

64. North Dakota Public Service Commission, "Electronic Record of July 20, 2015,
Work Session," July 20, 2015, https://psc.nd.gov/database/docket_file_list
.php?s_dept=PU&s_company_name=Dakota+Access%2C+LLC&docket
_viewPage=1&s_year_case=14&s_seq_num=842&s_doc=100.

65. North Dakota Public Service Commission, "Electronic Record of August 26,
2015, Work Session," August 26, 2015, https://psc.nd.gov/database/docket_file
_list.php?s_dept=PU&s_company_name=Dakota+Access%2C+LLC&docket
_viewPage=2&s_year_case=14&s_seq_num=842&s_doc=105.

66. Mike Nowatzki, "Company Advises Landowner of Court Action for Dakota
Access Pipeline Right-of-Way," *Bismarck Tribune*, September 15, 2015, http://
bismarcktribune.com/company-advises-landowner-of-court-action-for-dakota
-access-pipeline/article_d3276200-9588-57b7-a515-64ec2e997c90.html.

67. Amy Dalrymple, "S.D. Approves Major Pipeline but Official Calls Company
'Abusive,'" *Bismarck Tribune*, November 30, 2015, http://bismarcktribune.com

/news/state-and-regional/s-d-approves-major-pipeline-but-official-calls
-company-abusive/article_d2e9215d-66f2-5f3d-8ef5-52a2bd90654b.html.
See also South Dakota Public Utilities Commission, "Minutes of the Ad Hoc
Commission Meeting," September 24, 2015, https://puc.sd.gov/minutes/2015
/0924.aspx.

68. Three Affiliated Tribes, "Tribal Business Council Regular Meeting November
12th, 2015, Minutes," November 12, 2015, https://static1.squarespace.com/static
/5a5fab0832601e33d9f68fde/t/5b06c5b070a6ad2e494c0461/1527170509432
/2015-11-12+TBC+Minutes+Without+Closed+SessionCertified.pdf.

69. Three Affiliated Tribes, "Tribal Business Council Special Meeting December
2nd, 2015, Minutes," December 2, 2015, https://static1.squarespace.com/static
/5a5fab0832601e33d9f68fde/t/5b06c63188251b0847c1b3b0/1527170640938
/2015-12-02+TBC+Minutes+Without+Closed+Session+Certified.pdf.

70. Lauren Donovan, "Dakota Access Pipeline Files Condemnation Lawsuits,"
*Bismarck Tribune,* January 1, 2016, http://bismarcktribune.com/bakken/dakota
-access-pipeline-files-condemnation-lawsuits/article_e4473aea-3b7b-534c
-9110-7555ae86b6e6.html.

3. ORIGINS OF THE CAMP

1. Our Climate Voices, "Jasilyn Charger, Cheyenne River Sioux Tribe," January
18, 2019, https://www.ourclimatevoices.org/2019/jasilyncharger.

2. Cristina Maza, "Tribes Battle High Teen Suicide Rates on Native American
Reservations," *Christian Science Monitor,* April 13, 2015, https://www.csmonitor
.com/USA/USA-Update/2015/0413/Tribes-battle-high-teen-suicide-rates-on
-native-American-reservations; Julie Bosman, "Pine Ridge Indian Reservation
Struggles with Suicides among Its Young," *New York Times,* May 1, 2015, https://
www.nytimes.com/2015/05/02/us/pine-ridge-indian-reservation-struggles
-with-suicides-among-young-people.html.

3. Holly Hedegaard, Sally C. Curtin, and Margaret Warner, "Suicide Rates in the
United States Continue to Increase," NCHS *Data Brief* 309 (June 2018), https://
www.cdc.gov/nchs/data/databriefs/db309.pdf.

4. Caroline Jiang et al., "Racial and Gender Disparities in Suicide among Young
Adults Aged 18–24: United States, 2009–2013," Centers for Disease Control,
National Center for Health Statistics, September 2015, https://www.cdc.gov
/nchs/data/hestat/suicide/racial_and_gender_2009_2013.pdf.

5. Sari Horwitz, "The Hard Lives—And High Suicide Rate—of Native American Children on Reservations," *Washington Post,* March 9, 2014, https://www
.washingtonpost.com/world/national-security/the-hard-lives-and-high-suicide

-rate-of-native-american-children/2014/03/09/6e0ad9b2-9f03-11e3-b8d8
-94577ff66b28_story.html.

6. Jiang et al., "Racial and Gender Disparities in Suicide among Young Adults Aged 18–24."

7. North Dakota Department of Health, "North Dakota Suicide Prevention Plan 2017–2020," https://www.sprc.org/sites/default/files/ND_Suicide_Prevention _Plan_2017_to_2020.pdf (accessed October 2020).

8. Maza, "Tribes Battle High Teen Suicide Rates on Native American Reservations."

9. See, for example, Talli Nauman, "Tribal Members Continue Arrests of Truck Drivers: Cheyenne River Officials Call on Governor Daugaard to Reroute Oil Hauling Trucks," *Native Sun News*, April 7, 2014, https://www.indianz.com /News/2014/04/07/native-sun-news-cheyenne-river-11.asp.

10. Quoted in B. A. Morelli, "Rallies, Protests Begin Bakken Hearing," *Bismarck Tribune*, November 13, 2015, http://bismarcktribune.com/rallies-protests-begin -bakken-pipeline-hearing/article_0aeffa91-b7f4-5d61-b307-545a9ea5fa5d.html.

11. Dakota Access, LLC, "Formal Notice for Start of Construction," January 21, 2016, https://psc.nd.gov/database/documents/14-0842/145-010.pdf.

12. September 30 DAPL Meeting with SRST, https://earthjustice.org/sites/default /files/files/Ex6-J-Hasselman-Decl.pdf (accessed October 2020).

13. Congressional Research Service, "Oil and Natural Gas Pipelines: Role of the U.S. Army Corps of Engineers," June 28, 2017, https://www.everycrsreport.com/files /20170628_R44880_1105a52fd838d2e8d342c75e49199c8bcdeb6607.pdf.

14. Congressional Research Service, "Oil and Natural Gas Pipelines."

15. U.S. Army Corps of Engineers, "Frequently Asked Questions DAPL," May 3, 2016, http://www.nwo.usace.army.mil/Media/Fact-Sheets/Fact-Sheet-Article -View/Article/749823/frequently-asked-questions-dapl.

16. The White House, "Presidential Memorandum on Tribal Consultation," November 5, 2009, https://obamawhitehouse.archives.gov/the-press-office /memorandum-tribal-consultation-signed-president; Administration of William J. Clinton, "Executive Order 13175—Consultation and Coordination with Indian Tribal Governments," November 6, 2000, https://energy.gov/sites/prod/files /nepapub/nepa_documents/RedDont/Req-eo13175tribgovt.pdf; U.S. Army Corps of Engineers, "Frequently Asked Questions DAPL."

17. Letter from Wasté Win Young, Standing Rock Sioux Tribe Tribal Historic Preservation Officer, to Martha Chiefly, U.S. Army Corps of Engineers, February 15, 2015, https://puc.sd.gov/commission/dockets/HydrocarbonPipeline/2014 /HP14-002/rebuttal/ien/winltr3.pdf; letter from Wasté Win Young, Standing Rock Sioux Tribe Tribal Historic Preservation Officer, to Martha Chiefly, U.S.

Army Corps of Engineers, April 8, 2015, https://puc.sd.gov/commission/dockets /HydrocarbonPipeline/2014/HP14-002/rebuttal/ien/winltr1.pdf.

18. U.S. Army Corps of Engineers, "Frequently Asked Questions DAPL."

19. Congressional Research Service, "Oil and Natural Gas Pipelines."

20. Letter from David V. Chipman to Col. John W. Henderson, January 13, 2017, https://usace.contentdm.oclc.org/digital/collection/p16021coll5/id/1555.

21. Human Rights Watch, "The Human Right to Water: A Guide for First Nations Communities and Advocates," October 23, 2019, https://www.hrw.org/report /2019/10/23/human-right-water/guide-first-nations-communities-and -advocates.

22. Standing Rock Sioux Tribe v. U.S. Army Corps of Engineers, "Declaration of Dave Archambault II in Support of Motion for Preliminary Injunction," August 4, 2016, https://earthjustice.org/sites/default/files/press/2016/Declaration-of -Dave-Archambault-II.pdf.

23. Environmental Protection Agency, Office of Enforcement, *Report on Pollution Affecting Water Quality of the Cheyenne River System, Western South Dakota*, 1971, https://nepis.epa.gov/Exe/ZyNET.exe/9101PB9O.TXT?ZyActionD= ZyDocument&Client=EPA&Index=Prior+to+1976&Docs=&Query=&Time= &EndTime=&SearchMethod=1&TocRestrict=n&Toc=&TocEntry=&QField= &QFieldYear=&QFieldMonth=&QFieldDay=&IntQFieldOp=0&ExtQFieldOp =0&XmlQuery=&File=D%3A%5Czyfiles%5CIndex%20Data%5C70thru75 %5CTxt%5C00000024%5C9101PB9O.txt&User=ANONYMOUS& Password=anonymous&SortMethod=h%7C-&MaximumDocuments=1& FuzzyDegree=0&ImageQuality=r75g8/r75g8/x150y150g16/i425&Display =hpfr&DefSeekPage=x&SearchBack=ZyActionL&Back=ZyActionS&BackDesc =Results%20page&MaximumPages=1&ZyEntry=1&SeekPage=x&ZyPURL.

24. Maryalice Yakutchik, "Killer in the Water: Tracing Arsenic's Threats to Health in the Badlands," *Johns Hopkins Public Health*, Spring 2015, https://magazine .jhsph.edu/2015/spring/features/killer-in-the-water/index.html.

25. Charles Michael Ray, "Arsenic Pollution on the Cheyenne River Reservation," SDPB Radio, April 23, 2013, http://listen.sdpb.org/post/arsenic-pollution -cheyenne-river-reservation; Jennifer Ong et al., "Mercury, Autoimmunity, and Environmental Factors on Cheyenne River Sioux Tribal Lands," *Autoimmune Diseases*, 2014, https://www.ncbi.nlm.nih.gov/pmc/articles/PMC4017878.

26. Dakota Access, LLC, "Draft Environmental Assessment: Dakota Access Pipeline Project Crossings of Flowage Easements and Federal Lands," November 2015, http://www.nwo.usace.army.mil/Missions/Civil-Works/Planning/Project -Reports/Article/633496/dakota-access-pipeline-environmental-assessment.

27. Standing Rock Sioux Tribe v. U.S. Army Corps of Engineers, "Declaration of Dave Archambault II in Support of Motion for Preliminary Injunction."

28. Standing Rock Sioux Tribe v. U.S. Army Corps of Engineers, "Declaration of Dave Archambault II in Support of Motion for Preliminary Injunction"; Standing Rock Sioux Tribe, "Statement of Dave Archambault, II, Chairman, Standing Rock Sioux Tribe on Dakota Access Pipeline," February 5, 2016, https://www.facebook.com/permalink.php?story_fbid=1193260964035505&id=402298239798452&substory_index=0.

29. Joye Braun, Facebook post, February 21, 2016, https://www.facebook.com/joye.braun/posts/10154588444759057.

30. Joye Braun, Facebook post, February 25, 2016, https://www.facebook.com/joye.braun/posts/10154597222624057.

31. Quoted in Jessica Holdman, "Tribal Members Protest Dakota Access Pipeline," *Bismarck Tribune*, February 26, 2016, http://bismarcktribune.com/bakken/tribal-members-protest-dakota-access-pipeline/article_7c26cc47-9e1e-554e-863c-5770f25566ef.html.

32. Talli Nauman, "Standing Rock Sioux Tribe 'Pipeline Will Affect Future Generations': Tribe Diametrically Expresses Opposition," *Native Sun News*, March 14, 2016, http://www.indianz.com/News/2016/020668.asp.

33. Joye Braun, Facebook post, February 27, 2016, https://www.facebook.com/joye.braun/posts/10154601122049057.

34. Bikem Ekberzade, *Standing Rock: Greed, Oil and the Lakota's Struggle for Justice* (London: Zed Books, 2018).

35. Nick Estes and Jaskiran Dhillon, eds., *Standing with Standing Rock: Voices from the #NoDAPL Movement* (Minneapolis: University of Minnesota Press, 2019).

36. Earthjustice, "Webinar: How a Historic Grassroots Resistance and the Power of the Law Could Cancel the Dakota Access Pipeline," August 14, 2020, https://earthjustice.org/events/webinar-standing-rock-dakota-access-pipeline?utm_source=crm&utm_medium=email&utm_term=event&utm_campaign=200817_Events_DAPLwebinar_thanks&utm_content=HTMLBodyLink1&emci=4574937e-cee0-ea11-8b03-00155d0394bb&emdi=58941c34-abe1-ea11-8b03-00155d0394bb&ceid=156446.

37. Dakota Access, LLC, "Dakota Access Pipeline Project."

38. U.S. Army Corps of Engineers and Dakota Access, LLC, "Environmental Assessment: Dakota Access Pipeline Project, Crossings of Flowage Easements and Federal Lands," December 2015, http://www.nwo.usace.army.mil/Missions/Civil-Works/Planning/Project-Reports/Article/633496/dakota-access-pipeline-environmental-assessment.

39. Dakota Access, LLC, "Dakota Access Pipeline Project"; Estes, *Our History Is the Future.*

40. Standing Rock Sioux Tribe, "Resolution No. 406-15," September 2, 2015, https://www.facebook.com/StandingRockST/photos/a.422881167740159 /1193297920698476.

41. Quoted in "Standing Rock Sioux Tribe and Allies Work to Defeat the Dakota Access Pipeline," May 20, 2016, https://350pdx.org/dakota-access-oil-pipeline.

4. SEVENTH GENERATION RISING

1. Saul Elbein, "The Youth Group That Launched a Movement at Standing Rock," *New York Times Magazine*, January 31, 2017, https://www.nytimes.com/2017 /01/31/magazine/the-youth-group-that-launched-a-movement-at-standing -rock.html.

2. B. A. Morelli, "Iowa Regulators Formally Issue Bakken Pipeline Permit," *Bismarck Tribune*, April 9, 2016, http://bismarcktribune.com/bakken/iowa-regulators -formally-issue-bakken-pipeline-permit/article_6f9eb97d-6b8e-5f50-a2cd -d2559f98b83d.html.

3. Energy Transfer LP, "Dakota Access Pipeline."

4. Pipeline and Hazardous Materials Safety Administration, "Data and Statistics Overview," https://www.phmsa.dot.gov/data-and-statistics/pipeline/data-and -statistics-overview (updated March 4, 2020).

5. Sontag, "Where Oil and Politics Mix."

6. Chris Clarke, "North Dakota: The Oil Spill State," KCET, May 2, 2017, https:// www.kcet.org/shows/earth-focus/north-dakota-the-oil-spill-state.

7. Liz Hampton, "Sunoco, behind Protested Dakota Pipeline, Tops U.S. Crude Spill Charts," Reuters, September 23, 2016, https://www.reuters.com/article /us-usa-pipeline-nativeamericans-safety-i/sunoco-behind-protested-dakota -pipeline-tops-u-s-crude-spill-charts-idUSKCN11T1UW.

8. Energy Transfer/Sunoco Logistics Partners LP, "Annual Report Pursuant to Section 13 or 15(d) of the Securities Exchange Act of 1934," 2016, http://ir .energytransfer.com/phoenix.zhtml.

9. Dakota Access, LLC, "Formal Notice for Start of Construction," April 18, 2016, https://psc.nd.gov/database/documents/14-0842/160-010.pdf.

10. Chief Arvol Looking Horse, "Standing Rock Is Everywhere: One Year Later," *The Guardian*, February 22, 2018, https://www.theguardian.com/environment /climate-consensus-97-per-cent/2018/feb/22/standing-rock-is-everywhere -one-year-later.

11. Quoted in Braudie Blais-Billie, "6 Indigenous Activists on Why They're Fighting the Dakota Access Pipeline," *Fader*, September 9, 2016, http://www.thefader.com/2016/09/09/dakota-access-pipeline-protest-interviews.

12. "#RunForYourLife: NoDAPL Petition Letter to Army Corps of Engineers," *Indigenous Rising*, May 3, 2016, https://indigenousrising.org/runforyourlifenodapl-petition-letter-to-army-corps-of-engineers.

13. Elbein, "The Youth Group That Launched a Movement at Standing Rock."

14. Press release, "Lakota Youth Running 500 Miles in Opposition of Dakota Access Pipeline," *Indigenous Rising*, April 27, 2016, http://indigenousrising.org/lakota-youth-running-500-miles-in-opposition-of-dakota-access-pipeline.

15. "#RunForYourLife: NoDAPL Petition Letter to Army Corps of Engineers."

16. Estes, *Our History Is the Future*.

17. "One Year at Standing Rock," *Reveal*, April 10, 2017, https://www.youtube.com/watch?v=Yb9HHtye1Tk.

18. "One Year at Standing Rock," *Reveal*, April 10, 2017, https://www.youtube.com/watch?v=Yb9HHtye1Tk.

19. Quoted in "Native American Youth Run to Nation's Capital from North Dakota for Rezpect Our Water Campaign," *Last Real Indians*, July 16, 2016, https://lastrealindians.com/native-american-youth-run-to-nations-capital-from-north-dakota-for-rezpect-our-water-campaign.

20. Elbein, "The Youth Group That Launched a Movement at Standing Rock."

21. U.S. Army Corps of Engineers, "Final Environmental Assessment: Dakota Access Pipeline Project, Crossings of Flowage Easements and Federal Lands," 2016, http:cdm16021.contentdm.oclc.org/cdm/ref/collection/p16021coll7/id/2427.

22. Sacred Stone Camp, "Urgent Callout to Defend the Water and Stop Dakota Access Pipe . . . ," July 27, 2016, https://www.facebook.com/watch/?v=1747785488843815.

23. Standing Rock Sioux Tribe v. U.S. Army Corps of Engineers, "Complaint for Declaratory and Injunctive Relief," July 27, 2016, http://earthjustice.org/sites/default/files/files/3154%201%20complaint.pdf.

24. Quoted in Lauren Donovan, "Multiple Groups Join Pipeline Opposition," *Bismarck Tribune*, August 4, 2016, http://bismarcktribune.com/news/state-and-regional/multiple-groups-join-pipeline-opposition/article_a32fc5f4-e6db-5df6-9048-ec75d02386c1.html.

25. Congressional Research Service, "Oil and Natural Gas Pipelines."

26. Earthjustice, "In Conversation."

27. Dakota Access, LLC, "Dakota Access, LLC Pipeline Project Monthly Construction Status Report," July 2016, https://psc.nd.gov/database/documents/14 -0842/202-010.pdf.

28. Standing Rock Sioux Tribe v. U.S. Army Corps of Engineers, "Motion for Preliminary Injunction, Request for Expedited Hearing," August 4, 2016, https:// earthjustice.org/sites/default/files/files/Mtn-for-Preliminary-Injunction-and -Memo-in-Support.pdf.

29. Rezpect Our Water, "Native American Kids Standing Up against Big Oil Company!," https://www.facebook.com/ReZpectOurWater/videos /1097410266967934 (accessed January 2020).

30. Standing Rock Sioux Tribe v. U.S. Army Corps of Engineers, "Motion for Preliminary Injunction, Request for Expedited Hearing."

31. Abby Harlage, "This 21-Year-Old Native American Activist Got the Nation to Care about Standing Rock—and She's Just Getting Started," *Yahoo Life*, May 29, 2018, https://www.yahoo.com/lifestyle/21-year-old-native-american-activist -got-nation-care-standing-rock-shes-just-getting-started-220637722.html.

32. Unicorn Riot, "Black Snake Killaz: A #NoDAPL Story," April 17, 2017, https:// unicornriot.ninja/2017/black-snake-killaz-documentary-production-support -fund.

33. Dakota Access, LLC v. Dave Archambault et al., "Order Granting Plaintiff's Motion for Temporary Restraining Order," August 16, 2016, https://narf.org /nill/bulletins/federal/documents/dakota_access_v_archambault.html.

34. Unicorn Riot, "Land Defenders Storm Construction Site to Protect Water," August 15, 2016, http://www.unicornriot.ninja/?p=8319.

35. Quoted in "Video: Morton County Sheriff Kyle Kirchmeier," *Bismarck Tribune*, August 17, 2016, http://bismarcktribune.com/video/morton-county-sheriff -kyle-kirchmeier/youtube_540bbdb0-aacd-5820-a332-e19aec2ac375.html.

36. Quoted in Caroline Grueskin, "Construction Stops, Traffic Restricted Due to Dakota Access Pipeline Protest," *Bismarck Tribune*, August 17, 2016, http:// bismarcktribune.com/news/state-and-regional/construction-stops-traffic -restricted-due-to-dakota-access-pipeline-protest/article_80b8ef24-7bf3-507c -95f9-6292795a7ed4.html.

37. Lauren Donovan, "Sioux Chairman Calls for Removal of Highway Barriers," *Bismarck Tribune*, August 18, 2016, http://bismarcktribune.com/news/state -and-regional/sioux-chairman-calls-for-removal-of-highway-barriers/article _1845ea70-c075-5037-9f9c-52fa5a8d591a.html.

38. Quoted in "Protesters Celebrate 'Temporary' Victory," *Bismarck Tribune*, August 18, 2016, http://bismarcktribune.com/protesters-celebrate-temporary-victory/article_44e57ae3-b1c0-56d4-9962-8bc010f2ccc1.html.

39. Estes and Dhillon, *Standing with Standing Rock*.

40. "Views of Life at the Overflow Camp," *Bismarck Tribune*, August 30, 2016, https://bismarcktribune.com/gallery/views-of-life-at-the-overflow-camp/collection_7964a488-8240-54d3-a74d-3d342bb63997.html#21.

41. Dunbar-Ortiz, *An Indigenous Peoples' History of the United States*.

42. Dunbar-Ortiz, *An Indigenous Peoples' History of the United States*; Stephen L. Pevar, *The Rights of Indians and Tribes*, 4th ed. (Oxford: Oxford University Press, 2012).

43. Mark N. Fox, "The Mandan, Hidatsa, and Arikara Nation's Support for the Standing Rock Nation," August 22, 2016, http://media.graytvinc.com/documents/Standing+Rock+Support+Letter.pdf (site discontinued).

44. Kandi White, Facebook post, August 25, 2016, https://www.facebook.com/dallasgoldtooth/posts/10105639174765373.

45. Quoted in Lauren Donovan, "Negotiations Underway to Remove Protest Roadblock," *Bismarck Tribune*, August 31, 2016, http://bismarcktribune.com/news/state-and-regional/negotiations-underway-to-remove-protest-roadblock/article_727d3f6c-54dc-5695-9020-5978c4640748.html.

46. James E. Boasberg, "Responses of James E. Boasberg, Nominee to Be United States District Judge for the District of Columbia, to the Written Questions of Senator Jeff Sessions," https://www.judiciary.senate.gov/imo/media/doc/JamesBoasberg-QFRs.pdf (accessed November 2020).

47. Quoted in Lauren Donovan, "Protesters Vow to Maintain Occupation of Campsites," *Bismarck Tribune*, August 24, 2016, http://bismarcktribune.com/news/state-and-regional/protesters-vow-to-maintain-occupation-of-campsites/article_c196931b-7fcf-51e5-bb48-6527afa749e0.html.

48. Amnesty International, "Standing Rock," https://www.amnestyusa.org/standing-rock (accessed June 2020).

49. David Archambault II, "Opinion: Taking a Stand at Standing Rock," *New York Times*, August 24, 2016, https://www.nytimes.com/2016/08/25/opinion/taking-a-stand-at-standing-rock.html.

50. Tom Goldtooth et al., letter to President Obama, August 25, 2016, https://www.sierraclub.org/sites/www.sierraclub.org/files/blog/ED%20Letter%20President%20Obama%20Dakota%20Access%20Pipeline.pdf.

51. Estes, *Our History Is the Future*.

52. Elbein, "The Youth Group That Launched a Movement at Standing Rock."

53. Dakota Access, LLC, "Dakota Access Pipeline Monthly Construction Status Report, August 1, 2016 through August 31, 2016," September 8, 2016, https://psc.nd.gov/database/documents/14-0842/214-010.pdf.

54. Quoted in Caroline Grueskin, "Protesters Disrupt Second Dakota Access Pipeline Worksite," *Bismarck Tribune*, August 31, 2016, http://bismarcktribune.com/news/state-and-regional/protesters-disrupt-second-dakota-access-pipeline-worksite/article_94713f67-27f1-54ad-9c42-5133a9f0e7ac.html.

55. Standing Rock Sioux Tribe v. U.S. Army Corps of Engineers, "Transcript of Hearing on Preliminary Injunction before the Honorable James E. Boasberg," August 24, 2016, https://www.courtlistener.com/recap/gov.uscourts.dcd.180660/gov.uscourts.dcd.180660.27.0.pdf.

56. Standing Rock Sioux Tribe v. U.S. Army Corps of Engineers, "Declaration of Tim Mentz, Sr. in Support of Motion for Preliminary Injunction," August 11, 2016, https://earthjustice.org/sites/default/files/press/2016/Decl-of-T-Mentz-Sr.pdf.

57. Quoted in Amy Dalrymple, "Tribe Submits Evidence of Cultural Sites in Dakota Access Path," *Bismarck Tribune*, September 2, 2016, http://bismarcktribune.com/tribe-submits-evidence-of-cultural-sites-in-dakota-access-path/article_b987cebb-033d-525a-9f36-f18b36f17cd3.html.

5. MILITARIZATION OF THE RESPONSE

1. Amy Goodman, "Standing Rock Special: Historian Says Dakota Access Co. Attack Came on Anniv. of Whitestone Massacre," *Democracy Now!*, November 24, 2016, https://www.youtube.com/watch?v=2u1ROkldhkU.

2. Pekka Hämäläinen, *Lakota America: A New History of Indigenous Power* (New Haven: Yale University Press, 2019); Treuer, *The Heartbeat of Wounded Knee*.

3. Treuer, *The Heartbeat of Wounded Knee*.

4. Hämäläinen, *Lakota America*.

5. *Fort Laramie Treaty*, 15 Stat. 636, April 29, 1868, Art. 2.

6. Treuer, *The Heartbeat of Wounded Knee*.

7. Treuer, *The Heartbeat of Wounded Knee*.

8. Pevar, *The Rights of Indians and Tribes*.

9. Dunbar-Ortiz, *An Indigenous Peoples' History of the United States*; Treuer, *The Heartbeat of Wounded Knee*.

10. Treuer, *The Heartbeat of Wounded Knee*; Howard Zinn, *A People's History of the United States* (New York: Harper and Row, 1980).

11. Dunbar-Ortiz, *An Indigenous Peoples' History of the United States*, 189.

12. Estes, *Our History Is the Future*.

13. *Flood Control Act of 1944*, Pub. L. 78-534, 58 Stat. 887, 1944.

14. Gilio-Whitaker, *As Long as Grass Grows*.

15. The tribe initially received $12.3 million in compensation for its flooded lands, with an additional $90.6 million in the 1990s. "Impact of the Flood Control Act of 1944 on Indian Tribes along the Missouri River before the S. Comm. on Indian Affairs," 110th Cong. 4, November 1, 2007, https://www.indian.senate.gov/sites /default/files/upload/files/November12007.pdf; U.S. Senate, "Final Report and Recommendations of the Garrison Unit Joint Tribal Advisory Committee: Joint Hearing before the Select Committee on Indian Affairs," March 30, 1987, https:// babel.hathitrust.org/cgi/pt?id=pur1.32754074491261;view=1up;seq=12.

16. "Lawsuit Alleges Abuse at Indian Boarding Schools," *Sioux City Journal*, July 26, 2003, https://siouxcityjournal.com/news/local/education/lawsuit -alleges-abuse-at-indian-boarding-schools/article_531bdc51-0c20-5639-b26e -5344e0f7ccdf.html; Sharon Waxman, "Abuse Charges Hit Reservation," *Washington Post*, June 2, 2003, https://www.washingtonpost.com/archive/politics /2003/06/02/abuse-charges-hit-reservation/bcda861c-3476-4ad7-8989 -5a3a4c25b8ce; Charles Michael Ray, "Letters Detail Alleged Church Sex Abuse," SDPB Radio, April 7, 2013, https://listen.sdpb.org/post/letters-detail-alleged -church-sex-abuse. In 2010 South Dakota passed a law limiting legal recourse for victims who were abused at mission schools while they were run by the church. Patrick Anderson, "Native American Victims of Sex Abuse at Catholic Boarding Schools Fight for Justice," *Argus Leader*, May 16, 2019, https://www .argusleader.com/story/news/2019/05/16/native-american-sex-abuse-victims -catholic-boarding-schools-south-dakota/1158590001.

17. Treuer, *The Heartbeat of Wounded Knee*.

18. Means and Wolf, *Where White Men Fear to Tread*.

19. Dunbar-Ortiz, *An Indigenous Peoples' History of the United States*, 211–12.

20. Quoted in LeAnn Ackroth, "Protesters Break through Fence Line at Alternate Construction Site," *Bismarck Tribune*, September 3, 2016, https://bismarcktribune .com/news/local/protesters-break-through-fence-line-at-alternate-construction -site/article_31dfd79f-e065-540b-b99b-2fed90fbdd67.html.

21. "Guards Accused of Unleashing Dogs, Pepper-Spraying Oil Pipeline Protesters," *CBS News Wire*, September 5, 2016, https://wreg.com/2016/09/05/guards -accused-of-unleashing-dogs-pepper-spraying-oil-pipeline-protesters.

22. Amy Goodman and Denis Moynihan, "North Dakota vs. Amy Goodman: Journalism Is Not a Crime," *Democracy Now!*, September 15, 2016, https://www .democracynow.org/2016/9/15/north_dakota_vs_amy_goodman_journalism.

23. Bill McKibben, "A Pipeline Fight and America's Dark Past," *New Yorker*, September 6, 2016, https://www.newyorker.com/news/daily-comment/a-pipeline-fight-and-americas-dark-past.

24. Natural History Museum, "Archaeologists and Museums Denounce Destruction of Standing Rock Sioux Burial Grounds," September 21, 2016, http://thenaturalhistorymuseum.org/archaeologists-and-museums-respond-to-destruction-of-standing-rock-sioux-burial-grounds.

25. Elbein, "The Youth Group That Launched a Movement at Standing Rock."

26. Standing Rock Sioux Tribe v. U.S. Army Corps of Engineers, "Emergency Motion for a Temporary Restraining Order," September 4, 2016, https://earthjustice.org/sites/default/files/files/Motion-for-TRO-and-memo.pdf.

27. Quoted in Amy Dalrymple, "Use of Dogs at Pipeline Protest Criticized," *Bismarck Tribune*, September 6, 2016, https://bismarcktribune.com/news/state-and-regional/use-of-dogs-at-pipeline-protest-criticized/article_1f080ee1-21c9-5185-bc94-ec0708d7836c.html.

28. Quoted in Jessica Holdman, "Archambault Feelings Mixed on Judge's Ruling," *Bismarck Tribune*, September 6, 2016, http://bismarcktribune.com/news/state-and-regional/archambault-feelings-mixed-on-judge-s-ruling/article_15d176d3-9bcc-5647-92cf-91849ce56ca9.html.

29. "Journalist Amy Goodman Talks after DAPL Riot Charge Dismissed," *Bismarck Tribune*, October 17, 2016, https://bismarcktribune.com/video/journalist-amy-goodman-talks-after-dapl-riot-charge-dismissed/youtube_f36759c9-3399-50e9-a4c2-c69286c082ee.html.

30. Unicorn Riot, "20 Arrested during #NoDAPL Lockdown, Including 2 Unicorn Riot Journalists," September 13, 2016, https://unicornriot.ninja/2016/20-arrested-nodapl-lockdown-including-2-unicorn-riot-journalists.

31. Unicorn Riot, "20 Arrested during #NoDAPL Lockdown."

32. Jill Stein, Tweet, September 7, 2016, https://twitter.com/DrJillStein/status/773645480030969856.

33. "President Obama Dodges #NoDAPL Question as Native Youth Question His Commitment," Indianz.com, September 8, 2016, http://www.indianz.com/News/2016/09/08/president-obama-dodges-nodapl-question-a.asp.

34. Standing Rock Sioux Tribe v. U.S. Army Corps of Engineers, "Memorandum Opinion," September 9, 2016, https://earthjustice.org/sites/default/files/files/order-denying-PI.pdf.

35. U.S. Department of Justice, "Joint Statement from the Department of Justice, the Department of the Army and the Department of the Interior Regarding Standing Rock Sioux Tribe v. U.S. Army Corps of Engineers," September 9,

2016, https://www.justice.gov/opa/pr/joint-statement-department-justice
-department-army-and-department-interior-regarding-standing.

36. Standing Rock Sioux Tribe v. U.S. Army Corps of Engineers and Dakota Access,
LLP, "Emergency Motion for Injunction Pending Appeal," September 12, 2016,
https://earthjustice.org/sites/default/files/files/Mtn-for-Injunction-Pending
-Appeal.pdf.

37. Quoted in Amy Dalrymple, "Tribe Appeals Judge's Ruling, Seeks New Injunction," *Bismarck Tribune*, September 10, 2016, http://bismarcktribune.com/tribe
-appeals-judge-s-ruling-seeks-new-injunction/article_dbfc1538-2e96-5f9a-9ecd
-77224a0c1df0.html.

38. Standing Rock Sioux Tribe v. U.S. Army Corps of Engineers and Dakota Access,
LLP, "Emergency Motion for Injunction Pending Appeal."

39. Jack Healy and John Schwartz, "U.S. Suspends Construction on Part of North
Dakota Pipeline," *New York Times*, September 9, 2016, https://www.nytimes
.com/2016/09/10/us/judge-approves-construction-of-oil-pipeline-in-north
-dakota.html. See also Allysia Finley, "Opinion: Chief Obama and the Dakota
Pipeline," *Wall Street Journal*, September 13, 2016, https://www.wsj.com/articles
/chief-obama-and-the-dakota-pipeline-1473808024.

40. Energy Transfer, "Dakota Access Pipeline Project Update," September 13, 2016,
https://bloximages.chicago2.vip.townnews.com/bismarcktribune.com/content
/tncms/assets/v3/editorial/0/23/023a1dda-119b-5ea7-a5cc-86bc5b04c818
/57d805afeeea4.pdf.pdf.

41. Standing Rock Sioux Tribe, letter to Jo-Ellen Darcy, September 22, 2016, https://
usace.contentdm.oclc.org/digital/collection/p16021coll5/id/1636.

42. Nick Smith, "Department of Emergency Services Requests $6 Million for Pro-
test Response," *Bismarck Tribune*, September 14, 2016, http://bismarcktribune
.com/news/local/govt-and-politics/department-of-emergency-services
-requests-million-for-protest-response/article_063e8870-a1f2-573b-b09d
-90f5d9ac7033.html.

43. Nick Smith, "North Dakota Emergency Services Gets $6 Million Line of
Credit for Protest Response," *Bismarck Tribune*, September 31, 2016, http://
bismarcktribune.com/news/local/govt-and-politics/north-dakota-emergency
-services-gets-million-line-of-credit-for/article_ef76f408-8575-52cd-b898
-505721fb2a23.html.

44. Morton County Sheriff's Department, "News Release: Felony Charges Pursued
in DAPL Protest Activities," September 14, 2016, https://drive.google.com/file
/d/0B8MmtjOHKHiVdF9IOXZmWnE1Q28/view.

45. LaDonna Tamakawastewin Allard, Facebook post, September 11, 2016, https://www.facebook.com/earthw7/posts/10207476703821172.

46. "DAPL Civil Suit Dropped against Archambault, Council Members," *Indian Country Today*, May 19, 2017, https://newsmaven.io/indiancountrytoday/archive/dapl-civil-suit-dropped-against-archambault-council-members-nZdl37genUqDg1YEh_Mw_Q.

47. Nick Smith, "AG Determines Dakota Access, LLC Land Purchase Complies with Corporate Farming Law," *Bismarck Tribune*, November 22, 2016, https://bismarcktribune.com/news/local/govt-and-politics/ag-determines-dakota-access-llc-land-purchase-complies-with-corporate/article_da7db4a7-8bb6-5217-9af5-e6e67b98fdb8.html.

48. Alleen Brown, Will Parrish, and Alice Speri, "Leaked Documents Reveal Counterterrorism Tactics Used at Standing Rock to 'Defeat Pipeline Insurgencies,'" *The Intercept*, May 27, 2017, https://theintercept.com/2017/05/27/leaked-documents-reveal-security-firms-counterterrorism-tactics-at-standing-rock-to-defeat-pipeline-insurgencies.

49. Quoted in Brown, Parrish, and Speri, "Leaked Documents Reveal Counterterrorism Tactics"; John Porter, "TigerSwan DAPL SitRep 022," October 3, 2016, https://www.documentcloud.org/documents/3766413-Internal-TigerSwan-Situation-Report-2016-10-03.html.

50. LaDonna Tamakawastewin Allard, Facebook post, September 27, 2016, https://www.facebook.com/earthw7/posts/10207601154812369.

51. Clara Chaisson, "A Statue at Standing Rock Sends a Powerful Message of Resistance," NRDC, November 23, 2016, https://www.nrdc.org/onearth/statue-standing-rock-sends-powerful-message-resistance.

52. Dakota Access, LLC, "Dakota Access Pipeline Project: Monthly Construction Status Report," October 7, 2016, https://psc.nd.gov/database/documents/14-0842/220-010.pdf.

53. Quoted in "Law Enforcement Press Conference in Morton County," *Bismarck Tribune*, October 6, 2016, http://bismarcktribune.com/video/law-enforcement-press-conference-in-morton-county/youtube_341ab351-51ca-567d-83fc-4710f1b7aaeb.html.

54. John Floberg, Facebook post, September 29, 2016, https://www.facebook.com/jfloberg/posts/10155259931716978.

55. Cody Schulz, "An Update from the Morton County Commission Chairman," *Bismarck Tribune*, October 7, 2016, http://bismarcktribune.com/mandannews/local-news/an-update-from-the-morton-county-commission-chairman/article_31b11b9f-e08f-56c3-95f1-8ddcdcc27276.html.

56. "Corps, Federal Agencies Need to Take Action," *Bismarck Tribune*, October 9, 2016, http://bismarcktribune.com/news/opinion/editorial/corps-federal -agencies-need-to-take-action/article_c68725fe-4d31-56eb-a8b6-f01125afd648 .html.

57. Standing Rock Sioux Tribe v. United States Army Corps of Engineers and Dakota Access, LLC, "Order," October 9, 2016, https://earthjustice.org/sites /default/files/files/standing-rock_court-order-2016-10-09.pdf.

58. U.S. Department of Justice, "Joint Statement from Department of Justice, Department of the Army and Department of the Interior Regarding D.C. Circuit Court of Appeals Decision in Standing Rock Sioux Tribe v. U.S. Army Corps of Engineers," October 10, 2016, https://www.justice.gov/opa/pr/joint-statement -department-justice-department-army-and-department-interior-regarding-dc.

59. Mike Nowatzki, "Pipeline Protest Makes Ripples Nationally, Worldwide," *Bismarck Tribune*, October 15, 2016, http://bismarcktribune.com/news/state -and-regional/pipeline-protest-makes-ripples-nationally-worldwide/article _05066abc-5522-575d-b808-f698013e5e63.html.

60. Jenny Schlecht, "Five Senators Ask Obama to Halt Pipeline Construction," *Bismarck Tribune*, October 13, 2016, http://bismarcktribune.com/bakken/five -senators-ask-obama-to-halt-pipeline-construction/article_d99c85ee-49a7 -5cb4-ac0d-c77dfcaa3325.html.

61. Hilary C. Tompkins, "William C. Canby Jr. Lecture: Domestic Nations in the Age of 'Tribalism,'" Arizona State University Sandra Day O'Connor College of Law, October 24, 2019, https://mediasite.law.asu.edu/media/Play /7af11c1a551743618f045c40c5d7c9571d.

62. Tompkins, "William C. Canby Jr. Lecture."

63. Standing Rock Sioux Tribe v. U.S. Army Corps of Engineers, "Memorandum Opinion," September 9, 2016.

64. Hilary C. Tompkins, "65th Annual Institute: Working with Landscape-Scale Traditional Cultural Properties," Rocky Mountain Mineral Law Foundation, July 19, 2019, https://rmmlf.inreachce.com/Details/Information/3b240b1a -7647-4f23-bbf3-c245b3794608.

65. Tompkins: "William C. Canby Jr. Lecture" and "65th Annual Institute."

66. Caroline Grueskin, "Actress Pleads Not Guilty to Protest-Related Charges," *Bismarck Tribune*, October 19, 2016, http://bismarcktribune.com/news/state-and -regional/actress-pleads-not-guilty-to-protest-related-charges/article_2fa78387 -30bc-5440-979b-1ade208b281e.html; Shailene Woodley, "Shailene Woodley: The Truth about My Arrest," *Time*, October 20, 2016, http://time.com/4538557 /shailene-woodley-arrest-pipeline.

67. Caroline Grueskin and Blair Emerson, "27 Arrests Made at St. Anthony Protest Sites," *Bismarck Tribune,* October 10, 2016, http://bismarcktribune.com/news /state-and-regional/arrests-made-at-st-anthony-protest-sites/article_ba8d2aab -cf9c-5fa1-a268-46661bb51966.html.

68. Alleen Brown, Will Parrish, and Alice Speri, "The Battle of Treaty Camp," *The Intercept,* October 27, 2017, https://theintercept.com/2017/10/27/law -enforcement-descended-on-standing-rock-a-year-ago-and-changed-the-dapl -fight-forever.

69. Caroline Grueskin, "Questions Raised as Protest Policing Takes Proactive Approach," *Bismarck Tribune,* October 14, 2016, https://bismarcktribune.com /news/state-and-regional/questions-raised-as-protest-policing-takes-proactive -approach/article_d8cb61bf-6164-5972-9157-548c1b17e999.htm.

70. Julie Zeilinger, "What Really Happened at Standing Rock," MTV News, November 22, 2017, http://www.mtv.com/news/3048763/standing-rock-teen -activists/.

71. Evan Simon, "Meet the Youths at the Heart of the Standing Rock Protests against the Dakota Access Pipeline," ABC News, February 25, 2017, http://abcnews.go .com/US/meet-youth-heart-standing-rock-protests-dakota-access/story?id= 45719115; Phil McCausland, "More than 80 Dakota Access Pipeline Protesters Arrested, Some Pepper Sprayed," NBC News, October 22, 2016, https://www .nbcnews.com/storyline/dakota-pipeline-protests/more-80-dakota-access -pipeline-protesters-arrested-some-pepper-sprayed-n671281.

72. Brown, Parrish, and Speri, "The Battle of Treaty Camp."

73. Daniel A. Medina, "Tribe Asks DOJ to Intervene in Escalating Dakota Access Pipeline Protests," NBC News, October 24, 2016, https://www.nbcnews.com /news/us-news/amp/tribe-asks-doj-intervene-escalating-dakota-access -pipeline-protests-n671541.

74. Gilio-Whitaker, *As Long as Grass Grows.*

75. Quoted in Blake Nicholson and James Macpherson, "Company Asks Dakota Access Pipeline Protesters to Leave North Dakota Land," Associated Press, October 26, 2016, https://www.theglobeandmail.com/news/world/company -asks-pipeline-protesters-to-leave-north-dakota-land/article32531746/.

76. Estes, *Our History Is the Future.*

77. Alleen Brown, Will Parrish, and Alice Speri, "Police Used Private Security Air-craft for Surveillance in Standing Rock No-Fly Zone," *The Intercept,* September 29, 2017, https://theintercept.com/2017/09/29/standing-rock-dakota-access -pipeline-dapl-no-fly-zone-drones-tigerswan.

78. "Cheyenne River Sioux Chairman Brings Pipeline Opposition to Meeting with Obama," Free Speech Radio News, October 26, 2016, http://fsrn.org/2016/10/cheyenne-river-sioux-chairman-brings-pipeline-opposition-to-meeting-with-obama.

79. Quoted in Caroline Grueskin, "Tribal Chairman Criticizes Law Enforcement Response, Calls for Pipeline Reroute," Bismarck Tribune, October 29, 2016, https://bismarcktribune.com/news/state-and-regional/tribal-chairman-criticizes-law-enforcement-response-calls-for-pipeline-reroute/article_1bf1208f-b4d3-57fa-b9e2-6c69d7d85fc1.html.

80. Quoted in Forum News Service, "Negotiations between Protesters, Law Enforcement Break Down," Bismarck Tribune, October 26, 2016, http://bismarcktribune.com/news/state-and-regional/negotiations-between-protesters-law-enforcement-break-down/article_d1f7d849-5fdf-5076-ac9a-1a00016a7a71.html.

81. Grueskin, "Tribal Chairman Criticizes Law Enforcement Response."

82. Quoted in Forum News Service, "Jesse Jackson Joins Pipeline Protest Effort, FAA Issues 'No-Fly' Restriction," Bismarck Tribune, October 26, 2016, http://bismarcktribune.com/news/state-and-regional/jesse-jackson-joins-pipeline-protest-effort-faa-issues-no-fly/article_59bacc15-d626-560e-b4f5-d0562a4360d2.html.

83. Brown, Parrish, and Speri, "The Battle of Treaty Camp."

84. Quoted in Lauren Donovan, "Protesters, Law Enforcement Clash as Camp Cleared," Bismarck Tribune, October 27, 2016, http://bismarcktribune.com/news/local/mandan/protesters-law-enforcement-clash-as-camp-cleared/article_d8170db7-66f9-5f34-916a-35d40097e07c.html.

85. Sue Skalicky and Monica Davey, "Tension between Police and Standing Rock Protesters Reaches Boiling Point," New York Times, October 28, 2016, https://www.nytimes.com/2016/10/29/us/dakota-access-pipeline-protest.html.

86. Skalicky and Davey, "Tension between Police and Standing Rock Protesters Reaches Boiling Point."

87. Kandi White, Facebook post, October 27, 2016, https://www.facebook.com/dallasgoldtooth/posts/10105868129528193.

6. VICTORY ON THE HEELS OF VIOLENCE

1. Quoted in Grueskin, "Tribal Chairman Criticizes Law Enforcement Response."

2. Quoted in Nick Smith, "Officials, Protest Leaders at Odds over Law Enforcement Response," Bismarck Tribune, October 28, 2016, https://bismarcktribune

.com/news/local/govt-and-politics/officials-protest-leaders-at-odds-over-law
-enforcement-response/article_9551fddb-9a27-5887-b9c0-284d2a4113c0.html.

3. Brown, Parrish, and Speri, "Leaked Documents Reveal Counterterrorism Tactics."

4. Nick Smith, "State Approves $4M in Response to Protests," *Bismarck Tribune*, November 4, 2016, https://bismarcktribune.com/mandannews/local-news /state-approves-m-in-response-to-protests/article_88cd95c5-363e-5260-b17c -fdbcce38811d.html.

5. Will Parrish, "An Activist Stands Accused of Firing a Gun at Standing Rock. It Belonged to Her Lover—An FBI Informant," *The Intercept*, December 11, 2017, https://theintercept.com/2017/12/11/standing-rock-dakota-access-pipeline -fbi-informant-red-fawn-fallis.

6. Parrish, "An Activist Stands Accused of Firing a Gun at Standing Rock."

7. Blair Emerson, "Reporters Apprehended at Pipeline Protests," *Bismarck Tribune*, November 4, 2016, https://bismarcktribune.com/community/mandannews /local-news/reporters-apprehended-at-pipeline-protests/article_4dd9efcf-bd7c -5324-9e89-2d6d41276bf7.html.

8. Quoted in Amy Dalrymple, "At Least 7 Journalists Charged with Crimes during ND Pipeline Protests," *Bismarck Tribune*, November 5, 2016, https:// bismarcktribune.com/news/state-and-regional/at-least-journalists-charged -with-crimes-during-nd-pipeline-protests/article_64d2a5cc-f1f1-5873-87d0 -22b54f05e8aa.html.

9. Sam Levin and Nicky Woolf, "A Million People 'Check In' at Standing Rock on Facebook to Support Dakota Pipeline Protesters," *The Guardian*, October 31, 2016, https://www.theguardian.com/us-news/2016/oct/31/north-dakota -access-pipeline-protest-mass-facebook-check-in.

10. Merrit Kennedy, "More Than 1 Million 'Check In' on Facebook to Support the Standing Rock Sioux," NPR, November 1, 2016, https://www.npr.org/sections /thetwo-way/2016/11/01/500268879/more-than-a-million-check-in-on -facebook-to-support-the-standing-rock-sioux.

11. Quoted in "EXCLUSIVE: President Obama on Dakota Access Pipeline Protests: 'There's an Obligation for Authorities to Show Restraint,'" *NowThis*, November 1, 2016, https://twitter.com/nowthisnews/status/793641140184461313.

12. U.S. Army Corps of Engineers, "Dakota Access Pipeline FAQ's," https://www .usace.army.mil/Dakota-Access-Pipeline/FAQs (accessed June 2020).

13. Caroline Grueskin, "Burial Ground at Center of Police Confrontations Is Known Historical Site," *Bismarck Tribune*, November 13, 2016, https://bismarcktribune

.com/news/state-and-regional/burial-ground-at-center-of-police-confrontations
-is-known-historical/article_8a11a527-2119-58c4-a242-a04f3806a251.html.

14. Simon, "Meet the Youths At the Heart of the Standing Rock Protests against the Dakota Access Pipeline."

15. Lauren Donovan, "Cramer Says Pipeline Issue Will Be Moot by Trump's Inauguration," *Bismarck Tribune*, November 9, 2016, https://bismarcktribune.com /news/state-and-regional/cramer-says-pipeline-issue-will-be-moot-by-trump -s/article_37925efc-407e-5902-8890-ec5fe0b2464f.html.

16. Gilio-Whitaker, *As Long as Grass Grows*.

17. "Trump Alters the Outlook for Pipeline," *Bismarck Tribune*, November 13, 2016, https://bismarcktribune.com/news/opinion/editorial/trump-alters-the -outlook-for-pipeline/article_23272b30-c28f-57d2-883f-7579d6761e2b.html.

18. Alleen Brown, Will Parrish, and Alice Speri, "Standing Rock Documents Expose Inner Workings of 'Surveillance Industrial Complex,'" *The Intercept*, June 3, 2017, https://theintercept.com/2017/06/03/standing-rock-documents-expose-inner -workings-of-surveillance-industrial-complex.

19. John Porter, "TigerSwan DAPL SitRep 059," November 10, 2016, https://www .documentcloud.org/documents/3766419-Internal-TigerSwan-Situation-Report -2016-11-10.html.

20. Steven Mufson, "Trump Dumped His Stock in the Dakota Access Pipeline Owner over the Summer," *Washington Post*, November 23, 2016, https://www .washingtonpost.com/news/energy-environment/wp/2016/11/23/trump -dumped-his-stock-in-dakota-access-pipeline-owner-over-the-summer; Oliver Milman, "Dakota Access Pipeline Company and Donald Trump Have Close Financial Ties," *The Guardian*, October 26, 2016, https://www.theguardian .com/us-news/2016/oct/26/donald-trump-dakota-access-pipeline-investment -energy-transfer-partners.

21. Jordan Blum and David Hunn, "Pipeline Protests Put Kelcy Warren in the Spotlight and Bull's-Eye," *Houston Chronicle*, November 21, 2016, http://www .houstonchronicle.com/business/energy/article/Pipeline-protests-put-Kelcy -Warren-in-the-10628354.php.

22. Plumer, "The Battle over the Dakota Access Pipeline, Explained"; Mufson, "Trump Dumped His Stock in the Dakota Access Pipeline Owner over the Summer."

23. Quoted in Leonard, "The Billionaire behind the Dakota Access Pipeline Is a Little Lonely."

24. "CEO Confident Dakota Access Pipeline Will Be Completed under Trump Presidency," CBS News, November 11, 2016, https://www.cbsnews.com/news

/dakota-access-pipeline-energy-transfer-partners-ceo-kelcy-warren-breaks
-silence.

25. "Standing Rock Sioux Tribal Council Votes Unanimously to Ask Red Warrior Camp to Leave," KFYR-TV, https://www.kfyrtv.com/content/news/Standing -Rock-Sioux-Tribal-Council-votes-unanimously-to-ask-Red-Warrior-Camp-to -leave-401548985.html.

26. John Porter, "TigerSwan DAPL SitRep 067," November 18, 2016, https://www .documentcloud.org/documents/3766424-Internal-TigerSwan-Situation -Report-2016-11-18.html.

27. U.S. Department of the Army and U.S. Department of the Interior, "Statement Regarding the Dakota Access Pipeline," November 14, 2016, https://www.usace .army.mil/Media/News-Releases/News-Release-Article-View/Article/1003593 /statement-regarding-the-dakota-access-pipeline/.

28. Standing Rock Sioux Tribe v. United States Army Corps of Engineers and Dakota Access, LLC, "Dakota Access, LLC's Answer to Intervenor-Plaintiff Cheyenne River Sioux Tribe's First Amended Complaint for Declaratory and Injunctive Relief, and Cross-Claim against Defendant U.S. Army Corps of Engineers," November 15, 2016, https://earthjustice.org/sites/default/files/files/DAPL -answer-and-cross-claim.pdf.

29. Ryan Schleeter, "#NoDAPL Day of Action Draws Tens of Thousands, Lights Up Social Media," Greenpeace, November 16, 2016, https://www.greenpeace .org/usa/nodapl-day-action-draws-tens-thousands-lights-social-media.

30. See, for example, Alleen Brown, "Medics Describe How Police Sprayed Standing Rock Demonstrators with Tear Gas and Water Cannons," *The Intercept*, November 21, 2016, https://theintercept.com/2016/11/21/medics-describe -how-police-sprayed-standing-rock-demonstrators-with-tear-gas-and-water -cannons.

31. Estes, *Our History Is the Future*.

32. Standing Rock Medic and Healer Council at the Standing Rock Dakota Access Pipeline Camps, "Standing Rock: Critical Injuries after Police Attack with Water Cannons, Rubber Bullets in Freezing Temps," November 20, 2016, https://docs.google.com/document/d /11Aail5LREUaOwVCEMgOiQQAgeT8nF0Je1VZZO5Fkg8A/edit.

33. Jessica Holdman, "Explosion at Protest Site Bears Investigation," *Bismarck Tribune*, November 22, 2016, https://bismarcktribune.com/news/local/crime-and -courts/explosion-at-protest-site-bears-investigation/article_5f99fe4a-e1c3 -5640-b170-792c77c791e4.html.

34. Quoted in "Father of Activist Injured at Standing Rock Calls on Obama to Stop Dakota Access Pipeline Drilling," *Democracy Now!*, November 23, 2016, https://www.democracynow.org/2016/11/23/father_of_activist_injured_at_standing.

35. Colin Moynihan, "Cause of Severe Injury at Pipeline Protest Becomes New Point of Dispute," *New York Times*, November 24, 2016, https://www.nytimes.com/2016/11/24/us/dakota-pipeline-sophia-wilansky.html.

36. Blake Nicholson, "Injured Pipeline Protester Argues for Lawsuit to Proceed," AP News, February 26, 2019, https://apnews.com/07ee4ac65138435eaf3f123cc478bfb1.

37. Nicholson, "Injured Pipeline Protester Argues for Lawsuit to Proceed."

38. Quoted in Standing Rock Medic and Healer Council at the Standing Rock Dakota Access Pipeline Resistance Camps, "Press Release sw," November 22, 2016, https://docs.google.com/document/d/1sU15VLnlJlEdVB4H6SmLaQ2gQ25mtSjpFpVu4daGVTE/mobilebasic.

39. "Intel Group Email Thread," November 20, 2016, https://www.documentcloud.org/documents/3766489-Intel-Group-Email-Thread-2016-11-20.html.

40. Quoted in Brown, Will, and Speri, "Standing Rock Documents Expose Inner Workings of 'Surveillance Industrial Complex.'"

41. "The Morton County Sheriff's Department Is Holding a Press Conference in Response to Last Night's #DakotaAccessPipeline Protest at the Backwater Bridge," KFYR-TV, November 21, 2016, https://www.facebook.com/KFYRtv/videos/10154083083164103.

42. Defense Technology, "Instantaneous Blast Grenade OC, CN, CS, and Practice," http://www.defense-technology.com/on/demandware.static/-/Sites-DefenseTech-Library/default/dw1dd08d84/product-pdfs/less-lethal/Instantaneous_Blast_Grenade.pdf (accessed January 2020).

43. "Standing Rock Tribal Chairman Dave Archambault Discussing Backwater Bridge Incident Sunday," KFYR-TV, November 31, 2016, https://www.facebook.com/KFYRtv/videos/10154083007734103.

44. National Lawyers Guild, "Water Protector Legal Collective Files Suit for Excessive Force against Peaceful Protesters," November 28, 2016, https://www.nlg.org/water-protector-legal-collective-files-suit-for-excessive-force-against-peaceful-protesters.

45. Standing Rock Sioux Tribe, "Tribes Call on President Obama to Deny Easement, Investigate Pipeline Safety, and Protect Tribal Sovereignty," November 21, 2016, https://www.facebook.com/StandingRockst/photos/pcb.1442398579121741/1442398362455096.

46. "Violent Clashes Erupt over U.S. Oil Pipeline," CNN, November 24, 2016.

47. Editorial Board, "Power Imbalance at the Pipeline Protest," *New York Times*, November 23, 2016, https://www.nytimes.com/2016/11/23/opinion/power-imbalance-at-the-pipeline-protest.html.

48. John W. Henderson, letter to Chairman Dave Archambault II, November 25, 2016, https://www.facebook.com/photo.php?fbid=576967785830201.

49. James Cook, "Standing Rock: Camps Continue to Grow as Standoff Continue[s]," BBC News, December 2, 2016, https://www.bbc.com/news/world-us-canada-38191311.

50. Standing Rock Sioux Tribe, "Press Release: Army Corp Closes Public Access to Oceti Sakowin Camp on Dec. 5th," November 26, 2016, https://standwithstandingrock.net/army-corp-closes-public-access-oceti-sakowin-camp-dec-5th.

51. Julia Carrie Wong and Sam Levin, "North Dakota Governor Orders Evacuation of Standing Rock Protest Site," *The Guardian*, November 28, 2016, https://www.theguardian.com/us-news/2016/nov/28/north-dakota-access-pipeline-evacuation-order-standing-rock.

52. Standing Rock Sioux Tribe, "Press Release: Standing Rock Sioux Tribal Chairman Responds to Governor's Executive Order," November 28, 2016, http://standwithstandingrock.net/press-release-standing-rock-sioux-tribal-chairman-responds-governors-executive-order.

53. Bo Evans, "Dalrymple Holds Press Conference to Clarify Details of Emergency Evacuation Order of DAPL Protest Camps," KFYR-TV, November 30, 2016, https://www.kfyrtv.com/content/news/Dalrymple-hosts-press-conference-to-clarify-details-of-emergency-evacuation-order-of-DAPL-protest-camps-403830496.html.

54. Indigenous Environmental Network, "Press Conference: Response to Governor Dalrymple's Order to Evacuate the Oceti Sakowin Camp," November 28, 2016, https://www.facebook.com/ienearth/videos/10154177424030642.

55. Christopher Mele, "Veterans to Serve as 'Human Shields' for Dakota Pipeline Protesters," *New York Times*, November 29, 2016, https://www.nytimes.com/2016/11/29/us/veterans-to-serve-as-human-shields-for-pipeline-protesters.html.

56. Morton County Sheriff's Office, Facebook post, December 2, 2016, https://www.facebook.com/MortonCountySO/photos/a.162536147432065/367424520276559.

57. Quoted in Matt Petronzio, "How Young Native Americans Built and Sustained the #NoDAPL Movement," *Mashable*, December 7, 2016, https://mashable.com/2016/12/07/standing-rock-nodapl-youth/#VTeZSbN49qqG.

58. Joye Braun, Facebook video, December 4, 2016, https://www.facebook.com
    /joye.braun/videos/10155410882514057.
59. Joye Braun, Facebook video, December 4, 2016, https://www.facebook.com
    /joye.braun/videos/10155411093784057.
60. Quoted in Caroline Grueskin, "U.S. Army Denies Pipeline Easement in Win
    for Protesters," *Bismarck Tribune*, December 4, 2016, https://bismarcktribune
    .com/news/state-and-regional/u-s-army-denies-pipeline-easement-in-win-for
    -protesters/article_3de3e500-3ddf-594d-b52e-b0b66c8246b1.html.

7. FROM VICTORY TO EVICTION

1. Kandi White, "Update from North Dakota Monday December 5th," December 5,
   2016, https://www.facebook.com/kandi.mossett/videos/10154960667971844.
2. John W. Henderson, "Memorandum: Dakota Access LLC, Waiver Request,"
   August 3, 2016, https://usace.contentdm.oclc.org/digital/collection
   /p16021coll5/id/1670.
3. John W. Henderson, email to Scott A. Spellmon, "NWO Easement Recommen-
   dation and Unexecuted Easement with Exhibits," December 3, 2016, https://
   usace.contentdm.oclc.org/digital/collection/p16021coll5/id/1572.
4. Department of the Army, "Draft: Easement for Fuel Carrying Pipeline Right-of-
   Way," November 7, 2016, https://usace.contentdm.oclc.org/digital/collection
   /p16021coll5/id/1604.
5. Brian C. Deese, email to Lowry Crook, "Touch Base," December 2, 2016, https://
   usace.contentdm.oclc.org/digital/collection/p16021coll5/id/1578.
6. Kim Teehee et al., letter to President Barack Obama, November 28, 2016, http://
   www.usetinc.org/wp-content/uploads/bvenuti/WWS/2016/December
   %202016/December%202/Letter%20to%20the%20President%20re%20DAPL
   .11.28.16.pdf.
7. National Congress of American Indians, letter to President Barack Obama,
   "Urgent: Prevent Violence at Standing Rock, Deny Easement While Reconsid-
   ering Social Impacts of the Dakota Access Pipeline, OMB Guidance on Federal
   Infrastructure Permitting, Request for Meeting," November 27, 2016, https://
   usace.contentdm.oclc.org/digital/collection/p16021coll5/id/1586.
8. Hilary Tompkins, "Memorandum: Tribal Treaty and Environmental Statutory
   Implications of the Dakota Access Pipeline," December 4, 2016, https://www
   .eenews.net/assets/2017/02/21/document_ew_05.pdf.
9. Energy Transfer and Sunoco Logistics, "Energy Transfer Partners and Sunoco
   Logistics Partners Respond to the Statement from the Department of the Army,"
   *BusinessWire*, December 4, 2016, https://www.businesswire.com/news/home

/20161204005090/en/Energy-Transfer-Partners-Sunoco-Logistics-Partners
-Respond.

10. Standing Rock Sioux Tribe v. U.S. Army Corps of Engineers and Dakota Access, LLC, "Declaration of William S. Scherman in Support of Motion for Summary Judgment," December 5, 2016, https://earthjustice.org/sites/default/files/press /2016/3154-66-3-Dec-of-William-Scherman-ISO-MSJ.pdf.

11. Tompkins, "William C. Canby Jr. Lecture."

12. Kandi Mossett, Facebook post, December 5, 2016, https://www.facebook.com /kandi.mossett/posts/10154959805891844.

13. Our Revolution, Facebook video, "Veterans Ask for Forgiveness at Standing Rock," December 5, 2016, https://www.facebook.com/watch/?v= 1330615996990613.

14. Dave Archambault, "Chairman Update," December 5, 2016, https://www.youtube .com/watch?v=pe4aqRu5B_8; Standing Rock Sioux Tribe, "Standing Rock Chairman Calls for Water Protectors to Return Home," December 6, 2016, https://www.facebook.com/StandingRockST/photos/pb.402298239798452. -2207520000.1481183148./1464246836936915.

15. See, for example, LaDonna Tamakawastewin Allard, Facebook post, December 9, 2016, https://www.facebook.com/earthw7/posts/10208202870894895; Jasilyn Charger, Facebook live video, December 11, 2016, https://www.facebook .com/jasilyn.charger.5/videos/1173687419375394.

16. Quoted in Lauren Donovan and Nick Smith, "Archambault, Dalrymple Meet, Agree Barricaded Bridge Should Be Reopened," *Bismarck Tribune*, December 13, 2016, https://bismarcktribune.com/news/state-and-regional/archambault -dalrymple-meet-agree-barricaded-bridge-should-be-reopened/article _422bdfed-3731-563c-b925-8145cd35b43e.html.

17. Kandi White, Facebook post, January 1, 2017, https://www.facebook.com/kandi .mossett/posts/10155071352431844.

18. Dave Archambault II, email to Jo-Ellen Darcy and Lowry Crook, January 5, 2017, https://usace.contentdm.oclc.org/digital/collection/p16021coll5/id/1559.

19. Indigenous Rising Media, "Press Conference Update from the Headsmen of Oceti Sakowin," January 12, 2017, https://www.facebook.com /Indigenousrisingmedia/videos/1593510370665783; Dallas Goldtooth, "#NoDAPL Update 1/13—Meetings Today & Washington DC," January 13, 2017, https://www.facebook.com/dallasgoldtooth/videos/10106205704764713.

20. Caroline Grueskin and Jessica Holdman, "Backwater Bridge Declared Structurally Sound," *Bismarck Tribune*, January 12, 2017, https://bismarcktribune

.com/news/state-and-regional/backwater-bridge-declared-structurally-sound /article_41b7ddd0-4404-522b-810d-058852754b8c.html.

21. Indigenous Rising Media, "Update from Oceti Sakowin Camp Monday January 9th," January 9, 2017, https://www.facebook.com/Indigenousrisingmedia /videos/1590516797631807.

22. Water Protector Legal Collective, "WPLC Calls on Morton County to Remove Illegal Blockade of Hwy 1806 to Water Protector Camps," December 14, 2016, https://www.nlg.org/wplc-calls-on-morton-county-to-remove-illegal-blockade -of-hwy-1806-to-water-protector-camps.

23. Steve Horn, "TigerSwan, County Sheriff Sued over Road Blockade during Dakota Access Pipeline Protests," *Desmog*, October 26, 2018, https://www.desmogblog .com/2018/10/26/lawsuit-dakota-access-road-blockade; Thunderhawk et al. vs. County of Morton, Demand for Jury Trial, U.S. District Court, District of North Dakota, October 18, 2018, https://www.desmogblog.com/sites/beta .desmogblog.com/files/D.N.D.%2018-cv-00212%20dckt%20000001_000 %20filed%202018-10-18.pdf.

24. Dallas Goldtooth, Facebook post, March 16, 2017, https://www.facebook.com /dallasgoldtooth/posts/10106462655483413.

25. "From Keystone XL Pipeline to #DAPL: Jasilyn Charger, Water Protector from Cheyenne River Reservation," *Democracy Now!*, January 4, 2017, https://www .democracynow.org/2017/1/4/from_keystone_xl_pipeline_to_dapl.

26. Army Department, "Notice of Intent to Prepare an Environmental Impact Statement in Connection with Dakota Access, LLC's Request for an Easement to Cross Lake Oahe, North Dakota," January 18, 2017, https://www.federalregister .gov/documents/2017/01/18/2017-00937/notice-of-intent-to-prepare-an -environmental-impact-statement-in-connection-with-dakota-access-llcs; Standing Rock Sioux Tribe, "Standing Rock Sioux Tribe Welcomes Publication of Notice of Intent for EIS," January 18, 2017, https://standwithstandingrock .net/standing-rock-sioux-tribe-welcomes-publication-notice-intent-eis/ ?fbclid=IwAR2z7VDXekhF2OElQgDWme2fJLQfKwJvGziTkokPmlXfXA _xxONEgkMGDWE.

27. Kandi White, Facebook post, January 18, 2017, https://www.facebook.com /kandi.mossett/posts/10155131982436844.

28. Jo-Ellen Darcy, letter to Honorable Dave Archambault II, January 19, 2017, https://usace.contentdm.oclc.org/digital/collection/p16021coll5/id/1551.

29. Jenni Monet, "Standing Rock Tribal Council Approves Evacuation Order for All Camps," *Indian Country Today*, January 22, 2017, https://newsmaven.io

/indiancountrytoday/archive/standing-rock-tribal-council-approves-evacuation
-order-for-all-camps-gKgZSGp4Pk2wha8_Ra4e_Q.

30. Our Climate Voices, "Jasilyn Charger: Cheyenne River Sioux Tribe," January 18, 2019, https://www.ourclimatevoices.org/2019/jasilyncharger.

31. Elbein, "The Youth Group That Launched a Movement at Standing Rock."

32. Quoted in Our Climate Voices, "Jasilyn Charger."

33. White House Office of the Press Secretary, "Memorandum for the Secretary of the Army," January 24, 2017, https://earthjustice.org/sites/default/files/files /Construction-of-the-Dakota-Access-Pipeline.pdf.

34. "Trump: 'Haven't Had One Call' Complaining about Dakota Pipeline."

35. Quoted in "'Water Is Life, Water Is Sacred': Standing Rock's Bobbi Jean Three Legs Speaks Out against Trump," *Democracy Now!,* January 25, 2017, https:// www.democracynow.org/2017/1/25/water_is_life_water_is_sacred.

36. Quoted in "Trump Signs Orders Advancing Keystone, Dakota Access Pipelines," NBC News, January 24, 2017, https://www.nbcnews.com/politics/white-house /trump-sign-orders-advancing-keystone-dakota-access-pipelines-n711321.

37. Caroline Grueskin, "Archambault Says Trump Ignored Local Concerns," *Bismarck Tribune,* January 25, 2017, https://bismarcktribune.com/archambault-says-trump -ignored-local-concerns/article_f0715a7d-dde4-5116-9d29-b4322b4f2faf.html.

38. Earthjustice, "In Conversation."

39. Cecily Hilleary, "Native Americans Vow Legal Battle over Trump Pipeline Orders," VOA, January 24, 2017, https://www.voanews.com/usa/native -americans-vow-legal-battle-over-trump-pipeline-orders.

40. Kandi White, "Reaction Today January 24th on DAPL & Pipeline Decisions," January 24, 2017, https://www.facebook.com/kandi.mossett/videos /10155153826281844.

41. Quoted in Lauren Donovan, "Cleanup with Machines Is Emotional for Some," *Bismarck Tribune,* January 31, 2017, https://bismarcktribune.com/news/state -and-regional/cleanup-with-machines-is-emotional-for-some/article_932cda12 -a120-5319-8f1b-d0cc3124a39f.html.

42. See, for example, Lakota People's Law Project, "Last Child Camp: Words with Chase Iron Eyes," https://www.lakotalaw.org/resources/last-child-camp-words -with-chase-iron-eyes (accessed June 2020); Levi Rickert, "Chase Iron Eyes among 76 Arrested on Wednesday at Standing Rock Camp," Native News Online .net, February 1, 2017, https://nativenewsonline.net/currents/chase-iron-eyes -among-76-arrested-wednesday-standing-rock-camp.

43. Douglas W. Lamont, letter to Office of the Federal Register, February 7, 2017, https://earthjustice.org/sites/default/files/files/EIS-termination0.pdf, and

"Memorandum for Record: Compliance with Presidential Memorandum (January 24, 2017)," February 7, 2017, https://earthjustice.org/sites/default/files/files/Memo-Feb7-0.pdf; Department of the Army, "Notice of Termination of the Intent to Prepare an Environmental Impact Statement in Connection with Dakota Access, LLC's Request for an Easement to Cross Lake Oahe, North Dakota," February 7, 2017, https://earthjustice.org/sites/default/files/files/EIS-termination0.pdf.

44. Maria Cantwell and Bernard Sanders, letter to President Donald Trump, February 7, 2017, https://usace.contentdm.oclc.org/digital/collection/p16021coll5/id/1519.

45. U.S. Army Corps of Engineers, "Corps Grants Easement to Dakota Access, LLC," February 8, 2017, https://www.nwo.usace.army.mil/Media/News-Releases/Article/1077134/corps-grants-easement-to-dakota-access-llc; Department of the Army, "Easement for Fuel Carrying Pipeline Right-of-Way Located on Lake Oahe Project Morton and Emmons Counties, North Dakota," December 3, 2016, https://usace.contentdm.oclc.org/digital/collection/p16021coll5/id/1515.

46. John Porter, "TigerSwan DAPL SitRep 150," February 9, 2017, https://www.documentcloud.org/documents/3868794-Internal-TigerSwan-Situation-Report-2017-02-09.html.

47. Quoted in Indigenous Environmental Network, "Dept. of Army Announces Approval of DAPL Easement, IEN Response," https://www.ienearth.org/dept-of-army-announces-approval-of-dapl-easement (accessed January 2020).

48. Kandi White, Facebook post, February 8, 2017, https://www.facebook.com/kandi.mossett/posts/10155199965906844.

49. Standing Rock Sioux Tribe, "Standing Rock Denounces Army Easement Announcement, Vows Court Challenge," February 7, 2017, https://standwithstandingrock.net/standing-rock-denounces-army-easement-announcement-vows-court-challenge.

50. Quoted in Leonard, "The Billionaire behind the Dakota Access Pipeline Is a Little Lonely."

51. Associated Press, "Federal Judge Denies Tribes' Request to Block Work on Dakota Access Pipeline," CBS News, February 13, 2017, https://www.cbsnews.com/news/fight-against-dakota-access-pipeline-headed-again-to-court.

52. Standing Rock Sioux Tribe v. Dakota Access, LLC, "Plaintiff Standing Rock Sioux Tribe's Memorandum in Support of Its Motion for Partial Summary Judgement," February 14, 2017, https://earthjustice.org/sites/default/files/files/Memo-ISO-SRSTs-Mtn-for-PSJ.pdf.

53. Estes, *Our History Is the Future*, 53–54.

54. North Dakota Office of the Governor, "Burgum Issues Emergency Evacuation Order," February 15, 2017, https://www.governor.nd.gov/news/burgum-issues-emergency-evacuation-order.

55. Lauren Donovan and Caroline Grueskin, "Sacred Stone Camp Given Trespass Notice," *Bismarck Tribune*, February 17, 2017, https://bismarcktribune.com/news/state-and-regional/sacred-stone-camp-given-trespass-notice/article_b02f5c69-ae93-5c4f-91c8-dc651ee68a47.html.

56. "Live Feed," *Lakota People's Law Project*, February 22, 2017, https://www.facebook.com/LakotaPeoplesLawProject/videos/10154423675367029.

57. A confrontation in January 2019 at the Lincoln Memorial with high school students vaulted Nathan Phillips to national prominence.

58. Unicorn Riot, "Cam 2—Eviction of Main #NoDAPL Camp," February 22, 2017, https://www.facebook.com/unicornriot.ninja/videos/430839023916991.

59. Julian Brave NoiseCat, "Standing Rock Is Burning—But Our Resistance Isn't Over," *The Guardian*, February 23, 2017, https://www.theguardian.com/us-news/2017/feb/23/standing-rock-burning-dakota-access.

60. Jihan Hafiz, "A Closing Prayer for Standing Rock's Oceti Sakowin," *The Intercept*, February 25, 2017, https://theintercept.com/2017/02/25/video-a-closing-prayer-for-standing-rocks-oceti-sakowin.

## 8. THE STANDING ROCK LEGACY

1. "State Handled Evacuation in Smart Manner," *Bismarck Tribune*, February 24, 2017, https://bismarcktribune.com/news/opinion/editorial/state-handled-evacuation-in-smart-manner/article_b5f20845-8fe6-57b1-8dca-66009f76d1f8.html.

2. Kandi White, Facebook post, February 27, 2017, https://www.facebook.com/kandi.mossett/posts/10155259846501844.

3. "Unintended Consequences the Big Danger," *Bismarck Tribune*, January 26, 2017, https://bismarcktribune.com/news/opinion/editorial/unintended-consequences-the-big-danger/article_29df5341-b97d-57b3-ba89-5a189717349c.html.

4. Lloyd Omdahl, "Aura of Vengeance in Casino Proposal," *Bismarck Tribune*, March 12, 2017, https://bismarcktribune.com/news/opinion/editorial/columnists/aura-of-vengeance-in-casino-proposal/article_d09a6c9c-8847-5968-9dc0-d2659a6b4f92.html.

5. Zoe Carpenter and Tracie Williams, "PHOTOS: Since Standing Rock, 56 Bills Have Been Introduced in 30 States to Restrict Protests," *The Nation*, February

16, 2018, https://www.thenation.com/article/photos-since-standing-rock-56 -bills-have-been-introduced-in-30-states-to-restrict-protests.

6. International Center for Not-for-Profit Law, "US Protest Law Tracker," https:// www.icnl.org/usprotestlawtracker (accessed October 2020).

7. John Porter, "TigerSwan DAPL SitRep 158," February 17, 2017, https://www .documentcloud.org/documents/3868802-Internal-TigerSwan-Situation -Report-2017-02-17.html.

8. John Porter, "TigerSwan DAPL SitRep 165," February 24, 2017, https://www .documentcloud.org/documents/3868809-Internal-TigerSwan-Situation -Report-2017-02-24.html.

9. Noah Kirsch, "Dakota Pipeline Billionaire Slams Standing Rock Protests," *Forbes*, March 23, 2017, https://www.forbes.com/sites/noahkirsch/2017/03/23/kelcy -warren-dakota-access-pipeline-billionaire-slams-standing-rock/#6deea31376f8.

10. John Porter, "TigerSwan DAPL SitRep 176," March 7, 2017, https://www .documentcloud.org/documents/3940241-Internal-TigerSwan-Situation -Report-2017-03-07.html.

11. John Porter, "TigerSwan DAPL SitRep 182," March 13, 2017, https://www .documentcloud.org/documents/3940247-Internal-TigerSwan-Situation -Report-2017-03-13.html.

12. "Standing Rock Sioux Tribe Issues New Fact Sheet in Form of Q&A with Chairman," *Indian Country Today*, March 16, 2017, https://newsmaven.io /indiancountrytoday/archive/standing-rock-sioux-tribe-issues-new-fact-sheet -in-form-of-q-a-with-chairman-zet_N_-a_0i0Fsv10YhcYw.

13. LaDonna Tamakawastewin Allard, Facebook post, March 27, 2017, https:// www.facebook.com/earthw7/posts/10209101344836182.

14. LaDonna Tamakawastewin Allard, Facebook post, March 14, 2017, https:// www.facebook.com/CampOfTheSacredStone/posts/1868639826758380.

15. See, for example, Indigenous Environmental Network, "Indigenous Principles of Just Transition," https://www.ienearth.org/justtransition (accessed June 2020).

16. *Voices from Wounded Knee, 1973: In the Words of Participants* (Rooseveltown NY: Akwesaswe Notes, 1974); Zinn, *A People's History of the United States*.

17. Jenni Monet, "What Standing Rock Gave the World," *Yes! Magazine*, March 16, 2018, https://www.yesmagazine.org/issues/decolonize/what-standing-rock -gave-the-world-20180316.

18. Oliver Laughland and Tom Silverstone, "Liquid Genocide: Alcohol Destroyed Pine Ridge Reservation—Then They Fought Back," *The Guardian*, September 29,

2017, https://www.theguardian.com/society/2017/sep/29/pine-ridge-indian
-reservation-south-dakota.

19. "Indigenized Energy: Solar Power at Standing Rock," https://solve.mit.edu
/challenges/oceti-sakowin-solve-fellowship/solutions/2883 (accessed June
2020).

20. Estes and Jaskiran Dhillon, *Standing with Standing Rock*.

21. Jo Miles and Hugh MacMillan, "Who's Banking on the Dakota Access Pipeline?,"
*Common Dreams*, September 7, 2016, https://www.commondreams.org/views
/2016/09/07/whos-banking-dakota-access-pipeline.

22. Standing Rock Sioux Tribe, "Standing Rock Sioux Tribe Applauds BNP Paribas'
Decision to Divest from DAPL," April 5, 2017, https://www.pressenza.com
/2017/04/standing-rock-sioux-tribe-applauds-bnp-paribas-decision-to-divest
-from-dapl/.

23. Indigenous Environmental Network, "#DivestWellsFargo Mural Action,"
https://www.facebook.com/ienearth/videos/2065674563449359 (accessed
January 2020).

24. David Henry, "Citi Meeting Protest Prompts Apology on Pipeline Finance
Steps," Reuters, April 25, 2017, https://www.reuters.com/article/us-citigroup
-shareholder-meeting-idUSKBN17R20Y.

25. John Porter, "TigerSwan DAPL SitRep 228," April 28, 2017, https://www
.documentcloud.org/documents/3940282-Internal-TigerSwan-Situation
-Report-2017-04-28.html, and "TigerSwan DAPL SitRep 219," April 20, 2017,
https://www.documentcloud.org/documents/3940277-Internal-TigerSwan
-Situation-Report-2017-04-20.html.

26. "Indigenous Leader Kandi Mossett: 'It's Not OK for Our Women to Die
Because We Want to Protect Water,'" *Democracy Now!*, May 1, 2017, https://www
.democracynow.org/2017/5/1/indigenous_leader_kandi_mossett_its_not.

27. Robinson Meyer, "The Climate March's Big Tent Strategy Draws a Big Crowd,"
*The Atlantic*, April 30, 2017, https://www.theatlantic.com/science/archive/2017
/04/the-people-who-came-to-the-climate-march/524865.

28. See, for example, Department of the Interior, Bureau of Land Management,
"Methane and Waste Prevention Rule," https://www.blm.gov/programs/energy
-and-minerals/oil-and-gas/operations-and-production/methane-and-waste
-prevention-rule (accessed June 2020).

29. Barry Amundson, "Oil Spill in Far Northern ND Flows into Slough—Almost
300 Reported in State since Jan. 1," *Grand Forks Herald*, May 25, 2017, https://
www.grandforksherald.com/news/4273275-oil-spill-far-northern-nd-flows
-slough-almost-300-reported-state-jan-1.

30. Zak Cheney Rice, "The Dakota Access Pipeline Sprung 2 New Leaks," *Business Insider*, May 23, 2017, https://www.businessinsider.com/the-dakota-access -pipeline-sprung-2-new-leaks-2017-5.

31. Reuters, "The Controversial Dakota Access Pipeline Will Start Interstate Oil Delivery on May 14," *Fortune*, April 14, 2017, https://fortune.com/2017/04/14 /dakota-access-pipeline-interstate-delivery.

32. Global Witness, "Defenders of the Earth," July 13, 2017, https://www .globalwitness.org/en/campaigns/environmental-activists/defenders-earth.

33. John Porter, "TigerSwan DAPL SitRep 240," May 12, 2017, https://www .documentcloud.org/documents/3940294-Internal-TigerSwan-Situation -Report-2017-05-11.html.

34. John Porter, "TigerSwan DAPL SitRep 239," May 10, 2017, https://www .documentcloud.org/documents/3940293-Internal-TigerSwan-Situation -Report-2017-05-10.html, "TigerSwan DAPL SitRep," https://www .documentcloud.org/documents/3940291-Internal-TigerSwan-Situation-Report -2017-05-08.html (accessed November 2020), and "TigerSwan DAPL SitRep 238," May 9, 2017, https://www.documentcloud.org/documents/3940292-Internal -TigerSwan-Situation-Report-2017-05-09.html.

35. John Porter, "TigerSwan DAPL SitRep 233," May 4, 2017, https://www .documentcloud.org/documents/3940287-Internal-TigerSwan-Situation -Report-2017-05-04.html, and "TigerSwan DAPL SitRep 223," April 24, 2017, https://www.documentcloud.org/documents/3940281-Internal-TigerSwan -Situation-Report-2017-04-24.html.

36. John Porter, "TigerSwan DAPL SitRep 206," April 8, 2017, https://www .documentcloud.org/documents/3940267-Internal-TigerSwan-Situation -Report-2017-04-08.html.

37. "President Delivers Remarks on Infrastructure," C-SPAN, June 7, 2017, https:// www.c-span.org/video/?429651-1/president-pushes-infrastructure-agenda -cincinnati-ohio. See also "Trump Jokes Approvingly about Dakota Access Pipeline," *Washington Post*, June 7, 2017, https://www.washingtonpost.com /video/politics/trump-jokes-about-approving-dakota-access-pipeline/2017 /06/07/4eebd812-4bab-11e7-987c-42ab5745db2e_video.html.

EPILOGUE

1. Nadja Popovich, Livia Albeck-Ripka, and Kendra Pierre-Louis, "95 Environmental Rules Being Rolled Back under Trump," *New York Times*, December 21, 2019, https://www.nytimes.com/interactive/2019/climate/trump-environment -rollbacks.html; Maegan Vazquez, "Trump's Dismantling of Environmental

Regulations Unwinds 50 Years of Protections," CNN, January 25, 2020, https://www.cnn.com/2020/01/25/politics/trump-environmental-rollbacks-list/index.html.

2. Tompkins, "William C. Canby Jr. Lecture."

3. Tompkins, "65th Annual Institute."

4. Quoted in Leonard, "The Billionaire behind the Dakota Access Pipeline Is a Little Lonely."

5. "Dakota Access Pipeline Company Paid Mercenaries to Build Conspiracy Lawsuit against Environmentalists," *The Intercept*, November 15, 2017, https://theintercept.com/2017/11/15/dakota-access-pipeline-dapl-tigerswan-energy-transfer-partners-rico-lawsuit.

6. Department of the Interior, Bureau of Land Management, "Methane and Waste Prevention Rule."

7. United States Environmental Protection Agency, "EPA Issues Final Policy and Technical Amendments to the New Source Performance Standards for the Oil and Natural Gas Industry," https://www.epa.gov/controlling-air-pollution-oil-and-natural-gas-industry/epa-issues-final-policy-and-technical (accessed October 2020).

8. Coral Davenport, "Trump Eliminates Major Methane Rule, Even as Leaks Are Worsening," *New York Times*, August 13, 2020, https://www.nytimes.com/2020/08/13/climate/trump-methane.html.

9. Merrit Kennedy, "EPA Aims to Roll Back Limits on Methane Emissions from Oil and Gas Industry," NPR, August 29, 2019, https://www.npr.org/2019/08/29/755394353/epa-aims-to-roll-back-limits-on-methane-emissions-from-oil-and-gas-industry; Juliet Eilperin and Brady Dennis, "Trump Administration to Relax Restrictions on Methane, a Powerful Greenhouse Gas," *Washington Post*, August 29, 2019, https://www.washingtonpost.com/climate-environment/2019/08/29/trump-administration-reverse-limits-methane-powerful-greenhouse-gas; Popovich, Albeck-Ripka, and Pierre-Louis, "95 Environmental Rules Being Rolled Back under Trump."

10. Lenz, "Homegrown Stories Episode 10 with Lisa Finley DeVille."

11. Amy Dalrymple, "Fine Ordered for 2014 Fort Berthold Pipeline Spill," *Bismarck Tribune*, February 2, 2018, https://bismarcktribune.com/news/fine-ordered-for-fort-berthold-pipeline-spill/article_4011e3fd-3df3-5715-b5ec-073c6071c137.html.

12. Sam Levin, "'He's a Political Prisoner': Standing Rock Activists Face Years in Jail," *The Guardian*, June 22, 2018, https://www.theguardian.com/us-news/2018/jun/22/standing-rock-jailed-activists-water-protectors.

13. Amy Dalrymple, "Dakota Access Pipeline Credited with Making Bakken More Competitive in 2017," *Bismarck Tribune*, December 26, 2017, https:// bismarcktribune.com/news/state-and-regional/dakota-access-pipeline-credited -with-making-bakken-more-competitive-in/article_72390e9c-ba24-5d41-bd4c -8b4ea4d7528f.html.

14. Adam Willis, "With a Green Light in Illinois, Dakota Access Pipeline Clears Final Barrier to Double its Capacity," *Grand Forks Herald*, October 15, 2020, https://www.grandforksherald.com/business/energy-and-mining/6718963 -With-a-green-light-in-Illinois-Dakota-Access-Pipeline-clears-final-barrier-to -double-its-capacity.

15. Estes and Jaskiran Dhillon, *Standing with Standing Rock*.

16. "Donation from DAPL Company 'Unusual,' but a Win for ND Taxpayers, Officials Say," *Bismarck Tribune*, October 5, 2017, https://bismarcktribune.com/news /state-and-regional/donation-from-dapl-company-unusual-but-a-win-for-nd /article_810adc2e-971d-556d-aee4-89607fa62a95.html.

17. Alleen Brown, "Five Spills, Six Months in Operation," *The Intercept*, January 9, 2018, https://theintercept.com/2018/01/09/dakota-access-pipeline-leak -energy-transfer-partners.

18. Standing Rock Sioux Tribe v. U.S. Army Corps of Engineers, "Memorandum Opinion," June 14, 2017, https://earthjustice.org/sites/default/files/files/DAPL -order.pdf.

19. Standing Rock Sioux Tribe v. U.S. Army Corps of Engineers, "Memorandum in Support of Standing Rock Sioux Tribe's Motion for Summary Judgment on Remand," August 16, 2019, https://earthjustice.org/sites/default/files/files/srst -Remand-brief.pdf.

20. Standing Rock Sioux Tribe v. U.S. Army Corps of Engineers, "Consolidated Brief of Standing Rock Sioux Tribe, Cheyenne River Sioux Tribe, Oglala Sioux Tribe, and Yankton Sioux Tribe Regarding Remedy," May 20, 2020, https:// earthjustice.org/sites/default/files/files/3154-525-consol-brief-of-srst-crst_ost _yst-re-remedy.pdf.

21. Camp of the Sacred Stone, Facebook post by LaDonna Tamakawastewin Allard, February 20, 2020, https://www.facebook.com/CampOfTheSacredStone/posts /2589814577974231.

22. Quoted in "One Year at Standing Rock."

23. Zak Cheney-Rice, "South Dakota Gears Up to Crack Down on Keystone XL Protesters in 2020," *New York Magazine Intelligencer*, December 19, 2019, http:// nymag.com/intelligencer/2019/12/kristi-noem-south-dakota-riot-boosting .html.

24. Bill McKibben, *Eaarth: Making a Life on a Tough New Planet* (New York: St. Martin's Griffin, 2010).

25. Klein, *This Changes Everything.*

26. Harold C. Frazier, letter to TransCanada, "Keystone XL Pipeline—United States Update," July 12, 2018, https://twitter.com/CRSTChairman/status/1017544831566921728.

AFTERWORD

Epigraph: Indigenous Rising Media, Facebook video, July 8, 2020, https://www.facebook.com/Indigenousrisingmedia/videos/3105945992821721.

1. Jasilyn Charger, Facebook video, July 3, 2020, https://www.facebook.com/jasilyn.charger.5/videos/3078297088914408.

2. The White House, "Remarks by President Trump at South Dakota's 2020 Mount Rushmore Fireworks Celebration, Keystone, South Dakota," July 4, 2020, https://www.whitehouse.gov/briefings-statements/remarks-president-trump-south-dakotas-2020-mount-rushmore-fireworks-celebration-keystone-south-dakota.

3. Standing Rock Sioux Tribe v. U.S. Army Corps of Engineers, "Memorandum Opinion," March 25, 2020, https://earthjustice.org/sites/default/files/files/standing-rock-sj.pdf.

4. Standing Rock Sioux Tribe v. U.S. Army Corps of Engineers, "Memorandum Opinion," July 6, 2020, https://earthjustice.org/sites/default/files/files/standing_rock_sioux_tribe_v._army_corps_of_engineers.pdf.

5. Standing Rock Sioux Tribe v. U.S. Army Corps of Engineers, "Brief of Members of Congress as *Amici Curiae* in Support of Plaintiffs," May 20, 2020, https://www.documentcloud.org/documents/6896222-Amicus-Brief-of-Members-of-Congress-in-Support.html.

6. Alison Cagle, "Still Standing: Youth Activism and Legal Advocacy Work Hand in Hand in the Fight for Justice," Earthjustice, July 6, 2020, https://earthjustice.org/features/standing-rock-still-standing.

7. Earthjustice, "Webinar: How a Historic Grassroots Resistance and the Power of the Law Could Cancel the Dakota Access Pipeline."

8. Quoted in Earthjustice, "Judge Orders Dakota Access Pipeline to Shut Down," July 6, 2020, https://earthjustice.org/news/press/2020/judge-orders-dakota-access-pipeline-to-shut-down.

9. Energy Transfer Partners, "Energy Transfer Statement on Dakota Access Pipeline," July 6, 2020, https://twitter.com/JanHasselman/status/1280199370919403521/photo/1.

10. Standing Rock Sioux Tribe v. U.S. Army Corps of Engineers, "Dakota Access, LLC's Emergency Motion for Stay Pending Appeal," July 10, 2020, https://earthjustice.org/sites/default/files/files/dapl-dc-circuit-redacted-stay-motion-as-filed.pdf.

11. Hiroko Tabuchi and Brad Plumer, "Is This the End of New Pipelines?," *New York Times*, July 8, 2020, https://www.nytimes.com/2020/07/08/climate/dakota-access-keystone-atlantic-pipelines.html.

12. Yessenia Funes, "Indigenous Protests Are Blazing a New Trail for How to Beat Big Oil," *Gizmodo*, July 11, 2020, https://earther.gizmodo.com/indigenous-protests-are-blazing-a-new-trail-for-how-to-1844328315.

13. Amnesty International documented unnecessary and excessive use of force including sponge rounds, rubber bullets, tear gas, and pepper spray in response to the demonstrations in summer 2020. See Amnesty International, "USA: Law Enforcement Violated Black Lives Matter Protesters' Human Rights, Documents Acts of Police Violence and Excessive Force," August 4, 2020, https://www.amnesty.org/en/latest/news/2020/08/usa-law-enforcement-violated-black-lives-matter-protesters-human-rights/.

14. Indigenous Rising Media, Facebook video, July 8, 2020, https://www.facebook.com/Indigenousrisingmedia/videos/3105945992821721.

15. The White House, "Fact Sheet: President Biden Takes Executive Actions to Tackle the Climate Crisis at Home and Abroad, Create Jobs, and Restore Scientific Integrity Across Federal Government," January 27, 2021, https://www.whitehouse.gov/briefing-room/statements-releases/2021/01/27/fact-sheet-president-biden-takes-executive-actions-to-tackle-the-climate-crisis-at-home-and-abroad-create-jobs-and-restore-scientific-integrity-across-federal-government/; Juliet Eilperin, Brady Dennis, and Darryl Fears, "Biden to Place Environmental Justice at Center of Sweeping Climate Plan," *Washington Post*, January 27, 2021, https://www.washingtonpost.com/climate-environment/2021/01/26/biden-environmental-justice-climate/.

16. Julian Brave NoiseCat, "In Trump v. Biden, Native American Voters Played a Crucial Role; It's Time to Recognize That," NBC News, November 27, 2020, https://www.nbcnews.com/think/opinion/trump-v-biden-native-american-voters-played-crucial-role-it-ncna1249005.

17. The White House, "Memorandum on Tribal Consultation and Strengthening Nation-to-Nation Relationships," January 26, 2021, https://www.whitehouse.gov/briefing-room/presidential-actions/2021/01/26/memorandum-on-tribal-consultation-and-strengthening-nation-to-nation-relationships/.

18. Quoted in Rebecca Beitsch, "Biden Makes Historic Pick with Haaland for Interior Secretary," *The Hill*, December 17, 2020, https://thehill.com

/policy/energy-environment/529495-biden-names-haaland-as-interior
-secretary?fbclid=IwAR1Un29HIHELXIo3QKFz40nd2Ee9XykjjHSUtdQt6
IGG7qtbDTErrmNBD7Q.

19. Nina Lakhani, "'No More Broken Treaties': Indigenous Leaders Urge Biden to
Shut Down Dakota Access Pipeline," *The Guardian*, January 21, 2021, https://
www.theguardian.com/us-news/2021/jan/21/dakota-access-pipeline-joe-biden
-indigenous-environment.

20. Bill McKibben, "Joe Biden's Cancellation of the Keystone Pipeline is a Landmark
in the Climate Fight," *New Yorker*, January 21, 2021, https://www.newyorker.com
/news/daily-comment/joe-bidens-cancellation-of-the-keystone-pipeline-is
-a-landmark-in-the-climate-fight; David Blackmon, "First Keystone XL, Now
Dakota Access: Pipeline Politics Swirl Around Biden," *Forbes*, February 10, 2021,
https://www.forbes.com/sites/davidblackmon/2021/02/10/first-keystonexl
-now-dakota-access-pipeline-politics-swirl-around-biden/?sh=1807cc9e10c1.

21. Jodi Archambault, "How Covid-19 Threatens Native Languages," *New York Times*,
January 24, 2021, https://www.nytimes.com/2021/01/24/opinion/covid-lakota
-language.html?action=click&module=Opinion&pgtype=Homepage.

22. Letter from Indigenous women leaders to President-elect Biden, January 14, 2021,
https://d99d2e8d-06c9-433b-915d-f6e381b1acd4.usrfiles.com/ugd/d99d2e
_bac8dc29b9d54086a076b5aa6a3f5644.pdf.

23. Letter from chairman of the Standing Rock Sioux Tribe, chairman of the Cheyenne
River Sioux Tribe, president of the Oglala Sioux Tribe, and vice-chairman of the
Yankton Sioux Tribe to President-elect Biden, January 19, 2021, https://earthjustice
.org/sites/default/files/files/tribes_letter_to_presidential.elect_biden_re_dapl
.011921.final_.pdf; Letter from tribal organizations to President Biden, February 9,
2021, https://earthjustice.org/sites/default/files/files/joint-tribal-org-dapl-letter
-2_9_2021.pdf; Letter from Indigenous and environmental activists and creatives
to President Biden and Vice President Harris, https://earthjustice.org/sites
/default/files/files/letter-to-biden-harris-shutdown-dapl.pdf (accessed February
2021); Letter from members of Congress to President Biden, February 5, 2021,
https://earthjustice.org/sites/default/files/files/2.5.21-dapl-biden-letter.pdf.

24. Standing Rock Sioux Tribe v. U.S. Army Corps of Engineers, "Opinion of the
U.S. Court of Appeals for the District of Columbia Circuit," January 26, 2021,
https://earthjustice.org/sites/default/files/files/dc_cir_dapl_opinion.pdf.

25. Dave Kolpack, "Corps Wants Delay on Hearing to Shut Down Dakota Access
Line," AP News, February 8, 2021, https://apnews.com/article/technology
-courts-army-9019cee3ffc4f7f7ef1a03bdee5e33e2.

# Index

accidents, oil rig, 53

accidents, road, 26, 33, 42, 47–48, 53, 184

ACLU (American Civil Liberties Union), 101, 119, 231

addiction, 66, 203, 219, 232. *See also* alcohol use

AIM. *See* American Indian Movement (AIM)

air contamination, 32, 44, 49–50

Alberta tar sands, 70, 168, 239

Alcatraz Island occupation, 8

alcohol use: affecting families, 16–17, 63–64, 95, 232; at camps, 182, 194, 196; crimes related to, 26; deaths caused by, 17, 52; factors contributing to, 21; forbidden, 81, 82, 84, 221; liquor stores contributing to, 203; as social problem, 27, 66

Al Jazeera, 45

Allard, LaDonna: as activist, 3, 9, 89, 91–92, 140–41, 147, 151, 207, 240; background of, 80, 112, 115–16; black snake prophecy and, 11, 118, 225; camp beginnings and, 77–78, 81–82, 85, 95, 105, 125; camp closure and, 181, 189–90, 191, 196, 200–201, 205, 210; camp management by, 86, 119–21, 125–27, 130–31, 132, 153, 160, 175, 177–78; as environmental leader, 222; health of, 149–50, 178, 199, 227,

237; on impact of camp, 237–38; marriage of, 156, 221–22, 224–26; as mentor, 238; as organizer, 76, 79, 205; on pipeline decisions, 122, 163, 224–25, 237–38; projects of, 205, 221; racism toward, 123; sacred sites and, 71–72, 111–12, 146, 210, 224–26; surveillance of, 128–30, 226–27; as tribal historian, 71, 125, 130–31

Allard, Miles, 82, 125, 127, 156, 207, 210, 221, 225–26

All Nations Fire, 180

American Civil Liberties Union. *See* ACLU (American Civil Liberties Union)

American Horse, Dale "Happy," 106–7

American Indian Movement (AIM), 8, 87, 119, 203

Amnesty International, 103, 104

animals, dangers to, 25, 42–45, 75, 96, 227

Apache, 105

Archambault, Dave: as activist, 95–97, 98, 103; background of, 72; Barack Obama and, 104–5; camps and, 137, 138, 159–60, 175–76, 179, 182, 187, 190; connections of, 78, 84–85, 101; on cultural sites destruction, 117; DAPL opposed by, 72, 104; easement and, 186; EIS and, 148, 178, 180–81; environmental concerns of,

Archambault, Dave (*cont.*)
85; historical awareness of, 80; on law enforcement tactics, 155; in legal proceedings, 1, 126; pipeline decisions and, 122, 123, 151, 162–63, 174; press and, 119; at public forum, 89; as tribal chairman, 72, 75, 130, 143, 145, 168, 183–84, 199–200; tribal election and, 208, 222

Arikara, 15, 19–20, 168, 202

armored vehicles, 132, 136, 138, 140, 146, 191

Army Corps: activists and, 94, 151, 198; burial sites and, 146; camps and, 146, 159, 185–86, 188, 193; dams built by, 20–21, 85; EA and, 75–76, 172; easements and, 89, 91, 150–51, 161–63, 167, 171, 173; EIS and, 7, 10, 88, 89, 121–22, 173–74, 180–81, 209, 224, 236, 240–41; flooding caused by, 20–21, 85, 89–90, 114–15; land ownership issues and, 79–80, 98–99; in legal proceedings, 92, 126, 172, 187, 188; media and, 132; permits and, 72–74, 84, 85, 91, 171, 236, 240–41; pipeline route and, 6, 78–79; presidential influence on, 7, 134, 145, 147–49, 184, 209, 239–41; role of, 171

arsenic, 74

asthma, 50

Atlantic Coast Pipeline, 237

*Awake* (documentary), 207

Backwater Bridge barricade, 160, 174, 176, 179–80

Backwater Bridge conflict, 139, 143–45, 151–56, 175–76

Baker, Edmund, 39, 45–46, 49

Bakken cough, 53

Bakken pipeline. *See* DAPL (Dakota Access Pipeline)

Bakken region: crime in, 27–28; DAPL and, 41; health problems from, 53; as oil source, 3, 5–6, 18, 188–89, 210; oil spills in, 48; reservation on, 17, 19, 39; traffic problems from, 25–26, 70; tribal interest in, 22

Bald Eagle, Kalen: as activist, 66, 76, 182, 228–29; at camp, 82, 84, 87, 105, 128, 140, 150, 190, 191; as caretaker, 156–57, 232; family of, 65, 88, 156–57, 229–30; on front lines, 139, 158; Jasilyn Charger's relationship with, 64, 65–66, 196–97, 209–10, 230, 232; observations of, 75; seventh generation concept and, 90; surveillance of, 129–30, 229

Bank of America, 206

Bank of North Dakota, 123

Banks, Dennis, 101

BankTrack, 215–16

Barclays, 206

barricade. *See* blockade of Highway 1806

Battle of the Little Bighorn, 113

Bayou Bridge Pipeline, 231, 232

Bear Butte SD, 64

benzene, 44

BIA (Bureau of Indian Affairs), 3, 23–24, 123, 154–55, 189–90, 196

Biden, Joe, and administration, 10, 224, 238–41

Birdbear, Joletta, 53–54, 55–56, 89

Birdbear, Theodora, 53–54, 55–56

birds, dangers to, 42–43, 96

Bismarck ND, 6, 78–79, 114, 124, 173, 213

DACA (Deferred Action for Childhood Arrivals), 235

Dakota, 87, 88, 112

Dakota Access, LLC: construction by,
59, 94, 106, 132, 133, 182; EA prepared
by, 75; easements granted to, 90, 186;
EIS and, 122; financing for, 206; gift
to state from, 223; land acquisition
by, 54–55, 57–58, 84, 127–28, 137, 185;
in legal proceedings, 1, 96, 126, 151,
155–56, 173, 236–37, 239–41; money
offered by, 2–3; ownership of, 5, 41;
permits applied for, 41, 54, 73, 79,
86; pipeline routes of, 6; on safety
standards, 85–86; security company
hired by, 119, 150; strategy of, 92; trespassing policy of, 137; wealth of, 204

Dakota Access Pipeline. See DAPL
(Dakota Access Pipeline)

Dakota Resource Council, 42, 54, 79

Dakota Rural Action, 56

Dakota Uprising, 148

Dalrymple, Jack, 98, 120–21, 137, 138,
159–60, 175

dams, 20–21, 59, 73, 85, 114–15

DAPL (Dakota Access Pipeline):
approvals for, 58, 71; Biden administration and, 239–41; construction
of, 93, 106, 136–37; denials to, 7, 126,
151, 162–63, 167–68, 170–72, 180, 236;
economic effect of, 222; employment with, 184; as environmental
injustice, 6; as example, 9, 192, 216;
extent of, 4–6; financial support of,
205–6; justification for, 85–86; lacking permits, 236, 240–41; leaks and
spills of, 208, 223–24; location of,
69–70; in operation, 3, 10, 210, 240;
opposition to, 42, 54–56, 70–72, 76,
78–80, 97, 101, 104, 151, 183–84, 204,
226; planning for, 37, 41–42; private
security for, 137; support for, 56,
143, 151, 215, 237. See also black snake
prophecy

DAPL cough, 149–50, 178, 195, 227

Darcy, Jo-Ellen, 123, 178, 180–81

Dawes Act, 20, 114

Deese, Brian, 171

Defend the Sacred, 221

Defense Technologies, 155

Democracy Now!, 111

Deutsche Bank, 206

DeVille, Lisa: as activist against DAPL,
9, 16, 48, 53, 55–56, 89–90, 208, 218;
as activist against Keystone XL, 220;
as activist for community, 31–32, 54;
background of, 16–17, 21–23; camps
and, 101, 175; education of, 28, 30,
53; employment of, 15; family of, 28,
218–19; health of, 53; observations of,
environmental, 25, 43–44, 47, 49, 59,
216; observations of, social, 26–27,
35–36, 46, 50, 58, 92, 219–20; political
campaign of, 219; tribal elections
and, 217–18; in Washington DC, 199

DeVille, Maria, 199

DeVille, Michael, 28, 30, 32, 218

DeVille, Thomas, 28, 32, 218

DeVille, Walter: background of, 28;
community assessment by, 32;
health of, 53; helping campers, 101,
175; observations of, 26, 30, 36, 40,
47, 59, 216–17, 218, 219; volunteer firefighter work of, 47–48; work of, 29

Dewey, Myron, 207

DiCaprio, Leonardo, 207

divestment of fossil fuel industry, 184, 205–6

DNB (Norwegian bank), 206

Doctrine of Discovery, 4, 100, 147

dog attack, 112, 117–19, 172

Donaghy, Nicole, 42, 48, 56, 79

donations, 82, 99, 127, 161, 177, 200, 223

drones, 128, 137

drug use, 26, 27, 63, 67, 170, 182, 189, 194, 196, 219

drug use, forbidden, 81, 82, 84, 221

Dunbar-Ortiz, Roxane, 114, 117

EA (Environmental Assessment), 75, 78–79, 91, 92, 172, 218

Eagle, Glenna, 87, 95–96, 97

Eagle, Kathy, 47, 50, 51

Eagle Butte SD, 63, 65–68, 69, 194, 209

Eagles Nest Camp, 196

EarthFirst!, 215

Earthjustice, 78, 85, 86, 184, 236

EarthRights International, 215

easements: delayed, 150–51; denied, 7, 161–63, 167–68, 170–73; EIS and, 89; federal government and, 121, 134, 147–48, 156; granted, 7, 186–87; lacking, 240–41; obtained by DAPL, 2, 54, 57–58, 90, 127; as requirement, 73, 91; treaties affecting, 74

EIS (Environmental Impact Statement): allowed to proceed, 180–81; Army Corps and, 7, 10, 173–74; federal government and, 121, 208–9; lacking, 104, 236, 240–41; in progress, 10, 186–87, 240; purpose of, 92–93; recommended, 162, 172; requested, 73, 88, 89, 90, 122, 133, 176,

178; as requirement, 72, 148, 224, 230, 236; as unlikely, 186

Elbowoods ND, 21

election, presidential, 123, 131–32, 147–49, 227, 238–39

Emergency Management Assistance, 99, 137

eminent domain, 55, 58, 137

Enbridge Company and pipelines, 99, 231, 239, 240

Energy Policy Act, 46

Energy Transfers Partners. See ETP (Energy Transfer Partners)

Environmental Assessment. See EA (Environmental Assessment)

Environmental Impact Statement. See EIS (Environmental Impact Statement)

environmental justice, 6, 7, 8, 9, 10, 69, 78–79, 169, 238

Environmental Protection Agency. See EPA (Environmental Protection Agency)

environmental racism, 138

EPA (Environmental Protection Agency), 6, 16, 45, 46, 85, 86, 216, 218, 219, 223

Episcopal Church, 100, 198

ETP (Energy Transfer Partners): attitudes of, 173; background of, 41; connections of, 143, 149, 176, 184; on contamination by industry, 86; distrust toward, 163; economic effect of, 223; financial support of, 206; land acquisition by, 127; in legal proceedings, 151, 215–16; as pipeline builder, 5–6, 10, 42, 78, 223; plans of, 186, 237, 240; preliminary process done by, 54; security company and, 128, 197, 215–16; shares of, 122–23, 183, 197; tribes ignored by, 81

Facebook: fundraising over, 80–81; as organizational tool, 76, 79, 91–92, 161, 187, 222; as protest tool, 96, 135, 145, 169, 179, 184, 227; security company using, 119, 128–29; for self-expression, 131, 140, 167, 173, 178, 194, 200; as support tool, 67, 69; threats on, 124

Fallis, Red Fawn, 144, 237

farming, 19, 21, 112, 114, 202

FBI (Federal Bureau of Investigation), 27, 144, 154–55

Federal Aviation Administration, 137

Federal Register, 180

Federal Regulatory Commission, 209

Feinstein, Diane, 134

fines, 42, 45–46, 125, 144, 219

fires, 82, 180, 190

fires, sacred, 81, 84, 99, 100, 102, 162, 179, 190

fish, dangers to, 44, 75

Fish and Wildlife Service, 42

fishing rights, 8, 75, 172

Flag Avenue, 119

flaring, 46, 50, 53, 189, 216–17, 219

Floberg, John, 2, 132, 147, 162–63, 198, 222

Flood Control Act. See Pick-Sloan Plan

flooding, 20–21, 50, 59, 80, 85, 89, 115, 178–79, 219

Floyd, George, 235

Fonda, Jane, 157–58

Fort Berthold Protectors of Water and Earth Rights. See POWER (Protectors of Water and Earth Rights)

Fort Berthold Reservation: activism on, 192, 212–13; Army Corps projects and, 21–22; discrimination on, 23–24; environmental problems on, 5, 39, 52, 189; flooding on, 80; health issues on, 40, 50–53; history of, 20–21; oil industry and, 17–18, 19, 24–25, 32, 168, 218, 220; racism on, 39–40, 189; renewable energy research on, 201; significance of, 219; social conditions on, 25–28, 29–30, 70

Fort Laramie Treaty (1851), 2–3, 4, 20, 80, 98–99, 104, 113, 137, 139, 185

Fort Laramie Treaty (1868), 2–3, 4, 73–74, 80, 98–99, 104, 113–14, 137, 139, 185

Fort Rice ND, 133

Fort Yates ND, 77, 81, 112, 178, 221

Fox, Josh, 207

Fox, Mark: DAPL and, 42, 57, 58–59; Kandi White and, 169; in legal proceedings, 219; on oil production, 23, 40–41, 46, 218, 220–21; Standing Rock Reservation and, 59, 101–2; as tribal chairman, 36–37, 39; tribal election and, 212, 217–18

fracking: acceptance of, 15, 22, 30; activism against, 168–69, 220; animals affected by, 42–45; banned, 70, 220; description of, 17–18; environmental effects of, 5, 208; and frack socks, 49; humans affected by, 44–45, 49, 52–53, 189, 219–20; public relations about, 30; regulations for, 46–47, 212–13, 218; spills from, 90, 216–17; wastewater from, 39–40, 44–45, 47–48, 90, 218

hypothermia, 152, 153

Idle No More movement, 8
IEN (Indigenous Environmental
  Network): activists and, 69, 168–69,
  187, 197, 199; camps and, 160, 175,
  179; DAPL opposed by, 56, 104; false
  accusations and, 98, 182; Keystone
  XL opposed by, 208, 216, 239–40;
  renewable energy and, 201
IHS (Indian Health Service), 51–52
IIYC (International Indigenous Youth
  Council): awards for, 227–28; on
  front lines, 139, 153, 158–59; founding
  of, 102–3, 105; pipeline decisions
  and, 162; precautions taken by, 128,
  150; role of, 136, 161; supporting
  activists, 105–6; as targeted group,
  124, 209; violence against, 140; in
  Washington DC, 182
Illinois Commerce Commission, 58
improvised explosive devices, 154
Independence ND, 22, 30, 219
Indian Health Service. See IHS (Indian
  Health Service)
Indians of All Tribes, 8
Indigenized Energy, 205
Indigenous Climate March (2015), 69
Indigenous Environmental Network.
  See IEN (Indigenous Environmental
  Network)
Indigenous Rising Media, 169
infiltrators, 7, 129–30, 140, 150, 169–70
infrastructure projects, 33, 80
ING Bank, 206
injunctions, 93, 94, 103, 106, 118, 121,
  122, 133

Instantaneous Blast canisters, 155
The Intercept, 128–29, 148, 154–55, 170
International Center for Not-for-Profit
  Law, 195
International Indigenous Youth Coun-
  cil. See IIYC (International Indige-
  nous Youth Council)
Iowa, 54–55, 56, 84, 223–24
Iron Eyes, Chase, 185, 190
Iron Eyes, Tokata, 162
Island Girl (yacht), 33

Jackson, Jesse, 138
Jefferson, Thomas, 100
John, Moe, 97
Johnson v. McIntosh, 100
journalist arrests, 121, 144–45, 185, 191
J. P. Morgan Chase, 206
jurisdiction issues, 28, 46, 57, 72, 218
Just Transition, 201–2, 213–14

Kasowitz Benson Torres LLP, 215
Keystone Pipeline, 224
Keystone XL Pipeline: blocked, 238–
  40; border crossing by, 93; concerns
  about, 233; employment with, 184;
  in legal proceedings, 208, 216; opposition to, 8, 69, 70–71, 208, 220, 228–
  29, 230–31, 234, 238–40; support for,
  147–48, 183, 231, 239, 240
King, Martin Luther, Jr., 100
Kirchmeier, Kyle, 94, 97–98, 117, 119,
  132, 136, 138, 145, 155, 194
Klein, Naomi, 162

LaDuke, Winona, 84, 99
Lafleur-Vetter, Sara, 145

Mentz, Tim, 107

mercury, 52, 74–75

Meriam Report, 117

Merkley, Jeff, 207

Methane and Natural Gas Waste Rule, 208, 216, 238

methane gas, 16, 18, 216, 219

Meyer, Brenda, 127

Meyer, David, 127

MHA Nation: activists and, 16; environmental problems on, 20–21, 42, 217; as example, 207; health issues in, 51–53; history of, 19–20; hopes for, 217; legal standing of, 218; oil development on, 19, 22, 23–25, 46, 58–59, 173, 192; oil production by, 56–57; population of, 25; scandals in, 33–36; settlements for, 219; social conditions in, 189; supporting Standing Rock Sioux, 101–2, 185; tribes of, 15; water safety in, 47

MHA Times, 40, 217

Migratory Bird Treaty Act, 42–43, 96

mineral rights, 22, 24, 36

Missouri River: damming of, 20–21, 115; DAPL crossing, 4, 7, 73–74, 89, 224, 239, 241; description and importance of, 5, 9, 78, 81, 202, 213; as water source, 2, 74, 81, 85, 92, 204

Missouri River Resources, 24, 56–57

Mni Wiconi Pipeline, 202

Monet, Jenni, 185

Morgan Stanley, 206

Mount Rushmore, 3, 235–36

MS-13 (international criminal gang), 27

Mueller investigation, 227

murders, 34

Nakota, 87, 88

National Congress of American Indians, 172

National Environmental Policy Act. *See* NEPA (National Environmental Policy Act)

National Guard, 120–21, 132, 137, 144, 191

National Historic Preservation Act. *See* NHPA (National Historic Preservation Act)

National Lawyers Guild, 155

Nationwide Permit 12, 72–73

Native Nations March (2017), 197–99

NDN Collective, 222

NEPA (National Environmental Policy Act), 92, 188, 236

Ness, Ron, 222

New Source Performance Standards, 216, 223

New Town ND, 27, 28, 29, 33, 168, 188–89

*New York Times*, 33, 39, 49, 104, 122, 156, 183

NHPA (National Historic Preservation Act), 73, 92, 107, 121, 130, 133, 134–35

NODAPL, 177, 204

North Dakota: environmental damage in, 48; environmental disregard in, 45, 56, 223; history of, 111; hopes for, 213; oil production in, 10, 18–19, 79, 86, 208, 223; protests, response to, 98, 103; social conditions in, 26, 27, 29, 53; traffic deaths in, 25–26; tribal relations with, 22, 31, 121, 143, 146, 176, 180, 193, 195–96; weather in, 152, 159, 174–75, 178

North Dakota Agricultural Department, 126

racism, 39–40, 66, 123–24, 138, 157, 189, 213, 235, 237

Racketeer Influenced and Corrupt Organizations (RICO) Act, 215

radioactivity, 44, 48–49

rail transport, 37, 41, 80, 85–86

Rapid City SD, 66, 114

Red Warrior Camp, 99, 150, 215

relocation programs, 116, 124

Rencountre, Charles: "Not Afraid to Look," 8, 131, 200, 225–26

renewable energy, 201, 221

Rensch, Cassi Dee, 26

Republicans, 147–48, 149, 195, 208, 223

Respiratory Syncytial Virus. See RSV (Respiratory Syncytial Virus)

Reuters, 86

"Rezpect Our Water" campaign, 79

RICO Act. See Racketeer Influenced and Corrupt Organizations (RICO) Act

Rivers and Harbors Act, 72

roadblock on Highway 1806, 103–4, 121

roads and road conditions, 25–26, 32–33, 218, 220

Robert F. Kennedy Human Rights Award, 227–28

Romney, Mitt, 43

Rosebud Camp, 99, 176, 180, 181, 190, 193

Rosebud Reservation, 69, 116

royalties, 24, 25, 219

RSV (Respiratory Syncytial Virus), 50

Ruffalo, Mark, 138

"Run for Water" event, 79

run to Omaha NE, 87–90

run to Washington DC, 90–91, 93–95, 240

sacred sites, 92, 121, 126, 145

Sacred Stone Camp: closure of, 196; formation of, 77–78; government orders for, 181, 189–90; growth of, 95, 98; law enforcement and, 97–98; legacy of, 205, 210, 237–38; memories of, 200, 225–26, 237–38; misconceptions about, 200–201; opening of, 80–82, 83–84; outreach by, 84–85, 91–92, 222; population of, 119–20, 175, 176; purpose of, 131; security at, 130; structure of, 84; support for, 86–87, 101–2, 127, 131, 177–78; theft from, 201; traditional life at, 120, 157–58; veterans at, 161; winter preparations at, 126–27, 160

Sacred Stone Village, 205

Safe Drinking Water Act, 46

safe houses, 75–76

Sand Creek Massacre (1864), 177, 190

Sanders, Bernie, 104, 121, 134, 143, 186, 198, 199, 207

Sandpiper Pipeline, 99

Sarandon, Susan, 103

Save Our Aboriginal Rights (SOAR), 54

Schrader, Adam, 144–45

Schulz, Cody, 132

Seabrook Nuclear Power Plant, 10–11

Serck-Hanssen, Harald, 206

Seven Council Fires of the Sioux Nation. See Oceti Sakowin (Sioux Alliance)

Seventh Generation Camp, 196

seventh generation concept, 11, 90–91, 118, 228, 233, 238

Sierra Club, 104

silica and silicosis, 53

Silverton (security company), 119

Simmons, Marco, 215–16

Sioux Falls SD, 114

Sioux Tribe. *See* Cheyenne River Sioux Tribe; Dakota; Great Sioux Nation; Lakota; Nakota; Oceti Sakowin (Sioux Alliance); Standing Rock Sioux Tribe

Sitting Bull, 90, 163, 177

SLAPP. *See* Strategic Litigation against Public Participation (SLAPP)

smallpox, 19–20, 202

snow, yellow, 15, 30

SOAR. *See* Save Our Aboriginal Rights (SOAR)

solar energy, 201, 202, 204, 205

South Dakota, 51, 56, 67, 74, 90, 203, 229, 230, 231

South Dakota Public Utilities Commission, 58

sovereignty, 10, 24, 156, 167, 205

Speer, Robert, 186

Spione, James, 207

Spirit Lake Nation, 220

Standing Rock Reservation: activists visiting, 76; boundaries of, 4, 79–80; description of, 114; environmental damage to, 115; language groups on, 112; long-term focus of, 204–5; pipeline location near, 1, 5, 6, 59, 70, 73, 78–79; water protectors and, 6; water supply of, 70, 75

Standing Rock Sioux Tribe: budget of, 177, 200; camp cleanup by, 185; economic conditions of, 208; environmental movements and, 173–74; land ownership and, 74; in legal proceedings, 10, 92, 126, 187–88, 223–24, 236; legal rights of, 172; North Dakota government and,

103; Obama administration and, 7; pipeline opposition of, 7, 10, 71–72, 170–71, 183–84, 209, 224; treaties and, 4–5, 74

Stein, Jill, 121

Stenehjam, Wayne, 127–28

St. Francis Mission, 116

Stingrays (surveillance devices), 170

Strategic Litigation against Public Participation (SLAPP), 215

suicide, 63, 67, 68–69, 106, 194, 203, 230

Sunoco Logistics Partners, 86, 151

SWAT teams, 192

Taboo (rapper), 200

Takini SD, 229–30, 233, 238

tax revenues, 19, 22, 25, 41, 222–23

TC Energy. *See* TransCanada

tear gas, 146, 152, 153, 155, 195

telescope, protest against, 232

thermal power, 221

350.org, 104, 120

Three Legs, Bobbi Jean, 79, 87–88, 90–91, 94, 103, 240

Thundershield, Josephine, 69–70, 130, 152–53

Thunder Valley Community Development Corporation, 84, 184–85, 202, 203–4

TigerSwan: attitudes of, 186, 195–96, 197; background of, 128; in legal proceedings, 215; politics and, 148; tactics of, 7, 128–29, 150, 178, 207, 209

Tillerson, Rex, 176

Tilsen, Ken, 203

Tilsen, Nick, 84–85, 124–25, 185, 202, 203–4, 222, 235

Tioga ND, 86

water contamination, 44–45, 48–49, 52, 230

Water Protector Legal Collective, 155–56

water protectors: appearance of genuine, 130; arrests of, 8, 94–97, 136, 139, 140, 143–44, 176, 185, 192, 202; background of, 3–4; blockade and, 179–80; camps and, 83–84, 159–60, 174, 185, 190–91; concerns of, 149; Dave Archambault and, 175–76; false accusations about, 104, 194; front-line actions of, 94, 97–98, 111–12, 132, 135, 138–41, 146–47, 152–54, 158–59; health of, 149–50; infiltrators and, 170; legislation against, 195; lock-downs on machinery by, 106–7, 124–25; mentors for, 200; nonviolence of, 98, 99, 104, 119, 124, 170; Obama administration and, 171; optimism of, 241; pipeline decisions and, 161–63, 236; post-camp, 143–44, 203, 205; publicity for, 95–96, 118; racism against, 189; as role models, 235; surveillance of, 128–29, 148, 150, 209; threats against, 124–25; veterans and, 161, 162; violence against, 6–7, 117–18, 139–40, 146–47, 155–56, 191–92, 237; in Washington DC, 182, 198

water supply, 2, 6, 47, 70, 72, 74, 75, 76, 79

weapons, 7, 143–44, 146–47, 152–56, 191–92

weapons, forbidden, 81, 98, 161, 194

weigh station, 219–20

Wells Fargo, 206

White, Aiyana, 89, 169–70, 189, 192, 199, 202, 211, 213–14, 237

White, Kandi: as activist, 9, 89–90, 169, 179, 184, 187, 201–2, 205–9, 211–12, 234, 240; background of, 26, 47, 52, 168–69; Bakken region and, 188–89; camp closure and, 174–75, 182, 185, 188, 192, 201; camp life of, 86, 100–101, 160, 169–70, 178; concerns of, 50, 212–13; on false accusations, 194; family of, 211, 237; on front lines, 140, 143; health of, 52; heritage of, 213; life experience of, 213–15, 216; observations of, 25, 27, 29–30, 42, 47; as organizer, 79, 197–98, 199; on pipeline decisions, 58–59, 102, 167–68, 173, 180, 237–39; surveillance and, 145; tribal elections and, 212, 217; with veterans, 174; violence against, 140; in Washington DC, 182, 200

White, Loren, 199, 211, 213–14

White Clay NE, 203

White Eyes, Joseph: as activist, 71, 76–77, 103; at camp, 82, 175; character of, 74; on front lines, 102; Jasilyn Charger helped by, 63–64, 66; as organizer, 66–67, 69, 75, 79, 90–91; on runs, 87–88, 90–91, 240

Whitestone Massacre, 111

Wiconi (child), 93

Wilansky, Sophia, 154–55, 156, 158

Wilansky, Wayne, 154–55

Williams, Damon, 33, 37

Williams, Dave, 46, 56–57

Williston ND, 19, 27

Wilz, Greg, 103

Win, Ta'Sina Sapa, 97, 153, 184

wind energy, 201, 202, 221

Women's March (2017), 182

Wood, Michael A., Jr., 161

Woodley, Shailene, 93–94, 103, 135
Wounded Knee Massacre (1890), 177, 190, 203
Wounded Knee occupation (1973), 8, 203

Yakama Nation, 97
Yankton Reservation, 69
Yellow Fat, Dana: as activist, 95–97, 139–40; camp involvement of, 86–87, 181, 193–94; easement denial and, 162; family of, 199; legal actions and, 1, 126; as organizer, 81, 98; political views of, 148; racism observed by, 123–24; reflections of, 222; violence against, 178
Young, Phyllis, 87, 99, 115, 119, 163, 205, 221–22
Young, Wasté Win, 71–72
*yuwipi* (ceremony), 77